CONTROLLING ENVIRONMENTAL POLICY

SUSAN ROSE-ACKERMAN

CONTROLLING
ENVIRONMENTAL
POLICY

THE LIMITS OF PUBLIC LAW
IN GERMANY AND
THE UNITED STATES

Yale University Press
New Haven and London

Chapter 3 is reprinted, by permission, from Susan Rose-Ackerman, "Environmental Policy and Federal Structure: A Comparison of the United States and Germany," *Vanderbilt Law Review* 47: 1587–1622 (1994). Tables 2.4 and 2.5 are reprinted by permission from *International Environmental Affairs*.

Designed by Jill Breitbarth. Set in Ehrhardt and Futura typefaces by Keystone Typesetting, Inc., Orwigsburg, Pennsylvania.

Printed in the United States of America by BookCrafters, Inc., Chelsea, Michigan.

Library of Congress Cataloging-in-Publication Data

Rose-Ackerman, Susan.
    Controlling environmental policy : the limits of public law in
Germany and the United States / Susan Rose-Ackerman.
        p. cm.
    Includes bibliographical references and index.
    ISBN 0-300-06065-3 (alk. paper)
    1. Environmental law—Germany.   2. Judicial review of
administrative acts—Germany.   3. Environmental law—United States.
    4. Judicial review of administrative acts—United States.   I. Title.
    K3585.4.R67   1995
    344.43′046—dc20
    [344.30446]   94-40558
                                                          CIP

A catalogue record for this book is available from the British Library.

The paper in this book meets the guidelines for permanence and durability of the Committee on Production Guidelines for Book Longevity of the Council on Library Resources.

10 9 8 7 6 5 4 3 2 1

CONTENTS

PREFACE

I come to the study of German administrative law and environmental policy as an American "innocent abroad." As an economist with an appointment in a law school and a political science department, I have an interdisciplinary focus, but I am a newcomer to German studies. I began my work in 1990 by studying German and by reading English-language sources. I spent the 1991–1992 academic year consulting German-language and European Union sources and interviewing a number of knowledgeable people.

I soon discovered that the field of comparative administrative law was relatively underdeveloped and lacked a strong policy focus. This book represents a preliminary effort to fill the gap. I have tried to cast a fresh eye on the problem of administrative accountability and technocratic policy-making in Germany—an eye trained in American universities and used to studying American problems. While I have made an effort to understand the justifications for present German practice, I have not hesitated to recommend legal and policy changes. I use American law and policy to illuminate German environmental law, and German law and policy to permit a new view of American public law.

This project could not have been attempted without the generosity of the Guggenheim Foundation, the Fulbright Commission, and Yale University, all of which helped finance my stay in Berlin during the 1991–1992 school year. As a research professor at the Free University and as the spouse of a fellow at the Institute for Advanced Study in Berlin, I had excellent access to German library materials. I am especially grateful to the librarians of the Institute for their invaluable aid in finding source materials. My use of German texts was greatly helped by the research assistance of Ralf Diekmann, a young German lawyer. He located and read a good deal of material and discussed his findings with me in biweekly meetings. Back in New Haven, Walter Burrier, Charlotte Burrows, and Susan Helms helped with translation, and James Rossi assisted with other research tasks. Brennan Van Dyke, while clerking at the European Court of Human Rights in Strasbourg, helped me locate European Union documents. I, of course, remain responsible for my interpretations of both the German- and English-language materials.

My effort to understand German law and politics would have been impossible without the generosity of numerous people in Germany who consented to be interviewed. I spoke with a number of professors and lawyers specializing in administrative and environmental law, and I interviewed officials in Berlin, Bonn, and Brussels. Near the end of my stay in Germany, I interviewed three justices of the High Administrative Court in Berlin. I also spoke with two justices of the German Constitutional Court about my project. These people, who are listed in an appendix to this study, were immensely helpful in my effort to understand German law. My debt to them goes beyond the occasional footnote to these conversations in the text.

As usual, I owe a particular debt to my husband, Bruce Ackerman, who has been a constant sounding board for my ideas and a ready translator of incomprehensible German sentences. Seminars and conversations with my colleagues in the Yale Law School and the Political Science Department have helped me develop my thoughts. I want especially to thank E. Donald Elliott, Uwe Kischel, John Langbein, Jerry Mashaw, Jefferey Sellers, Rogers Smith, Ian Shapiro, and Spiros Simitis. Several other people also made very useful comments on the draft manuscript. I wish particularly to thank Eberhard Bohne, Michael Bothe, Winfried Brohm, David Currie, Sven Deimann, Michael Greve, Bernd Holznagel, Peter Katzenstein, Philip Kunig, Gertrude Lübbe-Wolff, Eckard Rehbinder, Fritz Scharpf, Wolfgang Seibel, Rudolf Steinberg, and Gerd Winter. While these readers saved me from numerous errors and misjudgments, they should, of course, not be implicated in my interpretations and conclusions.

ABBREVIATIONS

AbfG Abfallgesetz (Waste Avoidance and Management Act)
AbwAG Abwasserabgabengesetz (Effluent Charge Law)
APA Administrative Procedures Act
AtG Atomgesetz (Law Concerning the Peaceful Development of Nuclear Power and Protection against Its Dangers)
BauGB Baugesetzbuch (Town and Country Planning Code)
BBU Bundesverband Bürgerinitiativen Umweltschutz (German Association of Citizens' Initiatives for Environmental Protection)
BGBl Bundesgesetzblatt (Federal Law Gazette)
BImSchG Bundes-Immissionsschutzgesetz (Federal Law for Protection against Environmental Harms from Air Pollution, Noise, Vibrations, and Similar Factors)
BImSchV Verordnung zur Durchführung des Bundes-Immissionsschutzgesetz (Ordinance Designed to Implement the BImSchG)
BNatSchG Bundesnaturschutzgesetz (Federal Nature Protection Law)
BRD Bundesrepublik Deutschland
BUND Bund für Umwelt- und Naturschutz Deutschland (German Association for Environmental and Nature Protection)
BVerfGE Entscheidungen des Bundesverfassungsgerichts (Decisions of the Federal Constitutional Court)
BVerGG Bundesverfassungsgerichtsgesetz (Law Concerning the Federal Constitutional Court)
BVerwGE Entscheidungen des Bundesverwaltungsgerichts (Decisions of the Federal Administrative Court)
CAA Clean Air Act
CDU / CSU Christlich-Demokratische Union / Christlich-Soziale Union (Christian Democratic Party / Christian Social Union)
CERCLA Comprehensive Environmental Response, Compensation, and Liability Act

CFR   Code of Federal Regulations

ChemG   Chemikaliengesetz (Chemicals Law)

CWA   Clean Water Act

DDR   Deutsche Demokratische Republik (German Democratic Republic)

DIN   Deutsches Institut für Normung (German Institute for Norms)

DVBl   Deutsches Verwaltungsblatt (German Administrative Gazette)

EPA   Environmental Protection Agency

EC   European Community

ECJ   European Court of Justice

EEC   European Economic Community

EPA   Environmental Protection Agency

EU   European Union

FDP   Freie Demokratische Partei (Free Democratic Party)

FRG   Federal Republic of Germany (BRD)

FWPCA   Federal Water Pollution Control Act

GDR   German Democratic Republic (DDR)

GenTG   Gentechnikgesetz

GG   Grundgesetz (Basic Law of the Federal Republic of Germany)

GGO   Gemeinsame Geschäftsordnung der Bundesministerien (General Internal Rules of Procedure for the German Federal Ministries)

KTA   Kerntechnischer Ausschuß (Technical Committee on Atomic Power)

NJW   Neue Juristische Wochenschrift

NVwZ   Neue Zeitschrift für Verwaltungsrecht

OECD   Organization for Economic Cooperation and Development

OJ   Official Journal of the European Communities

PDS   Partei des Demokratischen Sozialismus (Party of Democratic Socialism)

PflSchG   Pflanzenschutzgesetz (Law for the Protection of Cultivated Plants)

TA-Lärm   Technische Anleitung zum Schutz gegen Lärm (Technical Guidance Document for Protection against Noise)

TA-Luft   Technische Anleitung zur Reinhaltung der Luft (Technical Guidance Document for the Prevention of Air Pollution)

SPD   Sozialdemokratische Partei (Social Democratic Party)

UGB   Umweltgesetzbuch (Environmental Law Code)

UIG   Umweltinformationsgesetz (Environmental Information Law)

UmweltHG   Umwelthaftungsgesetz (Environmental Liability Law)

UVPG   Gesetz über die Umweltverträglichkeitsprüfung (Law Concerning the Review of Environmental Impacts)

VDI   Verein Deutscher Ingenieure (Society of German Engineers)

VerpackVO   Verpackungsverordnung (Ordinance on the Avoidance of Packaging Waste)

VGH   Verwaltungsgerichtshof (Administrative Court)

VwVfG   Verwaltungsverfahrensgesetz (Administrative Procedures Act)

VwGO   Verwaltungsgerichtsordnung (Ordinance for the Administrative Courts)

WHG   Wasserhaushaltsgesetz (Water Resources Management Act)

WRMG   Wasch- und Reinigungsmittelgesetz (Act Concerning the Environmental Impact of Washing and Cleaning Products)

INTRODUCTION

Democratic governments must strike a balance between expertise and popular control while restraining the influence of narrow, organized groups. Achieving a balance is hardest and most important in areas such as environmental protection, where expertise is essential and where the interests of consumers, labor, industry, and local residents are opposed.

In balancing popular control and expertise, the central issue is not the preservation of individual rights but rather the conflict between democratic control and governmental competence. Individual rights are, of course, the other great subject of administrative law, and their preservation provides another check on both popular sovereignty and administrative discretion. A focus on rights, however, often overshadows the equally fundamental issue of making democratic values operational in modern states where hierarchy and expertise cannot be avoided.

This second issue is my focus here. By concentrating on environmental policy, I emphasize a regulatory issue that is politically salient and technically complex. In the United States the basic framework is provided by the Constitution as modified by the New Deal, the Administrative Procedures Act, and the social regulation of the seventies and eighties. In Germany the framework is established at the national level by the Basic Law, or Grundgesetz [GG],[1] as elaborated by administrative statutes and practices.[2]

Germany and the United States are both advanced capitalist economies governed by representative democracies. Public and private spending on environmental protection is high, and both countries are heavy users of energy.[3] Germany, however, is much smaller in area and population and is much more densely populated. Because Germany is embedded in the European continent, its economy depends heavily on cross-border trade.[4] Its membership in the European Union makes some of Germany's regulatory problems similar to those of a large American state. Conditions in other European countries affect the quality of Germany's air and water, and the competitiveness of its products depends on the stringency of its regulations compared with those elsewhere in Europe.[5]

1

Over and above differences in geography and size, the relation between law and policy differs in Germany and the United States. Under the German parliamentary system, the connection between legislative process and statutory implementation by the executive is much closer than in the American system of separation of powers. German administrative law focuses narrowly on complaints by individuals against the state for violating their rights. The broad policy issues raised in American courts arise only indirectly in German legal cases. Organized groups with policy agendas, such as environmental or consumer associations, can seldom obtain standing under German law.[6] Policy debates go on elsewhere—in the Bundestag, Länder (state) governments, and federal agencies.

In German theory, popular control is exercised by citizens when they vote for representatives affiliated with political parties. The parties engage in a process of "political will building" that produces legislation reflecting popular concerns. The bureaucracy is a professional, expert body that implements these statutes in accord with the law. Under this conventional model, the state rejects demands for open and accountable ministerial processes because giving outside groups a legally enforceable role may obstruct the democratic will.[7]

Yet, especially in the field of environmental policy-making, statutes do not resolve all the political and policy choices. Parliament delegates much policy-making to the executive. German public law has not squarely faced this reality.[8] Part of the problem lies in Germany's admirable postwar emphasis on individual rights. Part derives from venerable principles of public administration that assign independent authority to the bureaucracy to carry out the law.[9] Newly recognized environmental problems are forced into the preexisting framework, but the fit is sometimes awkward.

I argue that the German model of administrative law and policy should not be used uncritically as a template in the design of modern administrative practices, at least in those substantive areas where expertise and administrative discretion are required. The construction of systems of administrative law is of relevance as the newly democratic states of Eastern Europe seek to redesign their political systems and look to the West for models. I hope to demonstrate that in the concrete case of environmental policy, the German legal framework is inadequate and needs reform.[10] The strains on the German legal system in the environmental area are not the fault of unreasonable "green" activists or recalcitrant individual bureaucrats. The problems are grounded in German concepts relating the citizen and the state. Public policy is justified either as the result of lawmaking by the popularly elected coalition of governing parties or as a bargain crafted through negotiation of the affected interests.[11] Neither route to democratic legitimacy provides sufficient public accountability.

The American solution, of course, has its own problems, but the American judiciary, at least, recognizes the nature of the underlying difficulties. Judges and lawyers have accepted the policy-making role of regulatory agencies.[12] Unless set back by an overly literal-minded Supreme Court, the American model, though imperfect, can provide guidance even to new states that settle on a parliamentary form of government.[13] Bureaucratic policy-making is the inevitable consequence of the complex problems that face the modern state. It cannot be displaced onto the legislature or the judiciary, but it needs to be monitored both by these formal organs of state power and by ordinary citizens.[14] Although criticism of the American regulatory process is fashionable, it is a useful model for German reformers in its self-conscious recognition of policy-making as a legitimate bureaucratic activity.[15]

At the same time, a study of German administrative law provides an instructive lesson for America. Led by Justice Antonin Scalia, the Supreme Court has moved in the direction of German orthodoxy—away from monitoring the legitimacy of regulatory processes and toward an exclusive concentration on individual rights violations in concrete situations.[16] The German case serves as a warning against further movement in that direction. If German administrative law is inadequate in a parliamentary system, it would be even more problematic if extended to the American system with its frequent conflicts between the executive and legislative branches. American legal scholars who find regulatory rulemaking processes overly cumbersome and who criticize the intrusiveness of judicial review should test their conclusions against the German solution.

The first three chapters establish the context. I begin by comparing the basic structures of democratic government in the United States and Germany. The next chapter develops the policy-analytic justification for environmental protection programs and reviews the substantive law in Germany and the United States. Based on an economic analysis of environmental policy, I emphasize the similar pathologies of the substantive law in both countries. Finally, I introduce the political economy of regulatory federalism and show how both Germany and the United States fall short.

With this background, the next section describes German administrative law and its link to environmental policy-making. I explain how the German administrative process has adapted to the tension between its legal-bureaucratic traditions and the realities of modern technocratic policy-making. The limited role of the judiciary in reviewing executive policy-making is outlined, followed by a review of planning and licensing processes. These processes, which are similar to American procedures, show that German law has recognized the value of notice, hearings, and explanation in a subset of administrative procedures. These procedures are limited to a narrow range of projects mostly at the state and local levels. They could, however, guide reform of German administrative procedures at higher levels of the policy process.

In the concluding chapters I review existing reform efforts and propose some of my own. I summarize the most salient reforms under discussion in Germany and argue that they do not provide a fundamental solution to the weaknesses of administrative law. Next, I explore the role of the European Union in forcing Germany to confront some of the features of its public law system most in need of rethinking. The book concludes with proposals for reform of German administrative law and with lessons that the German case provides for America.

PART I THE CONTEXT

1

DEMOCRATIC GOVERNMENT
AND POLICY IMPLEMENTATION

Modern democratic states have sought to reconcile public account-ability and bureaucratic expertise in two different ways. At the most general level we can label these alternatives "presidential" and "parliamentary." Each has many variants, but given my interests, I focus on the American and German versions. My emphasis is on present political structures, not history or political culture. Of course, cultural differences could overwhelm institutional ones, and historical studies can help explain why the American and German governments are organized as they are.[1] Nevertheless, although historical and cultural forces may help explain intercountry differences in policy-making structures, they cannot be used to justify them. Institutions are malleable, and political structures are not inevitably determined by past events; reform of both the German and the American systems is possible in the light of substantive realities.

Germany and the United States have different concepts of democracy. Nevertheless, they face remarkably similar challenges in the administration of environmental policy. Legislatures in both countries have incentives to support environmental statutes that delegate policy-making authority to the executive. The complex, highly technical nature of environmental problems deters legislators from resolving all issues in the text of statutes. Wide areas of policy space are left to be filled in by public administrators.

The two countries differ sharply, however, in the types of constraints they impose on high-level bureaucrats. The German parliamentary system, with the same party coalition controlling both the executive and the legislature, creates few incentives for legislative oversight of the bureaucracy. The political structure gives the legislature no imperative to assign review responsibility to the courts. The American presidential system, in contrast, gives the legislature an incentive to monitor the bureaucracy or, if that is not possible, to create procedural constraints and to co-opt other institutions, such as the courts, into providing oversight.[2]

GERMANY

The public law system in the Federal Republic of Germany has five elements: a parliamentary system with strong political parties; a federalized administrative structure; a professional bureaucracy; reliance on the technical expertise of private groups; and strong protections for individual rights, enforced by the courts.

POLITICAL CONTROL OF THE EXECUTIVE

The Bundestag, or lower house, is directly elected. Party discipline, though not absolute, is strong. The governing coalition controls both the Bundestag and the executive.[3] Subject to substantive constitutional checks,[4] the "public interest" is whatever has been decided by the elected representatives.[5] Statutes should resolve the basic political and policy trade-offs.[6] Individuals who do not like these policies should focus on political action to change the governing coalition at either the federal or the Land level.

One way to do this is to found a new party. The proportional representation system facilitated the development of an active Green party, which has been represented in the Bundestag since the early eighties and has been included in several state coalition governments.[7] Since the Greens have never been part of the governing coalition at the federal level, their influence on policy has been indirect.[8] Nevertheless, the party's parliamentary base gives it the opportunity to raise environmental (and other) issues and to pressure the major parties. As its leaders have entered federal and Länder parliaments and become state cabinet ministers, the Green party has gained a measure of respectability and is an important force in publicizing and investigating environmental hazards.[9]

Federal laws, regulations, and administrative guidelines that are to be implemented by the Länder must receive the consent of the Bundesrat, or upper house.[10] The Bundesrat is not directly elected. Its members are state ministers with representation roughly in proportion to population.[11] The Bundesrat's veto power is a function of the Länder's central role in policy implementation.[12] In most areas of regulatory policy, the Federal Republic lacks direct enforcement authority, cannot threaten to take over the enforcement process, and has no regional offices. State and federal bureaucrats have similar status and pay scales. Financial support for the Länder mostly takes the form of revenue sharing and earmarked taxes.[13]

In spite of its indirect influence over enforcement, the federal bureaucracy issues numerous regulations and administrative guidelines. High-level administrative processes are, however, not subject to legally enforceable procedural constraints. The German Administrative Procedures Act (Verwaltungsverfahrensgesetz—VwVfG) does not apply to the policy-making activities of the federal ministries.

A superficial view would suggest that formal legal controls on bureaucratic policy-making are unnecessary in the German system because the parliament and the executive are controlled by the same party coalition and because the interests of the states are protected by the Bundesrat. Owing to strong party discipline and the generally similar interests of the governing parties, coherent, consistent legislation can be produced to resolve the major policy trade-offs. Any tendency for bureaucratic policy independence can be checked by the governing coalition acting through the cabinet or, if that fails, through the Bundestag and its standing committees.[14] The close connection between the executive and legislative branches permits the governing coalition to monitor bureaucratic activities without the need for judicial interference. Federal ministries are led by members of the coalition, and an individual ministry cannot stray too far from the wishes of the Bundestag majority.

Under this simple parliamentary model, a public official's job is technical and administrative, not political. Bureaucrats at all levels are impartial, professional servants of the state.[15] The ideal bureaucrat is not engaging in policy analysis with all its implications of trading off costs and benefits in a fair and efficient manner. Implementation is not meant to be creative. It involves following the orders of both federal and state political bodies.[16]

The reality is quite different—at least for environmental policy. Statutes do not always represent a clear and coherent response to a policy problem. Especially in highly technical areas, the federal bureaucracy drafts the statutes that it will then help implement.[17] The Chemicals Act of 1980 was drafted in secret by the federal ministries and established interest groups. Consumer and environmental groups had no role in its drafting. Within the Bundestag only the animal protection lobby was strong enough to change the draft to remove express endorsement of animal testing.[18] Similarly, when the Atomic Power Act was amended in 1976, the end result followed the draft proposed by the executive branch. The Bundestag was subject to pressure from both citizens' groups and industry; such pressure was ineffective, at least in part, because most legislators lacked the technical background to evaluate the text.[19] The political salience of environmental problems has enhanced the importance of the Bundestag in recent years, but the executive branch will remain dominant in technical areas as long as the Parliament lacks staff and expertise.[20]

POLICY IMPLEMENTATION

Environmental statutes are not precise policy-making documents; they are full of vague and undefined terms that must be interpreted before the acts can be implemented.[21] To avoid inconsistent state implementation and to head off interstate competition, the federal ministries must establish policies under the law. These may take the form of technical standards, but they in fact represent a mixture of technical and policy considerations. The old ideal of the impartial official no longer accurately describes reality. Many officials view their role in political and policy-making terms.[22] In order to fulfill these dual roles, however, the bureaucracy needs both social science expertise and open and accountable processes. Both are lacking.

Policy analysis is not well developed in Germany. Economists play a limited role in analyzing regulatory problems outside of explicitly "economic" areas, such as macroeconomic policy. Although cost-benefit analyses are frequently used in the assessment of individual projects, such as the construction of highways, rail lines, or canals, analyses are uncommon when the government issues regulations or administrative guidelines.[23]

In the Environmental Ministry, even though the minister is an economist, economists are all but invisible, and the ministry's technical advisory body (Umweltbundesamt) consists largely of scientists and engineers.[24] Nevertheless, the Ministry did recently sponsor an effort to assess environmental damages. The studies provide monetary estimates of the harm caused by a variety of pollution problems and attempt to measure Germans' willingness to pay to avoid environmental harm.[25] The studies demonstrate the feasibility of estimating damages, but they are not true cost-benefit analyses. They include no estimates of the marginal costs and marginal benefits of alternative levels of control. These studies are a useful first step, but they do not demonstrate that policy analysis is affecting policy-making. Even the complementary cost-benefit analyses performed by the Institute for Economic and Social Affairs in Bonn were mostly retrospective studies.[26] Nevertheless, these efforts at least indicate that some German scholars use the technique and that officials in the Environmental Ministry recognize its value.

On the procedural level, administrative law has not kept pace with the growing technical and political complexity of regulatory problems. The government's parliamentary structure gives the Bundestag majority little incentive to require the federal bureaucracy to accommodate outside groups or submit to judicial review. The formal law conceives of the bureaucracy's job as essentially administrative. Under this view, there is no need to give the public any general right of access to executive branch officials or to the information they possess.[27] Individuals have no general legal right to obtain information held by the government unless it directly relates to a suspected violation of their rights in the context of an administrative proceeding.[28]

In practice, organized groups play a key role in developing environmental policy. But the process of consultation is under the control of the ministry and does not give outsiders any legally enforceable claim to be heard. The government routinely consults advisory committees of experts and representatives of interest groups. A model of policy-making, in which decisions are made by consensus after closed-door negotiations, is especially prominent in the field of labor-management relations.[29] It extends beyond the negotiation of wage contracts to the setting of some types of health and safety standards.[30] In environmental policy-making, such processes are used in the development of technical standards. Environmental groups are generally consulted, but they are not part of the formal process. As a consequence, the Green party and environmental groups have challenged this method of policy-making, especially in the highly sensitive field of nuclear power.[31]

The role of public interest groups is ill defined. They have no right to intervene in bureaucratic processes or to challenge the outcome in court. They may proffer opinions, or even be formally consulted, but giving them legal rights to participate is viewed by some as undemocratic, because it would run the risk of undermining the legitimate choices of the political authorities.[32] Formal organizations (*Verbände*) as well as informal citizens' initiatives (*Bürgerinitiativen*) have the legal right to participate in certain planning and licensing processes. These proceedings are not, however, general policy-making exercises; they involve implementation of statutes only in particular, geographically limited cases.[33]

Germany has many private groups, but few have the technical capacity to mount a challenge to the conventional policy-making and standard-setting process.[34] Most are poorly staffed and funded. No organizations resemble the Environmental Defense Fund and the National Resources Defense Council in their ability to invest millions of dollars per year intervening in administrative processes and bringing lawsuits.[35]

Even the well-respected Öko-Institut, founded in 1977 to provide scientifically valid information for those opposing nuclear power, is a small organization. In 1989 it had only fifteen full-time and twenty-eight part-time employees working with a budget of DM 3.2 million (just under two million dollars).[36] Only the Green party, Greenpeace, and the World Wildlife Fund have sizable budgets and staff.[37] Some groups can call on a substantial number of volunteers, and they sometimes perform important monitoring and educational functions.[38] Nevertheless, their role in the administrative process is limited by their relative lack of resources and professionalism. Well-funded and technically competent private groups might arise if the administrative law system were changed to give them a more important function. The limited role of private charity in Germany, however, imposes a constraint. Instead, the state funds some environmental organizations directly, a practice that may limit their ability to act independently.[39]

Strong private environmental groups would be unnecessary if the Green party could provide a viable substitute. Under modern policy-making conditions, however, political party organization is not sufficient. Many environmental issues are resistant to the influence of small opposition parties because many technically complex policy decisions are made in administrative proceedings, rather than in the legislature. Opposition political parties have no formal influence over such decisions. Green activists can point to their role in the early eighties in helping generate popular support for a tough regulation that reduced sulfur dioxide emissions.[40] Such dramatic successes are few, however. Environmentalists' concentration on Green party affairs may have weakened the incorporation of environmental values into high-level bureaucratic policy-making.[41]

JUDICIAL REVIEW

The Bundestag majority has no incentive to permit the courts to review bureaucratic policy-making. An independent judiciary could make decisions that might be embarrassing to the governing coalition. Even limited review of bureaucratic procedures will have little appeal in a parliamentary system. Neither the cabinet nor the Bundestag majority can be expected to support judicially enforceable constraints on the policy-making process. Even in highly technical areas where Bundestag influence is attenuated, independent judicial review could have negative political consequences.

These political imperatives leave the courts with a narrow role in administrative law. Conventional legal doctrine supports the political dynamic outlined above. Operating under the assumption that the bureaucracy's policy-making activities are overseen by political actors, German law views the judiciary's task as preventing the state from running roughshod over individuals in its effort to pursue broad public goals. In reaction against the National Socialist period, German constitutional law facilitates individual complaints against the state at all levels.[42] It also gives juridical persons—for example, corporations, local governments, and labor unions—a status similar to that of individuals.[43]

Conventional public law permits third parties to challenge executive branch policies in court only if the individual's "subjective rights" have been violated.[44] Thus the same reasoning that deprives individuals and groups of the right to participate in forming general regulations and legal guidelines also excludes them from making direct legal challenges to these regulations in court. Judges are concerned that a more liberal standing policy would present them with highly political cases.[45] German courts refuse to hear general challenges to the competence of the bureaucracy. The private rights of action common in American law are lacking in Germany. People can defend their individual rights but cannot act as private attorneys general to help enforce the law.

Germany has a separate system of administrative courts with three layers that culminate in a Federal Administrative Court in Berlin.[46] Although the administrative courts mainly decide cases based on the violation of individual rights, individuals can also file so-called Normenkontrollverfahren challenging the legality of Land ordinances. However, such actions are only possible if the individual has suffered or expects to suffer harm from the implementation process. They are not designed to permit direct oversight of procedures. Further, German law does not permit similar actions by individuals challenging the legality of federal or state laws or of federal regulations and guidelines.[47] The

administrative court system is not meant to be "a super watchman over the activities of the administration to keep it within the law." Instead, the courts are to
be "the protectors and defenders of the rights of an individual against . . .
administrative excesses."[48] The individual is protected from the state but is not
encouraged to participate in policy-making except as a voter or as a participant
in a local planning or licensing process.[49]

The judicial inability to deal with the political and policy-making nature of
public administration and scientific expertise is highlighted when an administrative issue does get into court. The lower German administrative courts
have the authority to examine both law and facts and to carry out their own
investigation of the administrative action over and above the material presented
by the parties to the suit.[50] Although the judges cannot go into the expediency
of administrative actions, they can replace an illegal administrative determina-
tion with one of their own.[51] They can both void a decision that infringes on
individual rights and oblige the administration to act to preserve a right.[52] When
the challenged decision is within the normal discretion of the administrative
agency, the courts will not make the substantive decision themselves but will
return the issue to the agency with instructions to follow the law.[53] Lawsuits are
generally attempts to vindicate substantive rights and seldom directly challenge
the procedures used by executive agencies.

The lack of procedural standards for judging the policy-making process
discourages courts from hearing cases that would involve them in controversies.
If they did take such cases, they would have no way to restrict their inquiry to
the legitimacy of the procedures. Nevertheless, one should not suppose that
German courts have an easier way of distinguishing law from policy than do
their American counterparts. When German courts try to define such "legal"
concepts as "reliability" or "public interest," they face the same vexing questions of separating law from policy as do American courts.[54]

THE UNITED STATES

The most important structural features of the American system for
my purposes are the separation of powers, judicial oversight of the bureaucracy,
and federalism. The bureaucracy combines professionalism and political accountability and is relatively open to citizen and interest group influence. I
discuss the relations between Congress, the federal bureaucracy, the courts, and
outside groups in this chapter. The impact of federalism is the topic of chapter 3.

SEPARATION OF POWERS AND
CONTROL OF THE EXECUTIVE

Because the chief executive is elected by the citizens, he has a direct
relationship with the public rather than one mediated through the legislative
majority. As a consequence, the president and Congress are often at odds on

particular policy issues. Even when both are of the same party, legislative influence on the bureaucracy is not assured by the government structure. Divided government further exacerbates the problem of legislative control.

Congress has little incentive to pass coherent statutes. The weakness of political parties, the multiplication of subcommittees, and the large size of members' staffs give individual members of Congress independent operating room. Many disparate individuals and groups seek to contribute to legislative initiatives, and there are few institutional mechanisms that promote an organized, logical drafting process. Even when one party controls both the House and the Senate, the prospects for coherent, consistent legislation are dim. Laws are likely to require interpretation by the executive and the judiciary before they can be implemented. Such laws may, like the Clean Air Act, be very detailed and full of precise requirements and timetables. Taken as a whole, however, a statute is unlikely to provide a consistent solution to a policy problem.[55] Even the long and detailed regulatory statutes typical of the environmental field have left considerable policy-making work for the administration.[56]

Although the Supreme Court has asserted that Congress must make clear the basic aims of statutes, it has not seriously constrained the delegation of policy-making to federal and state agencies. Administrative decisions can involve political as well as technical considerations.[57] Agencies must be impartial in deciding cases involving particular individuals or firms, but subject to statutory constraints, the president's political program can be influential in defining policy.[58]

The American structure of government produces unclear and inconsistent statutes, but it also gives Congress an incentive to control bureaucratic efforts to implement policy under these statutes. Legislators seek accountable executive branch processes so that they will know what is happening and can try to influence the outcome. Direct oversight is a major focus of congressional activity.[59] This is not sufficient, however, when the issue is technically complex and the situation fast changing. In such cases Congress establishes bureaucratic procedures and then enlists the help of other oversight institutions and groups —from private environmental groups to the federal courts.

Congress regulates executive procedures by making them accountable and open to outside, nongovernmental groups. The Administrative Procedures Act (APA) outlines the procedures agencies must use when issuing regulations with the force of law and when adjudicating individual cases.[60] Regulations do not have legal force unless these procedures are followed, and many substantive regulatory statutes include additional requirements. Neither purely judicial nor purely legislative procedures are appropriate for policy-making within agencies. Courtroom procedures are inappropriate for assessing technocratic evidence in a bureaucratic context, and the legislative model ignores the need for coherent justifications of decisions. In an attempt to find a middle ground, APA informal rule-making processes require notice, an opportunity for interested parties and groups to comment, and a reasoned opinion accompanying the decision. Notice must appear in the Federal Register and must include a proposed rule and a statement of the "time, place, and nature" of public rule-making proceedings. Although under the APA the agency need not have a public oral hearing, such hearings are usually held for important issues and are required by many environmental statutes. Written material must be accepted from any interested person. As a consequence, industry associations, labor unions, and environmental groups all have access to the bureaucracy.[61] Rules must be accompanied by "a concise general statement of their basis and purpose." The Freedom of Information Act gives outsiders access to much of the information held by the government. This legal right provides important advantages for those wishing to participate in agency procedures or to challenge an outcome in court.[62]

However actively outsiders participate, the ultimate decision is in the hands of the executive branch. Organized groups and individuals can present data and opinions, but they have no decision-making authority.[63] In recent efforts to encourage regulatory negotiation, regulatory negotiation is seen as a supplement to, not substitute for, informal rulemaking.[64]

JUDICIAL REVIEW

Judicial review supplements direct congressional oversight. If Congress has not articulated clearly what it wants the executive to do, it may not wish to carry the entire burden of oversight itself. Rather, it often enlists the help of the courts. Congress permits the judiciary to review agency decisions for conformity with substantive statutes under an "arbitrary and capricious" standard and to oversee the adequacy of agency procedures.[65] In some cases the courts are instructed to employ a "substantial evidence" test, which permits more careful judicial consideration of the evidence.[66] American law does not generally permit de novo review.[67]

Independent oversight by the courts has few political costs for members of Congress. Unlike the German system, where legislature and regime are closely linked, critical assessments of bureaucratic policy-making and adverse court decisions produce little political fallout for America's independent legislators. Even those in the president's party are unlikely to suffer and may even benefit by using adverse judgments as springboards for their own oversight activities.

American law provides pre-enforcement review of regulations and permits suits by private organizations that will be affected by the result.[68] Claimed violations of individual rights are not central to the review of rulemaking. The courts' primary goals are to assure conformity with the statutory language and to be sure that proper procedures were followed. If a breach occurred, judges do not make the substantive policy decision themselves. They return the issue to the agency so that it can make a legally acceptable choice. Despite this show of restraint, courts have in fact influenced the way agencies operate. Even in recent years, when the Supreme Court has taken a conservative turn, the justices have required the good faith observance of administrative procedures.[69] This kind of judicial review contrasts sharply with the German case, where pre-enforcement review is unavailable and federal government policy-making procedures are generally not subject to judicial review. The U.S. Congress has played a central role in mandating this strong role for the courts. In the absence of constitutional language, the basic structure of American government gives the legislative branch an incentive to pass statutes giving the courts a key oversight role.

Individuals and groups are important players in court challenges. Congress has responded to its own relative impotence by giving outsiders access not only to the bureaucracy but also to the courts. Most environmental statutes include provisions for citizen suits, permitting private plaintiffs to sue either dischargers or the administrator of the Environmental Protection Agency to require compliance with the law.[70] Public interest groups count as "citizens" under such statutes. In enforcing the Federal Water Pollution Control Act, suits against dischargers who violate their permits are a staple of public interest law firms. The statute facilitates such suits by requiring the regulated firms to supply data on their discharges and by mandating that defendants pay the legal fees of successful plaintiffs.[71]

Current trends, however, suggest that the law is changing. Recent Supreme Court decisions seek to redefine administrative law along German lines, as a way to protect individual rights, rather than a method of bureaucratic control.[72] According to one author, these decisions represent a return "to an older private rights model of standing, which concentrates on the individualistic sphere rather than public law."[73] This is an unfortunate development.[74]

DELEGATION TO THE EXECUTIVE IN
GERMANY AND THE UNITED STATES

American reformers seek to improve the methods by which executive branch behavior is monitored and constrained. Some criticize the use of circulars and guidelines that circumvent the rulemaking process while others argue against unrealistic deadlines in statutes. Critics debate the proper timing and scope of judicial review and argue about the role of citizens' groups and public interest organizations in the administrative process and the courts. This debate, however, occurs within the framework of statutory procedural requirements and a history of judicial review. Political scientists point to Congress's lack of incentives to design optimal oversight structures but do not deny that the legislature has an incentive to provide some kind of administrative control.

The remarkable fact about the German system is that with a government structure different from that of the United States, it too has produced a set of environmental laws giving broad discretion to the federal executive and to the state governments that implement the law. German statutes do not appear to suffer from obvious internal inconsistencies, but they are vaguely and imprecisely worded, requiring policy-making by the administration. The substantive statutes impose few controls on high-level executive branch procedures and do not permit judicial review of administrative procedures and statutory interpretations. The procedural requirements that do exist cannot give rise to court challenges. Parliamentary oversight, though not unknown, is also less vigorous than in the American system precisely because of the strength of party ties. Only the opposition has a strong incentive to provide monitoring, and it has limited ability to do so.

The high levels of delegation in Germany and the United States are determined by the nature of environmental problems themselves. Although the details of the laws in each country can be explained by differing political coalitions and legal traditions, the basic fact of delegation comes from the highly technical nature of many environmental problems. Busy, untrained legislators are simply unable to write detailed laws that absolve bureaucrats of policy-making responsibility. Even if politicians could do so by improving their staff capabilities, such precision would be unwise given the fast-changing nature of the scientific and technical bases of policy. If one accepts this proposition, then the German democratic model fails in this instance to provide responsible government. The nature of the issue produces, and should produce, laws with substantial policy-making delegated to the executive. The German political system is not well equipped to deal with the consequences of this delegation. The American system produces poorly drafted statutes, but it does give legislators an incentive to establish accountable administrative procedures and involve the courts in oversight. These incentives are lacking in the German system. Nevertheless, the problem of legitimating and monitoring administrative discretion remains. Students of German politics and law should confront the weaknesses of the German administrative system head on. Comparative lawyers should take no comfort from the seeming "convergence" of German administrative law and the jurisprudence of America's Supreme Court. Such a convergence would imply an abdication of a judicial role that is of more, not less, importance in the modern, technocratic world.

2

PUBLIC POLICY ANALYSIS AND
THE PATHOLOGIES OF POLITICS

Relative to most other countries, the United States and Germany
have strong and reasonably comprehensive environmental statutes. Although
reunification has created special problems, Germany is an environmental leader
within the European Union.[1] American laws have had a measurable impact on
the environment[2] and are frequently used as models for reform proposals in the
European Union and the new states of eastern Europe. Many of Germany's
statutes, enacted during the seventies, were influenced by legislative activity in
the United States.[3]

Nevertheless, policy in Germany and the United States suffers from similar
weaknesses. The laws of both countries focus on fairness and feasibility, not on
the relation between means and ends. The harm to people and to the environment that generated public support is frequently forgotten when detailed statutory provisions and regulations are written.

EXTERNALITIES: AIR AND WATER POLLUTION

Externalities justify a government role in environmental policy. In
the absence of public controls, individuals and organizations use certain resources, such as air and water, as if they were free, when in fact they are scarce.
One person's use can interfere with others' enjoyment. Even when a resource,
such as open space, is priced in the market, that price may not take into account
all the benefits and costs of competing uses.[4]

Two simple examples will help illustrate the concept of externalities. The
first is sooty factory smoke that prevents a nearby laundry from drying its sheets
in the open air. The second is untreated industrial wastewater that interferes
with a downstream brewery's production process. The most straightforward
response to externalities of this type is to put prices on scarce environmental
resources. If the prices reflect the marginal social costs of air and water use, the
producers of soot and dirty water would efficiently incorporate these costs into
their production decisions. Just as firms use different ratios of capital to labor

18

depending on the relative value of these inputs compared to their relative costs, so too would firms select different levels of pollution depending on the relative costs of cleanup.

A pricing system is based on two premises. First, polluters have no property right to use air and water without cost. If they did have such a right, a reverse system—in which polluters are paid to reduce discharges rather than fined to clean them up—would be required. Such a system would obviously have very different distributive consequences, but it could also be designed to produce efficient results. However the property rights are distributed, price or subsidy systems can give dischargers the correct marginal incentives to reduce pollution.

Second, policymakers must be able to estimate the net social costs of pollution. Most environmental problems are not as straightforward as the dirty laundry and contaminated beer examples. Complex biological and chemical processes, occurring over time and space, intervene between the production of pollution and the harm it causes. Uncertainties of scientific knowledge and randomness in the world complicate the assessment of costs and benefits. Multiple causes produce single effects, and single causes produce multiple effects. Solving one environmental problem may create another. Sulfur dioxide can be reduced, for example, by shifting from coal-fired power plants to nuclear energy. But nuclear energy generates another set of safety and health concerns. Furthermore, much of the harm caused by environmental pollution is difficult to quantify in physical terms and even more difficult to translate into dollar values. For example, if policymakers wish to incorporate the harm to wild animals and plants, a measure of humans' willingness to pay will not be sufficient.[5]

These measurement problems suggest that it will frequently be impossible to set a price on pollution that reflects a confident assessment of its social costs. The practical difficulties of calculation do not, however, imply that one should abandon the attempt to link means and ends. Even if the data are weak, we do have considerable technical knowledge about the link between air and water pollution discharges at one location and subsequent air and water quality at another.[6] Research exists on the health risks of various levels and types of air pollution.[7] Ecological damage from air and water pollution has been studied, and this knowledge should guide policy.

What is left of means/end rationality in complex cases where data are imperfect and a simple pricing system is infeasible? Policymakers, using whatever information is at their disposal, may be able to establish rough tolerances for pollutant concentrations in the ambient air and water. They might specify a level of dissolved oxygen in a river sufficient to permit fish life or set an air quality standard that keeps respiratory diseases below a certain level.[8] These decisions are political/policy choices guided by technical considerations. Given models that link discharges to air and water quality, the remaining problem is the distribution of pollution loads across dischargers. A basic lesson of decades of economic analyses is that uniform controls are almost always inefficient. Even policies that aim for uniform air or water quality do not imply uniform controls on firms even within the same industry. Firms differ because of their geographical location and the age and quality of their plants and equipment. A power plant in the west has a different impact on the environment than one on the East Coast because of the long-range transport of pollutants. A fifty-year-old oil refinery will face higher cleanup costs than a brand new one. Furthermore, a firm's costs are much more easily gauged by its managers than by outside bureaucrats, who may receive biased information.

Rather than issue uniform standards, the public authority should auction off pollution licenses, which would be designed to meet the ambient air or water quality goal. Dischargers would bid for the licenses. As time passes, and economic conditions change, dischargers would trade licenses among themselves. If the location of the discharge affects its environmental impact, transfer prices could be set to reflect the impact of geography. Thus if a river faced oxygen depletion in one critical region, the licensing scheme could take account of that fact. For example, the right to discharge 10 pounds of waste upstream of the region could cost the same as the right to discharge 40 pounds where the river is under less stress.[9]

Tradable licenses have two basic features. First, the regulatory instrument is calibrated in units of pollution discharged. Dischargers can decide on the method of control—end-of-pipe treatment, process change, or output reduction. Second, the state determines the overall level of discharge for an entire air shed or river basin. The pollution reduction required of any particular discharger is not set by the state. Both features contribute to efficiency.

Command-and-control regulation that specifies the required technology lacks both of these features. But all claims to reasonable policy-making need not be abandoned, even in situations where a trading system is unworkable. An intermediate solution exists. Instead of specifying which techniques must be used, the state can limit itself to issuing discharge permits. Government and private research groups could advise companies about the range of technical possibilities, but the firms would make the ultimate choice.

THE DIFFICULTY OF COMPARING RESULTS

The most difficult part of comparative research is relating structural differences to outcomes. Even documenting the differences in environmental quality between Germany and the United States is a complex exercise. Putting regulatory standards on a single comparable scale is similarly problematic. Linking the stringency of national standards with the quality of the environment is a vexing task, especially in Germany, which must deal with other

TABLE 2.1a   Trends in Emissions of Air Pollutants: United States, 1970–1988, Selected Years (1975 = 100)

Year	Sulfur Dioxide	Nitrogen Oxides	Total Suspended Particulates	Carbon Monoxide	Hydrocarbons	Carbon Dioxide
1970	110	95	175	120	119	97*
1975	100	100	100	100	100	100
1980	90	106	80	95	101	111
1985	81	103	67	83	91	107
1988	80	103	65	77	84	115

Source: Data from Organization for Economic Cooperation and Development, 1991a.
*1971 data.

TABLE 2.1b   Trends in Emissions of Air Pollutants: Germany, 1970–1988, Selected Years (1975 = 100)

Year	Sulfur Dioxide	Nitrogen Oxides	Total Suspended Particulates	Carbon Monoxide	Hydrocarbons	Carbon Dioxide
1970	112	93	182	104	103	104*
1975	100	100	100	100	100	100
1980	96	116	81	86	98	109
1985	72	115	62	64	93	104
1988	37	111	50	63	93	103

Source: See table 2.1a.
*1971 data.

countries' pollutants as well as its own. Finally, relating administrative and political reform to improvements in environmental quality is not possible given existing information.[10]

Air pollution, an area where relatively good data exist, illustrates the difficulties of comparing results. Tables 2.1a and 2.1b show trends in emissions of six major air pollutants in the United States and Germany. For four of the six, emission levels decreased faster in Germany than in the United States. The most striking difference is in the discharge of sulfur dioxide. In Germany the level in 1988 was 37 percent of the level in 1975, but in the United States the level in 1988 was 80 percent of the level in 1975. Table 2.2 compares emissions of sulfur dioxide (SO_2) and nitrogen oxides (NO_x) in 1988 for Germany and the United States. In 1988 sulfur and nitrogen oxide emissions per capita in western Germany were considerably below those in the United States. One can change the relative ranking of Germany and the United States, however, by changing the basis of comparison—the United States discharged less per square kilometer than the Federal Republic did.[11] Once one recognizes that the population

TABLE 2.2   Emission Levels of Sulphur Dioxide and Nitrogen Oxides, 1988

| | Reference Data | | | SO_2 Emission Levels | | | NO_x Emission Levels | | |
| | Population | Fossil Fuel Use | | | | | | | |
Country	millions	(1)	(2)	(3)	(4)	(5)	(3)	(4)	(5)
FRG	62*	9,364	151	1,250	133	20	2,850	304	46
GDR	16*	3,733	228	5,250	1,406	320	670	179	41
USA	247	69,145	280	20,700	299	84	19,800	286	80

Source: Adapted from Umweltbundesamt, 1992b:258–259. The German sulfur dioxide and nitrogen oxide emissions data are from *Strategies and Policies for Air Pollution Abatement: 1990 Major Review,* UN Publ. No. E.91.II.E.29 (ECE/EB.AIR/27). The United States data are from Organization for Economic Cooperation and Development 1991. The OECD publication reports slightly different figures for the FRG: 1,237 kilotons per annum of sulfur dioxide and 2,859 of nitrogen dioxide.
Note: 1 = quadrillion joules per annum
          2 = billion joules per annum per capita
          3 = kilotons per annum
          4 = kilograms per trillion joules per annum
          5 = kilograms per annum per capita
*1989 data.

density of the United States is about 14 percent of the population density of Germany, the United States' advantage seems even higher.[12] But neither summary discharge measure is especially revealing; better would be a frequency function of per capita exposures for each country recording the proportion of the population exposed to different levels of ambient air quality. Per capita numbers are misleading because if people live densely, they all breathe the same air. Air quality is not improved if the population of a city increases by a million people, a change which would lead to a sharp drop in emissions per capita.

The comparisons are also skewed by the timing of policy initiatives. In 1983 Germany introduced a major regulation that reduced sulfur dioxide emissions from power plants and other large sources. The United States acted only in 1990. Full implementation will reduce the intercountry differences. If the population of the United States does not change, annual per capita discharges would be 36.2 kg by the year 2000.[13]

The control of emissions is not the ultimate goal, however.[14] One needs to calculate the relation between discharges and ambient air quality and then estimate the resulting environmental damage. Making such links is difficult. The ambient concentrations in the United States of the six major air pollutants are presented in tables 2.3a and 2.3b.[15] With a few exceptions, especially for ozone in the late 1980s, all show a steady downward trend. Figure 2.1 demonstrates a similar result for western Germany. The figure lacks trend data for ozone, which has only recently become a concern of German policymakers.[16] The main intercountry differences are for suspended particulates and possibly sulfur dioxide.[17]

Concentrations of sulfur dioxide in western Germany have not declined as much as emissions because of heavy discharges from eastern Germany and neighboring countries. In 1989 western Germany produced 360.7 kt of atmospheric sulfur. It exported an estimated 190.2 kt and imported 374 kt. Subtracting the exports and adding the imports yields 544.5 kt of atmospheric sulfur in western Germany. If these numbers are representative, every kiloton of discharge reduction within the western Länder produces only a .47 kt reduction in that region. (The ratio between exports and domestic production of sulfur pollutants is 190.2/360.7=.53.) A similar pattern holds for nitrogen oxides.[18] Given the importance of long-range transport in producing acid rain, Germany's efforts to reduce emissions in the western states will not benefit its citizens very much.

Both Germany and the United States have standards for ambient air quality and for emissions. The ambient standards listed in table 2.4 have a different status in each country. In the United States they are part of legally binding State Implementation Plans (SIPs). In western Germany they have less practical relevance since ambient standards are usually met as a by-product of the country's emission standards.[19] The emissions standards listed in table 2.5 show that Germany had stronger requirements for dischargers than did the United States before the passage of the American Clean Air Act Amendments of 1990.[20]

The links between emission levels and legal requirements and between emissions and air quality are difficult to measure. In spite of improvements in environmental quality, the marginal impact of German and American laws cannot be measured precisely. Nevertheless, examination of the statutes in both countries demonstrates that they suffer from similar structural failures.

POLICY FAILURES

Environmental policy is presumably motivated by a desire to improve the quality of life for humans and to save endangered ecosystems. Sometimes, however, these fundamental goals are forgotten in the process of drafting statutes. Laws that politicians claim are groundbreaking attempts to deal with pressing environmental problems contain deeply entrenched irrationalities. The pathologies of program design are remarkably similar in Germany and the United States. Both countries' statutes suffer from excessive uniformity and the wrong kind of variability.

UNIFORMITY

The hallmark of many pollution problems is variability, but political pressures frequently produce calls for uniform treatment of industries in different parts of the country. Many people argue that it is unfair for industrial competitors to face different standards. The "level playing field" is frequently invoked even though pollution discharges should be valued differently if they have differing impacts on the world. The effect of pollution on the natural world

TABLE 2.3a   Ambient Concentrations of Criteria Air Pollutants in the United States, 1975–1988

Year	Sulfur Dioxide (ppm)	Carbon Monoxide (ppm)	Ozone (ppm)	Nitrogen Dioxide (ppm)	Total Suspended Particulates (μg/m³)	Lead (mg/m³)
1975	0.0154	11.96	0.153	0.029	61.9	1.04
1976	0.0156	11.32	0.153	0.029	62.8	1.05
1977	0.0138	10.66	0.155	0.029	62.9	1.16
1978	0.0126	10.07	0.156	0.029	62.4	1.04
1979	0.0120	9.07	0.134	0.026	63.1	0.77
1980	0.0109	8.52	0.136	0.025	64.2	0.61
1981	0.0104	8.25	0.127	0.025	60.3	0.48
1982	0.0096	7.86	0.125	0.024	50.1	0.49
1983	0.0092	7.77	0.137	0.024	49.7	0.39
1984	0.0094	7.72	0.124	0.024	51.2	0.35
1985	0.0088	7.03	0.123	0.024	48.8	0.23
1986	0.0085	7.00	0.118	0.024	48.6	0.13
1987	0.0083	6.64	0.125	0.024	49.7	0.10
1988	0.0084	6.56	0.136	0.024	50.5	0.08

Source: U.S. Council of Environmental Quality 1991, table 40.

Notes: ppm = parts per million

μg/m³ = micrograms per cubic meter

mg/m³ = milligrams per cubic meter

Sulfur dioxide and nitrogen dioxide records are arithmetic means. Carbon monoxide and ozone records are second maximum readings over 8- and 24-hour periods, respectively. TSP records are geometric means. Lead records are maximum quarterly recordings. Data represent composite averages from all sites in the nationwide monitoring network.

depends not only on the level of a firm's discharge, but also on factors such as the time and place of the discharge and the number and location of other polluters.

Excessive uniformity is a result of regulatory statutes' over-developed fondness for technological fixes. Social scientists have frequently criticized the technological bias of environmental statutes. It is common for statutes to require use of "the best available technology" or "the best practicable technology," as if the policy problem were essentially an engineering exercise. The engineer searches the literature or the industrial landscape to find what is "available" either on paper or in practice and creates standards on that basis. Practicability appears to mean what is already in use as well as what could be put into use without driving firms out of business.[21] Environmental benefits seldom influence the calculation.[22]

The political imperative toward uniformity fits well with the professional bias of engineers who favor technical standards that can be applied uniformly to all firms.[23] Technology and politics seem to have found a happy accommoda-

TABLE 2.3b   Trends in Ambient Concentrations of Criteria Air Pollutants in the United
States, 1975–1988 (1975 = 100)

Year	Sulfur Dioxide	Carbon Monoxide	Ozone	Nitrogen Dioxide	Total Suspended Particulates	Lead
1975	100	100	100	100	100	100
1976	101	95	100	100	101	101
1977	90	89	101	100	102	112
1978	82	84	102	100	101	100
1979	78	76	88	90	102	74
1980	71	71	89	86	104	59
1981	68	69	83	86	97	46
1982	62	66	82	83	81	47
1983	60	65	90	83	80	38
1984	61	65	81	83	83	34
1985	57	59	80	83	79	22
1986	55	59	77	83	79	12
1987	54	56	82	83	80	10
1988	55	55	89	83	82	8

Source: Calculated from table 2.3a.

tion. Forgotten in this conjunction is what ought to be the goal of policy in the first place: cost-effective improvements in the environment.

United States environmental statutes contain numerous examples of this failure. The Clean Water Act set federal standards on an industry-by-industry basis. Although the differential impact of pollution at different locations has received marginal consideration, uniform treatment of firms in the same industry is the rule.[24] Under the air pollution statute new stationary sources must meet national technical standards regardless of location. In addition, the federal government sets uniform standards for emissions from new cars.[25] Cars driven in the countryside presently face the same standards as cars driven in densely populated areas.[26]

One break with this pattern of uniformity was mandated in 1990 when a limited experiment with tradable pollution permits for sulfur dioxide was included in the amendments to the Clean Air Act. The plan goes beyond previous attempts to reduce costs through market-like schemes. It permits low-cost dischargers to sell pollution rights and treat their waste gases at a higher level than high-cost ones.[27] Control of smog and ozone is also subject to regional variations under the 1990 amendments.[28] Automobile drivers in California, and perhaps the Northeast, will face higher emission standards than the rest of the country.[29] Regional trading systems for nitrogen oxides and air toxics are being instituted in some areas.[30] In addition, the Environmental Protection Agency

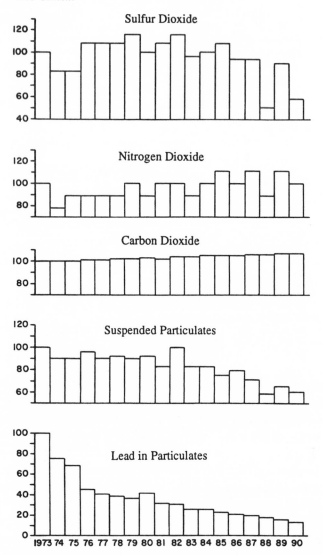

FIGURE 2.1.   Trends in Ambient Air Pollution in the Federal Republic of Germany, 1973–1990 (1973 = 100)

Source: Umweltbundesamt (1992b) p. 187.

may incorporate trading schemes into the implementation of the Clean Water Act.[31]

In Germany the link between environmental benefits and the licensing and standard-setting process is very weak.[32] Although German statutes begin with broad statements of environmental purposes, regulation generally involves licensing enterprises on the basis of individualized judgments and technical

TABLE 2.4   Ambient Air Quality Standards and Recommendations, 1988 ($\mu g/m^3$)

Pollutant	European Community[a]	The Netherlands[a]	USA	Germany[a]	Poland[a]	Sweden[a]
Nitrogen dioxide						
½-hour				80/200[b]	200	
1-hour	200	135				110/190[c]
24-hour					100	75/100[c]
annual			100		16	50[c]
Sulfur dioxide						
½-hour				140/400[b]	600	
1-hour	250/350[d]	830				750
3-hour			1,300			
24-hour	100/130[d]	250	365		200	300
winter						
annual	80/120[d]		80		32	60/100
Carbon dioxide						
½-hour				10,000/30,000[b]	5,000	
1-hour			40,000			
8-hour		6,000/15,000[e]	10,000			6,000/10,000[c]
24-hour					1,000	
annual					120	
Total suspended particulates[g]						
24-hour	250[f]	90	150	150/300[b]	120	150–260[f]
winter	130[f]					
annual	80[f]		50		50	60–75[f]
Lead (Pb)						
24-hour		2.0		2.0	1.0	
quarterly			1.5			
annual	2.0	0.5			0.2	0.5–1.0[c]

Source: Pratt 1992, Table 2. Based on International Energy Agency, *Emissions Controls in Electricity Generation and Industry* (Paris: OECD, 1988).

[a]The European standards are typically statistical such that the monitored 98th percentile value should not exceed the standard.

[b]Many of the German standards are two-tiered in that certain measures are required if the lower value is exceeded, and further measures if the higher value is exceeded.

[c]Recommendation.

[d]The EC sulfur dioxide standards depend upon the smoke level.

[e]The higher value is temporarily allowed until the year 2000, when a major fraction of the automobile fleet will have catalytic converters.

[f]The EC particulate standards are for "smoke" while the Swedish standards are for "soot."

[g]Particulate matter less than 10 micrometers in diameter.

guidelines. Using licenses as the basic control method emphasizes technical fixes. The guidelines are engineering documents that articulate the "state of the art."[33]

The Immission Control Act (*Bundes-Immissionsschutzgesetz*) provides for re-

TABLE 2.5 Emissions Standards, 1988 (mg/m³)

| Country | Fuel[a] | New Combustion Facilities | | Existing Power Plants | | Coal-Fired Capacity with Flue-Gas Controls | |
		Sulfur Dioxide	Nitrogen	Sulfur Dioxide	Oxides	1988	2000
W. Germany	S	400	200	400	200	40	85
	L	400	150	400	150	—	—
	G	35	100	—	100	—	—
Netherlands	S	400	400	400	1000	40	100
	L	400	300	400	700	—	—
	G	200	200	800	500	—	—
Sweden (all)		80–270	135–535	120–240	—	50	50[b]
Poland[c]	S	200–650	35–150	410–1540	35–495	—	—
	L	170–1250	90–120	1720	120–160	—	—
	G	—	35–85	—	60–145	—	—
USA	S	1240	475–620	—[d]	—[d]	20	30
	L	920	350–570	—	—	—	—
	G	1135	285	—	—	—	—

Source: Pratt 1992, Table 3. Based on International Energy Agency, *Emissions Controls in Electricity Generation and Industry* (Paris: OECD, 1988).
[a]S = solid fuel, L = liquid fuel, G = gaseous fuel.
[b]Swedish sulfur dioxide control strategy relies upon fluidized bed.
[c]The Polish standards are expressed in units of grams per gigajoule and will be phased in with stricter standards to take effect in 1997.
[d]None for plants built prior to 1971.

gional planning, but in practice this portion of the law does not constrain polluter behavior, and the plans lack the force of law.[34] The statute instructs the authorities to base licenses on both emissions and immissions (ambient air quality). In principle, if ambient air standards are exceeded, no new licenses can be issued, and existing dischargers can be ordered to cut back their emissions.[35] However, the implementing guidelines define the "assessment area" narrowly so that state and local authorities need focus only on the individual plant seeking a license. The size of the assessment area depends on the stack height of the source and cannot exceed a circle with a radius of 12.5 kms.[36] For most pollutants such a limitation means that emissions are the only relevant basis on which to set standards. Thus, in practice, licensing at the Länder level, using federal technical guidelines, suppresses concern for the environmental impact of pollution loads. Standard-setting and licensing processes ignore the relation between overall discharges and environmental quality at particular locations.

The control of acid rain illustrates the German fixation on engineering solutions. In 1983 the government introduced stronger controls on sulfur dioxide and nitrogen dioxide from coal-fired power plants, partly as a result of public outcry over damage to the trees (called *Waldsterben*, or "forest death") in southern Germany's Black Forest. The controls took the form of a legal regulation issued under the Immission Control Act.[37] The regulation led to a large reduction in ambient concentrations in the Ruhr. The program was a resounding success as long as the measure was reductions in emissions achieved through engineering controls. Although the policy was based on an analysis by the Council of Environmental Experts,[38] the end result was inefficient. The emphasis on technological "fixes" for dischargers, though it required new treatment measures, did not address the complex relation between forest damage and discharges from power plants.[39] The regulation is tough in the technical sense. It explicitly incorporates norms promulgated by the private German Institute for Norms[40] and included in government administrative guidelines.[41] The resultant large reduction in sulfur dioxide emissions, however, did little to help the German forests.[42] The policy may have had other justifications, such as reducing health risks and limiting damage to historical monuments, but one of the major arguments for action was inconsistent with the facts. The prevailing westerly winds seldom carry pollutants from the heavily polluted Ruhr valley south toward the Black Forest, and acid rain is, in any case, only one cause of forest damage.[43]

Another example of excess uniformity is the effluent fees that German companies are required to pay for wastewater discharges. Some view this program as a model for American reform efforts.[44] The fees, however, are not true prices; they are automatically imposed fines. Bureaucratic command-and-control regulations still play a central role. Water discharge permits issued under the Federal Water Act are based in the first instance on technical feasibility and the noxiousness of the wastewater. If ambient water quality does not meet Land guidelines, the authorities may require additional controls or deny a license entirely.[45] Dischargers pay fees based on estimates of the "noxiousness" of their wastes according to a formula contained in the Effluent Charge Act.[46] For industrial dischargers the fee depends only on wastewater characteristics.[47] Dischargers that comply with the relevant technical standards pay reduced fees.[48] The price schedule thus induces firms to comply with technical standards, but it bears no relation to the marginal impact of discharges on ambient water quality.[49]

VARIABILITY

Uniformity is not the only problem. Variability can be as counterproductive. In environmental statutes, variability often involves special treatment for certain dischargers, independent of their impact on the environment. Such variability generally increases the costs and lowers the benefits of environmental protection. Three forms are common: favoring old sources over new sources, favoring old industrial regions over undeveloped areas, and favoring one industry over another.

In both the United States and Germany there is a conflict between existing dischargers and potential entrants. The potential entrants, since they do not yet exist, cannot defend their interests. More stringent controls are frequently imposed on new plants or products. Many American observers have pointed out that this burdens new investment and keeps old plants in operation longer.[50] As a consequence, stringent controls on new plants may result in higher levels of pollution than would no regulation at all, and they are certainly less efficient than regulation that does not discriminate by date of investment. This same situation exists in Germany. New investments that will pollute the air must be licensed, and new chemicals, approved. Existing firms and substances are also regulated, but they have more time to comply with the standards imposed on new entrants.[51]

Interregional competition generates the second form of variability. Clean regions may be required to remain cleaner than dirty areas that must improve to comply with the law. It may, of course, sometimes be desirable to prohibit or limit industrial development in order to promote recreation and tourism, but a general rule limiting the development of clean regions is simplistic. Some observers have suggested that the real goal of such provisions is the preservation of jobs in old industrial areas. As an example, they point to the American law that requires states that exceed federal ambient air standards to prevent significant deterioration of air quality. This prevents undeveloped areas from competing with dirty areas for industrial investment through policies that offer a break on pollution control.[52] Germany, with a dearth of undeveloped regions, does not face this policy pathology. Nevertheless, in seeking to integrate the territory of the old German Democratic Republic it faces an analogous problem—whether to relax pollution control rules in the new Länder in order to encourage investment.[53]

Finally, powerful industries or groups may be able to mold the law and its enforcement to suit themselves. Thus in Germany the nuclear power industry benefited from the public outcry over acid rain.[54] Both farming interests and the chemical industry have a privileged position in the implementation of German environmental laws.[55] The chemical industry played an important role in negotiations leading to passage of the Chemical Law, and it successfully pushed for different treatment of old and new chemicals. For chemical hazards affecting workers, however, the influence of firms has been countered by that of labor unions.[56] The German nature protection and water laws contain language giving agriculture special treatment. It is unlikely that many farmers will be required to give up their land in order to protect nature,[57] and agricultural runoff remains an important source of water pollution.[58]

In the regulation of pesticides in the United States, farmers and pesticides manufacturers have both had a powerful impact on the law.[59] Although the United States has successfully reduced water pollution from point sources, more than half of the remaining pollution comes from non-point sources, including agricultural runoff.[60] A Senate bill to reauthorize the Clean Water Act addresses this problem by mixing state programs with federal guidelines. In hearings on the bill, agricultural interests supported a voluntary state-run approach whereas environmental groups argued for federal mandatory requirements.[61]

National and local protectionist concerns also play a role. If locally produced inputs, such as soft coal, are more polluting than inputs from other countries or states, policy may be biased against the substitution of clean for dirty inputs. For example, sulfur dioxide emissions can be reduced either by installing scrubbers on coal-fired power plants or by switching to low-sulfur coal. American policies requiring scrubbers favored high-sulfur coal producers over less polluting alternatives.[62] Recent amendments to the law, however, have reduced the special treatment for high-sulfur Appalachian coal.[63] German air pollution policy has accommodated the interests of German coal producers through subsidies and differential treatment of oil and natural gas on the one hand and coal on the other.[64] The European Union faces similar political pressures. The directive dealing with pollution from large combustion plants, for example, makes a special exception for high-sulfur Spanish coal.[65]

ENVIRONMENTAL POLICY-MAKING
IN POLITICAL PERSPECTIVE

Environmental policy depends not only on statutory language but also on political will. During the eighties the implementation of environmental laws was in the hands of right-of-center governments in both Germany and the United States. With the exception of Jimmy Carter's presidency, Republicans controlled the White House from 1969 to 1992 in the United States. In Germany environmental policy has been overseen by a coalition of Christian Democrats and Free Democrats (CDU/CSU/FDP). The impact of these conservative governments is not immediately obvious from data on pollution discharges or ambient air and water quality. In both countries measures of air pollution fell over the period. We cannot know what left-of-center governments might have accomplished, but at least the politics of the eighties did not reverse earlier environmental gains. Nevertheless, in order to assess the independent impact of the administrative process and judicial review in the chapters that follow, we need to understand the political context in which recent policy was made.

THE UNITED STATES

The United States established the Environmental Protection Agency (EPA) in 1971 after Richard Nixon became president. The agency consolidated fifteen different environmental programs. During the seventies, under Nixon, Ford, and Carter, considerable progress was made in implementing the newly passed statutes, but gaps remained and many deadlines were not met. The inaction and incompetence of the Environmental Protection Agency in the early eighties under Ronald Reagan's first administrator, Anne Gorsuch Burford, have been well documented. Burford was eventually cited for contempt of Congress in December 1982, and she resigned in March 1983.[66]

The Reagan administration's strategy was to encourage inaction by regulatory agencies, such as the EPA, that imposed costs on business. This was done by appointing people committed to supporting Reagan's ideology even if they were not well informed about the programs of the agencies in which they served.[67] If no one was available who fit these criteria, the administration failed to appoint anyone.[68] Overall the Reagan record was weak. Early in the new administration the EPA did issue final rules concerning aspects of water pollution. By 1984, however, it had made less progress on air quality. The backlog of State Implementation Plans was quickly approved, but only one revision to the National Ambient Air Quality Standards had been proposed or made final by 1984. The administration was also slow in issuing New Source Performance Standards, and little progress was made under the Resource Conservation and Recovery Act.[69]

In the early 1980s enforcement activities were reorganized and downgraded.[70] A General Accounting Office study found widespread violation of water pollution permits over an eighteen-month period beginning in October 1980. Over the same period formal EPA enforcement actions declined by 41 percent.[71] Inaction went together with budget and personnel cuts. Between 1981 and 1983 the budget of the Environmental Protection Agency fell from $1.35 billion to $1.04 billion, and the number of full-time employees fell by fifteen hundred. By 1984 the EPA budget was no greater in real terms than it was in 1972, in spite of vastly increased responsibilities. The EPA's research and development budget fell by more than half in real terms between 1981 and 1984.[72]

After March 1983, when William Ruckelshaus took over as head of the EPA, funding increased and agency morale improved. Ruckelshaus made an effort to improve the administration's environmental image. He gave a speech urging the enforcement staff to stop being "pussycats" and become "gorillas in the closet" of state officials.[73] Due to congressional budget increases, there were more federal inspections and enforcement actions in Reagan's second term.[74] An anti-regulation president faced severe constraints from a Congress that supported environmental values.

George Bush supported a larger EPA budget and appointed a committed environmentalist as head of the EPA. The Bush administration was deeply involved in the passage of Clean Air Act Amendments of 1990. But by the end of his term, the president's commitment to environmental values was being questioned as a result of quarrels between the EPA and the White House. The EPA administrator was weak relative to more conservative policymakers around the president.[75] Still, enforcement continued at a relatively high level.[76]

Despite a conservative bias and shifting commitments to environmental policy during the twelve years of Republican control, the nation continued to spend billions of dollars of public and private money on environmental cleanup. Although some administration policymakers wished to reduce regulation irrespective of the benefits foregone, others worked to improve the efficiency of environmental regulation.[77] Nevertheless, the overall outlines of environmental law continued to lack basic rationality checks.

GERMANY

Germany did not establish its Federal Environmental Ministry (*Bundesumweltministerium*) until the aftermath of the Chernobyl accident in 1986. Before 1986, responsibility for environmental affairs was spread over several ministries but was concentrated in the Interior Ministry.[78] German federal ministries are inherently weaker than American executive departments. The nature of the German federal system gives little implementation authority to central ministries, and these ministries generally have small staffs and little research capacity.[79] The United States EPA's budget was $6.7 billion in fiscal year 1994.[80] Its staff totaled 14,000 in 1987.[81] Germany's Federal Environmental Ministry had 850 employees in 1991, with another 600 working at an associated research agency, the *Umweltbundesamt*.[82] The ministry's budget in 1991 was DM 1.7 billion (about $1 billion).[83] Thus the German federal government employs one-tenth of those employed in the United States in a country with a population one-fourth of the United States'. The main reasons for the differences in budget and employment, beyond the smaller size of the German economy and population, are the different tasks performed by the two governments. The Environmental Ministry's budget does not include the proceeds of the German tax on water pollution discharges, which is used for water quality projects. Furthermore, although both countries rely on state governments to carry out enforcement responsibilities, the degree of state responsibility is much higher in Germany. On the other side of the ledger, the EPA's budget is bloated by the Superfund for hazardous waste cleanup and by the presence of state aid for water pollution control. If these sums are eliminated, the remaining budget is $3.7 billion, comparable to the German total.[84]

Even after Germany established its Environmental Ministry, some regulatory programs with environmental mandates and grant programs with environmental purposes were not moved to the new ministry.[85] Its only important spending authority is a program to support experimental projects.[86] Thus the German agency has no important constituency that benefits financially from its activities. Federal support for pollution control mostly takes the form of tax benefits, low-interest loans, and revenue sharing—forms of aid that require little federal discretion.[87]

Studies of the Environmental Ministry suggest that its head is a relatively weak member of the cabinet. Unlike the ministers of finance and national defense, the environmental minister has no power to block proposals supported by a majority of the cabinet. Some observers claim that federal environmental policymakers have been weak and ineffective.[88] Attempts to assess the impact of the ministry, however, are complicated by the fact that the first minister, appointed in 1986, had no background in environmental affairs and so would have faced difficulties no matter what structural weaknesses he faced.[89]

Some scholars have suggested that the existence of the Environmental Ministry has actually lowered the level of environmental concern within the German government. The Interior and Agricultural Ministries may now find it easier to ignore environmental matters than when these ministries included environmentally focused divisions. Environmental interests outside government may concentrate their efforts on influencing policy within the Environmental Ministry when the important decisions are being made elsewhere.[90]

In spite of this organizational weakness, conservative governments have been relatively aggressive environmental regulators throughout the 1980s and early 1990s. Perhaps the most assertive pro-environmental action occurred soon after the conservative coalition took office. It illustrates how the German "Party-state" can respond quickly to political pressures. The first Christian Democrat Minister of the Interior surprised his critics by taking a strong stand on environmental issues. One of his first acts was to promulgate the tough regulation that limits sulfur dioxide emissions from large combustion plants, which had been in the planning stage for five years.[91] The Christian Democrats' interest in the environment was encouraged by the political challenge posed by the Green party.[92] The Green party's agenda attained respectability in 1983 when the Greens first entered the Bundestag with 28 of the 520 delegates. The Greens supported strengthened air pollution regulations, echoing broad public concern for the damage caused to German forests by acid rain.

The case illustrates the strengths and weaknesses of the German system. On the plus side, the system of proportional representation gives a range of ideological positions a voice within the political system.[93] The spectrum of political ideologies is broader than in the American first-past-the-post system. Even a minority party, not part of the governing coalition, can have influence if it supports a popular policy. Mere responsiveness is not sufficient, however. On the negative side, the system does not guarantee a reasonable government response. As we have seen, the new regulation satisfied a political outcry but was poorly designed to deal with the problem that caused the public agitation. The reliance on political parties as the central route by which popular opinion influences policy choices is insufficient in many areas of environmental law.

Technical choices are not just esoteric details that can be safely delegated to impartial experts. They are the heart of environmental policy itself.[94]

CONCLUSION

Comparison of substantive environmental law in Germany and the United States permits two conclusions. First, the data are insufficient to permit a quantitative comparison of environmental policies in the two countries. Linking policy to results and then making cross-national evaluations is a complex exercise. Even for air pollution, where figures are available on discharges and ambient quality, it is impossible to balance the net benefits of German and American environmental law. In other areas the data are much weaker. For example, two American studies—one on hazardous waste policy and one concerning toxic substances—concluded that the data on harms and cleanup costs had serious inadequacies.[95] Germany has no better data on benefits and costs. Without basic data, provided in comparable form, no firm conclusions are possible.

Second, even lacking a strong data base, the logic of the analysis suggests that there are deep-seated deficiencies in the rationality of existing statutes. Estimates from the United States confirm this suspicion. A study of water pollution policy found that even if costs were 20 percent lower than the estimates and benefits were 20 percent higher, the costs would still outweigh the benefits.[96] According to one author, the estimated cost of complying with the Clean Air Act was approximately $50 billion in 1990. Benefit measures are extremely uncertain. Whatever their level, the gains achieved could have been accomplished much more cheaply.[97] The situation seems to be no better in Germany. Its laws suffer from the same failure to develop cost-minimizing solutions. Conservative governments in both Germany and the United States, in spite of their rhetoric of efficiency and the market, were uninterested in fundamental reform.

The first conclusion is at least in part a consequence of the second. Twenty years of environmental policy-making have failed to build up a strong knowledge base that would permit intercountry comparisons and an analysis of the impact of past policies. The failure to emphasize the rational connection of means to ends has made it increasingly difficult to achieve reasonable reforms. If Germany and the United States wish to move toward policies more focused on providing benefits at reasonable costs, they will have to support research that can provide the background for such reforms. They will need to monitor discharges, ambient air and water quality, and harm to humans and nature more carefully, and they must develop improved models that link these pieces of the puzzle. Both countries have adequate knowledge about technical treatment possibilities. Such information is essential background material, but it is only one element of a responsible policy-making process.

Germany and the United States have strong environmental laws backed up by vigorous enforcement and substantial public support. They are viewed as world leaders. Yet the policy record of both countries is full of failures. These failures are not just familiar examples of business interests manipulating the political and policy-making process for their own purposes. Rather, they represent fundamental structural weaknesses that produce statutes poorly designed to produce benefits while minimizing costs.

3

POLLUTION AND FEDERALISM

The assignment of tasks to the appropriate level of government is an important aspect of environmental policy design. Because the costs and benefits of pollution control are closely tied to geography, political solutions should reflect the underlying spatial structure of environmental problems. These solutions should not only incorporate the long-distance effects of air and water pollution, but also take account of the mobility of economic actors and the resource base of governments. Although both Germany and the United States have recognized the complex geographical character of environmental problems, neither has adequately matched problems to government structures. To oversimplify, Germany seems too decentralized and the United States too centralized.

There are three general types of environmental problems. Global issues have no complex geographical component. Regional issues arise when political boundaries do not coincide with the pollution's impact. In contrast, the environmental effects of local issues are confined within existing governmental borders.

GLOBAL AND REGIONAL PROBLEMS

Global problems occur when the benefits of environmental protection depend on the world-wide level of beneficial or harmful substances, not on their geographical distribution. No pollution problem fits this category perfectly, but the depletion of the ozone layer and global warming come close.[1] So too does protection of endangered species if one perceives risks to the entire world from a decline in the variety of life-forms.[2]

Global problems can be described in apocalyptic terms, but their economic properties are simple. Once scientific estimates of the link between discharges and damages are made, policymakers must set a global level of allowable discharge and design a system to distribute costs among the responsible parties and deep pockets of the world.[3] One possible solution is a system of pollution rights by which the generators of harmful substances either purchase the right to discharge limited amounts or engage in cleanup activities.[4] If some dischargers are located in poor countries or otherwise seem especially worthy, these countries can receive pollution rights that they can use for their own producers or sell on the world market.[5] Although many scientific issues remain unresolved and the political problems are complex and often intractable, the economic analysis is clear-cut.

Greater political and analytic difficulties occur when pollution damages depend on geography, meteorology, or the properties of bodies of water. Most air and water pollution falls into this category. It is not enough to know the total volume of sulfur dioxide discharged into the air or domestic sewage into the water. One must also know where the wind and water carry discharges, how they combine with other pollutants, and how the populations of people, trees, and wildlife are distributed relative to the distribution of pollution. The optimal level of cleanup may vary by location.[6] The distribution of causes and effects over space does not respect political boundaries.

Economic theory provides a straightforward but unrealistic answer to regional pollution problems: draw "optimal" jurisdictional boundaries. Because the states have little incentive to consider benefits and costs that out-of-state residents suffer, the central government should create special purpose authorities with jurisdictional boundaries designed to internalize external effects.[7] For example, a single authority should regulate upstream and downstream water users. Dischargers and breathers in a single air basin should be included in the same jurisdiction.

As a practical matter, this principle leads to an unmanageable number of overlapping governmental entities, forcing a search for second-best solutions. Federal matching-grant programs are one option. Without creating new government authorities or redrawing boundaries, grants could give states and localities an incentive to take responsibility for the external effects of their pollution.[8] Conversely, instead of subsidizing pollution control, the federal government could tax interstate emissions. Managing interstate externalities thus provides a normative argument for incentive-based cooperative federalism.

Implementing matching-grant programs or tax systems under this principle would be a complex enterprise. The federal government cannot simply set a single matching rate or unit tax. Most interstate externalities are asymmetric. One group of states (upstream polluters or energy-producing states, for example) imposes costs on other states (downstream water users or energy-using states) without reciprocation. This circumstance means that states should face different tax or matching rates depending on the degree of interstate externality.

LOCAL PROBLEMS

Local problems are confined within existing political boundaries. At first glance it seems obvious that decision-making authority should devolve to low-level governments for such problems as noise, local parks, and waste dumps. Each community weighs the costs and benefits of various levels of environmental protection and chooses the one that fits its tastes and pocketbook.

Devolution must, however, be done with care. The national government must establish a framework for local decision-making processes and must act when the benefits of standardized solutions outweigh the advantages of local control. Economies of scale in production and the mobility of regulated firms and households may require centralized policy-making.

Consider, first, economies of scale. Federal action may be justified if the costs of diverse local rules outweigh the benefits. Uniform national regulation may produce economies of scale of production and distribution for firms with national markets. Federal preemption may also reduce search costs for firms seeking new production and distribution locations. The argument for centralized standards is strengthened if local governments use idiosyncratic rules to favor local producers at the expense of citizens and national corporations.[9] Federal product standards need not, however, entirely preempt local restrictions. Thus a federal standard on the noise produced by motorcycles or power tools could be combined with local rules limiting nighttime use and restricting the places where noise may be produced. Local governments would, however, be prohibited from making rules that directly contradict the federal standard.

Second, consider mobility and its interaction with property rights. Efficient plant-location choices require a uniform system of property rules, but state and local environmental regulations can affect entitlements. To illustrate the problem, suppose one local government levies a tax on those who generate loud noises. The tax is levied per decibel of noise produced per hour. A second town directly regulates the level of noise and imposes fines on violators. Consider a noise producer that would meet the second town's standard in whichever town it locates.[10] If the noise producer is mobile and can shift towns without cost, it will locate in the second town. It avoids the tax levied in the first town with no change in noise produced. From the standpoint of efficiency, the firm should be indifferent between the two towns, but in fact it is not. The different policy tools chosen affect location decisions in inefficient ways. Even though the first town's noise fee is levied on a per-decibel basis, it acts like a tax on locating in the first town. To avoid such outcomes, the central government should specify the type of policy (that is, charges or standards) and leave it to local governments to decide on the appropriate level. Otherwise local governments would be deciding both the level of noise and the property entitlements of noise producers.

This problem of property entitlements has been generally ignored in the debate over whether jurisdictions are in a race to the bottom or a race to the top when they use regulatory policy to compete for business. Most theoretical work on interjurisdictional competition assumes that the basic policy instrument has been fixed a priori. Jurisdictions are free to decide only on its level.[11] For example, if effluent fees are the policy tool, each local government decides what fee to set. Each community trades off environmental cleanliness against jobs in a way that reflects the preferences of its residents. Under strong competitive assumptions for both communities and businesses, the result of interjurisdictional competition will be an efficient allocation of jobs and pollution loads.[12] If, however, some communities set standards for individual firms while others use effluent fees, the efficiency of the final result is compromised as firms seek to avoid paying fees.

If the problem being regulated is pervasive, however, land rents in the first community, which imposes charges, will fall to reflect its more expensive regulatory environment. Land rents will adjust so that marginal producers are indifferent between the two communities. This result, although an equilibrium, will not generally be efficient. The differing land rents will produce divergent investment choices for businesses and residents in each town even if the underlying real economic factors are equivalent. Only a lump-sum tax in the second town, or a subsidy in the first, would succeed in neutralizing the impact, and it seems unlikely that towns would be able to coordinate their efforts to set the correct fees and subsidies.

The ability of states to act as "laboratories" may also be undermined by firms' preferences for standards versus equally restrictive fees.[13] Supporters of decentralized regulatory policy point to the advantage of encouraging experimentation at state and local levels. New ideas can be tested on a small scale, and other jurisdictions can copy successful initiatives. This view of federalism can be criticized on a number of grounds,[14] but it is especially problematic in the face of interjurisdictional business mobility. A state-level property rights solution that reduces the profits of firms cannot receive a fair test under such conditions. Businesses will fail to locate in the experimenting jurisdiction, not because the implementation strategy is inefficient or ineffective, but simply because they earn lower profits than in a jurisdiction using equally stringent command-and-control regulation.

In principle, this problem with market schemes could be corrected through appropriate lump sum transfers, but once again, it seems highly unlikely that jurisdictions will take steps to assure that businesses earn the same level of excess profits everywhere. Without such a compensatory policy, land rents will fall in the experimenting jurisdiction to counter the increased cost of doing business there, but such a shift in prices will hamper efforts to evaluate the policy experiment in efficiency terms. The behavior of firms will reflect both the efficiency benefits of the new policy and its impact on property entitlements.

Unfortunately, the debate over the efficacy of interjurisdictional competition cannot be resolved simply by requiring the central government to determine a background regulatory framework. Suppose, for example, that the federal government mandates effluent fees, but permits individual states to select the fee levels. This strategy will solve the problem of interjurisdictional differences in property entitlements, but it may not avoid a race to the bottom. A "prisoners' dilemma" may still operate in which individually rational actions produce a result that is worse for state governments than a uniform national fee.[15]

To see how this can happen, consider a case where excess profits exist. Interjurisdictional competition favors relatively mobile groups in this situation.[16] Business firms that can invest in any state have a bargaining advantage over immobile citizens. Firms with little fixed capital, or companies that can credibly threaten to go out of business, also have a political advantage over ordinary voters. Governments may try to outdo each other in offering low levels of environmental regulation. If one government charges a low fee for waste disposal and another requires waste generators to pay high fees, mobile waste producers will flock to the low-cost jurisdiction. The transfer will continue until wages, land rents, and other costs in the low-fee jurisdiction rise enough to compensate for the cost advantage in waste disposal. Thus state and local officials may support federal laws that limit interstate competition. Because states will also have an incentive to undercut each other at the implementation stage, state officials may also support federal enforcement efforts.

Some argue, however, that interjurisdictional competition over environmental standards is likely to be efficient when cross-border externalities do not exist.[17] Several existing theoretical models produce this result.[18] The most important feature of these models is the lack of excess profits in equilibrium. Thus in these models, interjurisdictional differences simply reflect differences in preferences. If businesses do not operate in a perfectly competitive business environment, however, some of their excess profits can be transferred to local jurisdictions in the form of higher levels of environmental quality. Although a tax on excess profits or a lump sum tax on the firm would have superior social welfare properties, such levies may—for reasons of internal state politics—be infeasible. Interjurisdictional competition will, however, prevent such a transfer of rents. A community that attempts to impose high levels of protection will find that firms will locate elsewhere if not given a corresponding benefit in some other form, for example, lower wages or taxes.[19]

Waste disposal and recycling policy illustrate how local problems can become national issues because of interjurisdictional interactions. As long as waste does not seep into ground water or get converted to air pollution through incineration, waste disposal remains a local problem.[20] The basic market failure is the ease with which people can dispose of waste unlawfully without being caught. In most jurisdictions the state has responded to the difficulty of catching litterers, not by beefing up the police force, but by providing free trash and garbage pickup, at least for households. Unregulated trash disposal is curbed, but without forcing consumers, and therefore retailers and manufacturers, to recognize the cost of disposal or recycling.

Charging households and firms based on the volume and type of waste they produce creates an incentive for illegal dumping. If a community adopts a strict, well-enforced law against illegal dumping, trash haulers may simply cross jurisdictional borders. A local problem then becomes an interjurisdictional one.[21] Thus a fee system may need to be national or international in scope to be effective, and it must include a comprehensive attack on illegal dumping. If such a program is not politically possible, there may be no realistic alternative to free, publicly provided trash pickup.

Recycling requirements and policies that force producers, retailers, and customers to internalize the cost of waste disposal can supplement trash pickup. Although the costs are borne locally and vary among communities, efficiency may be served by uniform national packaging standards or deposit and return requirements. Thus the central government would set packaging standards or levy taxes based on each product's waste content and ease of disposal. Local communities could provide supplemental programs as long as they did not generate illegal interjurisdictional hauling. In areas with high population density it will often be inefficient to dispose of waste close to its point of origin. Thus trash exporting would be permitted so long as it was approved by the importing municipality.

MIXED CASES

Many situations do not fit neatly into a single category. The most salient mixed cases involve nature conservation, nuclear power, and abandoned hazardous waste sites. Nature conservation implicates broad environmental concerns when it requires the preservation of the habitat of an endangered species or of land that aids in flood control, water supply, or the absorption of pollutants. In such cases the decision should not be made by local planning bodies since they are unlikely to weigh global concerns adequately. Yet moving policy-making to high-level governments risks possible scapegoating—making local communities bear the cost of a global policy. Thus small communities should be able to present evidence of localized costs and benefits to higher levels of government. We need innovative techniques to compensate hard-hit localities if conservation decisions are to be made on ecological grounds.

The regulation of nuclear power is too complex an issue to be dealt with adequately here. Neighbors of nuclear power plants would be most seriously harmed by an accident, but they also benefit from jobs at the plant. A major accident would have an impact far beyond jurisdictional borders, but inexpensive power also has broad-based benefits. Some people object to nuclear power on principle without concern for whether they will be directly affected by possible accidents. At a technical level, there are only so many ways of building a safe nuclear power plant. Centrally articulated standards can save time and money—though again, fine-tuning is needed to accommodate local conditions. If plants are built, neighbors should be indemnified for the excess risk that they must bear.

Abandoned hazardous waste sites pose special problems. Here the principal argument for federal responsibility is based on distributive justice, not efficiency. The only efficiency claim is technocratic: the central government can convene experts to set overall standards for waste site cleanups more cheaply than can the multitude of local units. Distributive justice involves considerations of intergenerational equity. Old sites represent external costs imposed on current residents by past economic activities. Although the problems of hazardous waste are usually locally based, it is unfair for nearby residents to bear the costs of cleanup. After all, locals often did not know of the risk, and in most cases the hazardous material came from outside the neighborhood. Why should existing residents and businesses be required to pay for cleanup to make the health prospects of residents equal to those of others who had the good luck to be located in clean areas?[22] Furthermore, if a local area attempts to finance cleanups by raising taxes, it discourages new businesses and residents.

CONSTITUTIONAL STRUCTURE

The division of regulatory authority in Germany and the United States does not accurately mirror the political and economic concerns raised above. The laws of both nations acknowledge the interjurisdictional nature of many pollution problems, but the actual division of authority contains many questionable features. Some of these issues have implications for German and American constitutional law.

THE U.S. CONSTITUTION

The U.S. Constitution does not detail the assignment of responsibilities to levels of government. The Tenth Amendment reads simply: "The powers not delegated to the United States by the Constitution, nor prohibited by it to the States, are reserved to the States respectively, or to the people." This sentence has not produced a jurisprudence of regulatory federalism. The Supreme Court is permissive. It has invoked the Interstate Commerce Clause to justify a wide range of federal regulation even in cases where the interstate impact is indirect.[23] Federal regulation of the environment has seldom raised constitutional issus.[24] Comprehensive federal statutes control air and water pollution; laws on waste, pesticides, drinking water, and the protection of land and endangered species give the federal government an important role.[25]

The link between federalism and the environment has recently been raised in three areas of constitutional law. First, the federal courts have invoked the Commerce Clause to strike down state laws that impose special burdens on the disposal of out-of-state waste or that favor in-state producers of polluting products. Building on an earlier case dealing with solid waste, the Supreme Court outlawed state taxes or fees that require out-of-state waste generators to pay higher rates.[26] Differential charges must be linked to differences in costs of handling such waste. The Court also held unconstitutional the state regulations that required landfills to accept only locally generated waste and that required all local waste to be handled by local facilities.[27] Waste is to be treated like any other article of commerce.

Providing special benefits to in-state firms is also suspect. A federal district court struck down as an interference with interstate commerce an Illinois regulatory statute that favored local high-sulfur coal.[28] The act was passed after the federal Clean Air Act was amended in 1990 to remove the favorable treatment of high-sulfur coal. The Constitution permits the federal government to favor regional interests as it did under the Clean Air Act Amendments of 1977.[29] The federal district court held, however, that states cannot take such action on their own. Nevertheless, direct subsidies to a state's industry appear to be permissible, and if the state becomes a "market participant" by opening its own landfill or disposal facility, it can do as it likes.[30]

Second, the status of state common law nuisance suits has been questioned in cases challenging the preemptive power of the federal Clean Water Act. A series of cases involving suits by the State of Illinois against the City of Milwaukee concluded that the Clean Water Act preempted federal and state common law actions between parties in different states.[31] A subsequent case argued that suits brought under the law of the discharger's state are permitted and that these suits need not be brought in the courts of the discharger's state. Thus in one situation that was before the Supreme Court, a New York discharger could be sued for common law nuisance under the law of New York in Vermont courts.[32]

The decisions in these first two areas of constitutional law limit the states' ability to isolate themselves from the rest of the nation, and they establish the preemptive effect of federal statutes. No case explicitly considers the substantive division of tasks between federal and state governments or challenges the federal government's ability to regulate the environment. Commerce Clause jurisprudence has not addressed interregional differences in the substance of problems—differences that may require interstate cooperation rather than federal uniformity.

The third category does touch on the subject of interstate cooperation, and its link to federal power. A federal statute requires that states either form regional interstate compacts to handle the disposal of low-level nuclear waste or dispose of it within their borders.[33] State officials engineered passage of the law. The original act imposed no sanctions on states that failed to comply. After several years of experience with this act, the states themselves proposed that Congress pass a tougher measure containing federally enforceable incentives and penalties. In a recent case challenging the constitutionality of this statute, the Supreme Court invoked the Tenth Amendment to limit federal power. The Court upheld the sanctions supported by the states. However, the Court found unconstitutional on federalism grounds a provision that ordered uncooperative states to accept ownership of internally generated waste. This "take title" provision, the Court reasoned, "crossed the line distinguishing encouragement from coercion."[34]

Justice Byron White in dissent objected to the decision on the ground that the "Act was very much the product of cooperative federalism, in which the States bargained among themselves to achieve compromises for Congress to sanction."[35] White's dissent would have been reasonable if he had been correct. If the states asked to be bound by a federal statute *ex ante,* they should not be able to renege *ex post.* A study of the act's legislative history suggests that Justice White's claim, though true for the other two sanctions upheld by the Court, does not apply to the "take title" provision. According to one study, the provision was added on the floor of the Senate on the last day of the 99th Congress. It had been proposed by the Nuclear Regulatory Commission in hearings but had not been formally approved by either the House or the Senate committees and was not part of the states' proposal.[36] Although the Court stated that the consent of state officials is not sufficient to lend constitutional legitimacy to a federal law, the provision in question did not, in fact, provide a sharp test of this claim.[37]

The Supreme Court has not clearly worked out the limits of federal and state power over environmental issues. Federal courts seem to give state common law greater deference than state statutes, perhaps because state statutes more explicitly favor in-state interests. States cannot favor in-state over out-of-state coal producers or waste generators, but states can provide direct subsidies, and federal statutes can have disparate state or regional impacts. Although coercive federal restrictions on the states are unconstitutional, the Court has not clearly articulated the distinction between coercive conditions and those that merely provide incentives.

THE GERMAN GRUNDGESETZ

In contrast to the U.S. Constitution, the German Grundgesetz explicitly assigns responsibilities and financing sources to different categories of federal and state control. Nuclear power, real estate and housing law, waste disposal, air purification, and noise abatement fall into one category,[38] and land distribution, regional planning, water, hunting, nature conservation, and landscape management fall into another.[39] In the first group concurrent legislative authority exists. The Länder can legislate so long as the federal government has not. The federal government can legislate when states might be tempted to impose costs on each other.[40] For the second group, the Grundgesetz permits only federal framework laws that give the Länder discretion to fill in the legislative details with their own statutes.[41]

The constitutional distinction contains anomalies not justified on the basis of the nature of the substantive environmental problems. Water quality should fall into the concurrent category. Noise control should be in the framework group unless interjurisdictional competition is thought to be a serious problem. Similarly, nature conservation should distinguish between locally beneficial projects and those supporting the preservation of species and biodiversity. Waste disposal is also a mixed case, because it can have local, regional, and national impacts. The Bundestag and the Constitutional Court could use the general language of the Grundgesetz to make these distinctions, but so far these bodies have not done so.[42]

In fact, so far as the question has been raised at all in the environmental area, the judicial response has been disappointing. The German constitution explicitly requires the federal government to administer the federal waterways used for inland shipping.[43] The Constitutional Court held that federal jurisdiction extended only to commerce between the German Länder, not to the control of water pollution and water supply.[44] Yet the justification for a federal presence is the same in both cases—the costs that one Land may impose on another and on the nation as a whole. Water pollution control is subsumed under the federal authority to promulgate framework statutes concerning the "water regime," the weakest form of federal legislative authority.[45] This was done even though a number of long, heavily industrialized rivers flow through several Länder and foreign countries.

In practice, the anomalies are not as serious as the constitutional text might imply. On one hand, the waste disposal law is more like a framework law than a detailed program of control. On the other hand, the federal water law is stringent and detailed, and a separate federal statute levies taxes on dischargers. Although the constitutional authority is weak, the federal government does oversee cooperative planning,[46] and century-old associations of water users control both the water quality and use of a number of rivers.[47] Furthermore, international bodies deal with German water quality issues. For example, there is a Convention for the Protection of the Rhine (*Rheinschutzübereinkommen*), and Germany and the Czech Republic have established an International Commission for the Protection of the Elbe.[48]

The Grundgesetz makes the Länder responsible for the day-to-day implementation of most federal regulatory statutes. Although the federal government can exercise some control over the Länder, there is no possibility of federal takeover.[49] This institutional structure gives the Länder considerable freedom to shape federal requirements to fit their priorities. In the United States the states are also heavily involved in the administration of federal environmental laws. Nevertheless, states may choose not to become involved, and conversely the federal government can judge a state incapable of effective administration and federalize implementation. Some view this freedom to refuse involvement as a cornerstone of American federalism, which enhances state power. The German situation casts doubt on this claim. The German Länder are powerful precisely because the federal government has no choice but to implement its statutes through the states.

The German federal government faces constitutional limits on its authority to make grants to the states. The Grundgesetz establishes overall conditions for allocating revenue that take account of interstate differences in fiscal resources.[50] The Constitutional Court ruled in the mid-seventies that imposing conditions on federal grants would violate the freedom of decision of federation members.[51] In 1986 the Constitutional Court held that portions of a federal law apportioning revenue from taxes on corporate income and wages had not adequately considered variations in the tax bases of state governments.[52] In a reunited Germany the old formulas inadequately reflect the diverse situations of the Länder. The fiscal constitution, based on revenue-sharing principles, may limit the scope of federal grants earmarked for specific purposes, such as the cleanup of old dumps. Nevertheless, the 1986 case does recognize the constitutionality of supplementary federal payments (*Bundesergänzungszuweisungen*) to take account of the special burdens of individual Länder.[53]

The current debate over the German constitution has done little to advance the discussion of German federalism. While some argue that environmental protection should be included in the Grundgesetz as a goal of the German state, many combine this position with support for further devolution of authority to state and local governments.[54] There appears to be little recognition of the tension between the solution of large-scale environmental problems and the parochial concerns of small-scale governments. That tension is blurred because of the presence of the Green party in Land coalition governments and parliaments at a time when the party is weak nationally. Environmentalists who support greater decentralization may be extrapolating too easily from the current situation in which the Länder appear, on balance, greener than the federal government. These advocates are looking at political configurations without considering the underlying nature of the substantive problems. In an interdependent Europe additional delegation of environmental responsibilities to the Länder seems ill advised.

LOCAL CONTROLS OVER REGIONAL PROBLEMS

The environmental policies of Germany and the United States often ignore the regional character of pollution. The scope of the problem and the jurisdictional level are mismatched. Pollution with regional and national impact is frequently regulated by state and local officials who have no incentive to look outside their jurisdiction. Even when a national statute guides lower-level enforcement, implementation by state and local officials may ignore the policy's broader impact. Conversely, federal statutes can be overly rigid and insensitive to differing state and local conditions. Both countries experience both problems, but over-delegation is especially prevalent in Germany, and excessive rigidity is widespread in the United States.

In Germany relatively weak federal control of implementation makes the problem of cross-border effects especially serious. Land officials have considerable discretion in setting enforcement priorities.[55] Even when a strong federal role is justified, implementation is largely left to the states and localities. The possibility for exceptions favoring local interests is great even when the environmental harm crosses jurisdictional borders.

Local control is especially notable in implementing air pollution policy where the federal law is vague and state governments have failed to promulgate clear enforcement guidelines. According to one study, this led in the seventies to "management by exception," in which lower-level governments gave special treatment to favored firms.[56] While central government guidelines and regulations strengthened air pollution requirements in the eighties, case-by-case licensing processes remain open to local influence. Water pollution policy is better organized at the state level, but subsidies for water pollution control do not necessarily reflect the costs of pollution.[57]

The German emphasis on licensing in both water and air pollution control combines with federalism to encourage a case-by-case approach. Ambient conditions are supposed to play a role in the licensing process, but, in practice, state and local officials lack strong incentives to look outside their own borders. The federal government has issued technical guidelines that have presumptive force covering air pollution, noise, and solid waste. This practice can counteract local incentives to be overly lenient or excessively strict, but it is not the route to cost-efficient policies. The guidelines may lead state and local officials to be "tough," but that is quite different from considering the systemic impact of decisions on national and international environmental quality.

In the past German observers have argued that an "implementation deficit" exists in environmental laws.[58] This deficit may have resulted from the attempts of individual Länder to benefit economically at the expense of others. That criticism is currently blunted by the existence of the Green Party as a coalition partner in some state and local governments. Some people now claim that enforcement is too vigorous in certain Länder.[59] Whatever the bias, it is in any case inconsistent.

Federal control is stronger in the United States, and regional offices of the Environmental Protection Agency play a central role.[60] Nevertheless, even here state implementation creates problems of interregional consistency and risks underregulation of interjurisdictional effects. For example, the focus on State Implementation Plans under the Clean Air Act invites state officials to take a parochial view. While the amendments of 1990 put more emphasis on the control of pollutants that cross state boundaries, it remains to be seen if the new provisions are sufficient.[61] A study of the administration of the Clean Air Act found that overly stringent federal regulations were administered flexibly by lower-level governments and federal district courts.[62] The centralized nature of federal policy-making produced strains on the lower rungs of the government ladder. These were resolved ad hoc and often were premised on avoiding the shutdown of an important employer.

In the past, the Clean Water Act provided federal matching funds to state and local governments for water pollution projects. Such matching grants could have been designed to induce local governments to account for the costs their sewage imposes on downstream communities. In practice, the matching rate never bore any relation to the degree to which costs were externalized.[63] Studies of the location and effectiveness of sewage treatment plants suggest that efficient improvements in water quality seldom determined where and when subsidized plants were built. The days of large-scale grants for sewage treatment plant construction are over, but current policy has not corrected these deficiencies.[64]

In Germany too much decentralization has led the federal government to try to induce lower-level licensing authorities to impose high standards. Unable to enforce strong regional plans effectively, especially for air pollution, federal authorities have to rely on technical standards to guide these licensing activities. Even the subsidies provided by federal revenue sharing and tax benefits are subject to the implementation priorities of lower-level governments.[65] In the United States, over-centralization has produced stringent, legally binding regulations for new air pollution sources and industries that pollute the water.[66] These uniform rules are often poorly adapted to individual air basins and watersheds, and the exceptions permitted by state officials and federal courts are unlikely to reflect the differential cost-benefit trade-offs.[67]

HAZARDOUS WASTE AND RECYCLING

Even if an environmental issue is locally based, destructive competition and serious inequities can result from giving too much authority to state and local governments. Hazardous waste policy in Germany provides an instructive comparison to the American regulatory structure; United States policy is criticized for excessive rigidity, but the German solution is too decentralized. German recycling policy, in contrast, is too heavily controlled by the federal government.

Destructive interstate competition in the United States is a well-recognized problem. It has been extensively discussed in the context of state business taxes and investment aids, and it applies to environmental policy as well.[68] One of the ironies of the Reagan administration's efforts to devolve regulatory authority to the states was the occasional opposition of state officials. For example, governors welcomed devolution of regulatory authority from the EPA but argued that "successful delegation of programs can only be accomplished with strong technical and financial assistance from EPA, a national presence of EPA in standards setting and resolving interstate pollution problems, and strong federal research."[69] These officials recognized the benefits of avoiding destructive interstate competition by using a strong federal presence to tie their hands.

This idea is a basic principle behind the federal Superfund law mandating the cleanup of existing hazardous waste sites.[70] Superfund—financed by a special national tax on waste producers—pays for cleanup if the responsible parties cannot be found.[71] Waste sites usually affect only nearby residents, making a strong federal role seem unjustified. Nevertheless, any state that tried to move vigorously would burden its taxpayers and induce potentially liable firms to relocate. Thus few states would act on their own. Federal intervention is also justified on distributive justice grounds. Because of these considerations, one cannot reform the much-criticized federal law by arguing for devolution to lower levels of government; reform must instead focus on the design of the statute.

An alternative to the cumbersome Superfund process would be a law placing liability on waste producers but leaving local communities the authority to decide whether to take the cash or engage in cleanup. One could retain the current Superfund, under which the federal government provides backup funding if the waste producers cannot be found or are unable to pay. In other words, the federal government would establish the basic rights to compensation and let communities decide how to balance health risks against an influx of cash.[72] Such a program would limit the federal government to restraining interstate competition and equalizing financial capacities. Because the risks are local, their reduction would be a local choice. Although a federal role is justified, the American response is overly centralized.

Germany has no federal equivalent of Superfund, and its liability law makes it difficult to extract cleanup funds from those who generated waste in the past.[73] The federal law permits municipal waste treatment facilities to reject hazardous waste, but it does not mandate a solution to the problems of disposal and the cleanup of old dump sites. Voluntary private cleanup efforts occur for sites in need of permits for future development. Land owners or past operators of waste disposal facilities can be held strictly liable for cleanup costs. Thus some cleanups take place under threat of state coercion. However, those who generated the waste and new owners who lack knowledge of the site's characteristics escape liability. Frequently no one with the requisite funds can be held legally responsible for cleanup. In response, some Länder levy taxes or charge licensing fees to generate cleanup funds.[74] Fees paid by the current generators of hazardous waste are combined with general public revenues to produce funds used to clean up old sites.[75]

The decentralized nature of German hazardous waste policy permits states to make different judgments about the importance of tackling the problems of old waste sites and newly generated waste. Subject to federal minimum standards, each Land can balance the costs and benefits in its own way. This structure appears desirable, given the local nature of the benefits; however, decentralization creates inequities among the Länder that the more centralized American process avoids. Some observers claim that state authorities form coalitions with waste producers that overlook the interests of ordinary citizens.[76] Waste producers have bargaining power because they can threaten to leave the state or cut back on expansion plans. This may be a problem in some Länder, but it does not seem to be the major disadvantage of Germany policy. Inequity appears to be a more serious problem than the threats of mobile business interests to relocate. Rich states can collect cleanup funds from individuals and generators more easily than poor ones with little industrial base and many waste sites.[77] Interregional inequities have become more acute with reunification. Before 1989, much western waste was dumped in East Germany. The new eastern Länder now contain this waste but have no wealthy producers to finance a cleanup.[78]

Recognizing this problem, the federal government has sought ways around the possible constitutional limits on earmarked grants to the Länder.[79] Thus far, the response has been ad hoc. The federal government has financed cleanup programs through special project grants and through the transitional Treuhandanstalt, which is organizing the privatization of the east.[80] But these initiatives are only stopgaps. Clearly, Germany needs to find ways to avoid the severe distributive inequities produced by the combination of its federal structure and a liability system that relieves past generators of responsibility.

German recycling policy presents a different type of problem. Germany is putting highly restrictive regulations into place throughout the country. The regulations impose a stringent set of requirements. An ordinance requires both packaging manufacturers and product distributors to take back and recycle transport packaging materials.[81] Product distributors are required to accept returned packaging or participate in a private system that collects packaging from households.[82] The ordinance includes quotas, which rise over time, for the amount of packaging collected and for the percentage to be recycled.[83] A private company called *Duales System Deutschland* (DSD) has the exclusive right to collect and recycle products marked with the *Grüne Punkt* symbol. The DSD, financed by fees on industry, operates in 95 percent of German cities and districts.[84]

The system is reducing the tonnage of packaging materials.[85] It has recently come under attack, however, both because of the DSD's monopoly power and because of the program's expense and rigidity.[86] Though it is a monopoly, the DSD has been a money loser that was bailed out by several large companies in the summer of 1993.[87] Monopoly complaints come both from small recyclers that accuse the DSD of overcharging for waste and from those who accuse the firm of inefficient waste collection practices.[88] Much of the waste collected has been exported to other countries, and critics charge that the nation is not meeting its recycling targets.[89] The federal environmental minister is seeking to reduce the quotas for recycling and to make other changes in the ordinance.[90]

The program is both too centralized and too decentralized. The law inefficiently limits the disposal and recycling choices of the Länder and manufacturers at the same time that it fails to impose uniform federal packaging standards where they would be efficient.[91] The regulations have the advantage of giving producers a clear duty with respect to packaging. But the ordinance lacks flexibility. It rules out a whole range of potentially cost-effective alternatives for waste collection. The quotas in the law appear to bear little relation to the relative benefits of recycling versus other methods of disposal.

RESPONDING TO GLOBAL PROBLEMS

Both Germany and the United States recognize the global nature of ozone depletion in the upper atmosphere, global warming, and biodiversity. Ozone depletion has proved the easiest to resolve, and an international protocol with some bite promises to ameliorate the problem.[92] New evidence on the existence of an ozone hole over the northern temperate zone has spurred Germany, the European Union, and the United States to announce faster schedules to eliminate the production of chemicals that deplete the ozone layer.[93] The international protocol was amended in late 1992.[94] The American chemical industry supported the original protocol because unilateral American restrictions on the use of these chemicals had hurt their competitiveness.[95] The industry wanted global restrictions imposed to level the playing field.[96] The case is an example of how national regulation of a global problem, while pointless as a long-run strategy, can turn opponents of regulation into political allies.[97]

The problems of global warming and biodiversity are proving more difficult to resolve. Both are plagued by vexing empirical problems that complicate the policy debate. While global warming is a relatively well defined phenomenon, biodiversity is a catch word for a range of concerns, from the preservation of individual species to the management of threatened ecosystems. Furthermore, even if scientific conflicts over the extent of species depletion could be resolved, deep conflicts over values complicate the search for international solutions. A final source of dispute is the distribution of costs, with developing countries arguing that they should not have to bear the costs of their late development.

Both global warming and biodiversity were on the agenda of the Rio Conference in 1992 organized by the United Nations. The Convention on Climate Change signed at the Conference has neither clear timetables nor goals for reducing the level of greenhouse gases.[98] American negotiators reportedly feared that such timetables would have more legal force in the United States than elsewhere. However, in the aftermath of this agreement both the European Union and the United States have set goals of reducing their own carbon dioxide levels to 1990 levels by the year 2000.[99] It is not clear, however, what these goals mean. In the United States the Clinton administration proposed only voluntary compliance programs for substances that contribute to global warming.[100] The German cabinet has committed itself to reducing carbon dioxide emissions to 75 percent of 1987 levels by 2005. But this is a goal, not a legally binding condition.[101]

Furthermore, stronger measures, not required by the convention, such as taxes on carbon are unlikely in the near future. The United States has not endorsed a carbon tax, and the European Union's backing for a carbon tax is conditional on the agreement of all members of the Organization for Economic Cooperation and Development (OECD).[102] The German environmental minister supports a carbon tax only in the framework of such a broad initiative.[103] The fear of competitive losses prevents any group of countries from acting independently, and international institutions are not strong enough to impose a solution.

More progress was made on biodiversity. Germany signed the biodiversity treaty at the Rio Conference, though the United States did not. The Clinton administration signed the treaty in June 1993.[104] The Bush administration's concerns that the treaty might harm intellectual property rights were apparently exaggerated, because the Industrial Biotechnology Association, representing 80 percent of the industry, endorsed the accord.[105] This may be another case of an industry that fears unilateral American action favoring an international agreement that imposes similar restrictions on all producers.[106]

The mixed record on the greenhouse effect and biodiversity suggests that global problems imposing heavy costs on advanced countries will be difficult to solve. Limits on greenhouse gases will raise energy costs worldwide. Although the immediate costs will fall heavily on newly developing countries, such as China, all users of fossil fuels will be affected. These costs could be substantial if stringent limits are imposed. Efforts to subsidize poorer countries would further increase the burden on wealthier ones.

In contrast, preserving species by preserving tropical rain forests is a perfect political issue for industrially developed countries. Germany has no tropical rain forests, and the United States has only small enclaves in outlying areas. Political actors can claim great concern but make it clear that global cooperation is necessary.[107] If such cooperation is not forthcoming, then little need be done at home.[108] Possible unilateral responses, such as limiting the import of tropical woods, have the advantage of being supported by domestic competitors.[109] Even when a global treaty is signed, it will impose only marginal costs on major industrial powers.

CONCLUSION

The U.S. constitutional structure places few constraints on the assignment of environmental responsibilities to different levels of government. As a result, strong federal statutes exist in most areas of environmental protection. The German constitution is more specific in assigning environmental responsibilities and mandates that states administer most federal regulatory programs. The constitutional assignment of environmental responsibilities to government levels in Germany is inefficient in that it fails to adequately account for the geographical extent of pollution problems.

Both countries' statutes fail to recognize the complex regional and interregional character of air and water pollution. Existing jurisdictional boundaries are given excessive weight in policy design and implementation. In the United States federal laws frequently impose too much uniformity on the country in the form of treatment requirements or discharge levels. The German focus on licenses and on state and local control of implementation creates particular difficulties in dealing with pollution that crosses political borders.

Turning to local problems, the cleanup of existing hazardous waste sites shows how a seemingly local problem can require national intervention. The U.S. solution recognizes these national concerns but does so in a cumbersome, rigid, and costly way. The German solution places too much responsibility for cleanup on state governments. Recycling policy is a counter-example to my general claim that Germany is too decentralized. Germany is much farther along the recycling path than the United States, but it has designed an excessively standardized scheme.

The failure of the international community to deal sensibly with global problems cannot be blamed on either Germany or the United States, although the involvement of both countries is necessary for further progress. International cooperation may be facilitated by U.S. statutes that give industry an incentive to seek global solutions. This possibility provides a political-economic justification for domestic policies that would otherwise appear ineffective.

In short, the constitutional and statutory assignment of environmental responsibilities in both countries leaves much to be desired. Germany puts too much emphasis on implementation by state and local governments, the United States too little. Yet the underlying problems are more subtle than this simple generalization. Existing political jurisdictions are not well fitted to the reality of many environmental problems. Both countries need to recognize more fully the complex regional and interjurisdictional character of pollution.

PART II   THE GERMAN CASE

4

GERMAN ENVIRONMENTAL
POLICY-MAKING PROCESSES

German public law recognizes the need to give bureaucrats discretion to resolve individual cases fairly. The legitimacy of delegating policy-making to the executive is not so readily accepted.[1] Yet delegation is omnipresent in policy areas where scientific expertise is needed to make concrete policy choices. Science and politics cannot be neatly separated. German officials issue broad-based regulations and guidelines that take account of the lack of specificity of many statutes. Between 1949 and 1987 Germany enacted 3,990 statutes and 12,639 regulations with the force of law, more than one per day.[2] Regulatory guidelines with less legal force are also common. In 1982 alone, state and federal governments issued 5,000 administrative guidelines, more than 13 per day.[3]

THE CONSTITUTIONAL FRAMEWORK

Unlike the U.S. Constitution, the Grundgesetz explicitly limits the executive's regulatory activity. The German notion of separation of powers (*Gewaltenteilung*) assigns governmental tasks to the legislature, the executive, and the judiciary.[4] The doctrine emphasizes controls and restraints on the exercise of public power.[5]

Before a regulation can be issued, the Grundgesetz requires the Bundestag to delegate regulatory authority in the statutory language. After the Bundesregierung proposes a regulation, the Bundesrat must approve it if the Länder will be involved in its implementation. The Bundesrat must also approve administrative guidelines that regulate state administration of federal laws. These constraints on the federal bureaucracy are all external. They do not directly affect the internal practice of the ministries. Judicial review seldom concerns ministerial processes. Once the Constitutional Court accepts the constitutionality of a substantive government action, it inquires no further into the procedural details.

"CONTENT, PURPOSE, AND SCOPE" OF REGULATIONS

The government can only promulgate regulations with legal force (*Rechtsverordnungen*) if the authorizing statute articulates their "content, purpose, and scope."[6] The German courts give this principle more significance than the corresponding "nondelegation doctrine" under American law, by requiring that the outcome be foreseeable from the statutory language. In practice, however, the courts permit wide delegation in technically complex areas, such as environmental law. The Constitutional Court considers the legislative plan to determine whether delegation is needed. If it is, it looks to the statutory scheme, not just to the clause authorizing the regulation, to determine whether the delegation is sufficiently clear. The legal empowerment need not be detailed but can be in the form of general standards of valuation.[7]

The German focus on individual rights in administrative law has influenced recent cases developing these ideas. The Constitutional Court has accepted general clauses delegating authority if they permit the government to take account of the special circumstances of individual cases.[8] If delegation to the executive may violate individuals' rights, then the Court requires greater clarity in the statutory language.[9]

The ambiguities of these judicial formulas reveal an underlying tension between legislative accountability and executive discretion. In the environmental area, where the justifications for delegation are especially strong, the courts have left the legislature free to draft open-ended statutes. Judicial opinions have accepted the necessity of statutory terms that are not precisely defined (*unbestimmter Rechtsbegriff*). In a recent case, for example, the Federal Administrative Court held that the phrase "revival of landscape" (*Belebung des Landschaftsbilds*) in the federal and Bavarian nature protection acts did not violate the nondelegation doctrine.[10] Because the Bundestag does not have the capacity to make detailed environmental policy choices, the permissiveness of the delegation doctrine as applied to environmental statutes leaves the administration with a remarkably free hand given the lack of legally enforceable constraints on its procedures.

BUNDESRAT AND BUNDESTAG APPROVAL

The Grundgesetz requires Bundesrat approval for regulations implemented by the Länder and for many statutes as well.[11] The Constitutional Court has broadly interpreted this requirement.[12] As a consequence, more than half of all federal laws go through this body, and given the importance of the Länder in administering federal statutes, almost all legal regulations are sent to the Bundesrat for approval.[13]

When the Länder administer a federal statute, the constitution also permits the federal government to issue guidelines or general administrative rules (*Verwaltungsvorschriften*) so long as the Bundesrat votes its consent.[14] Unlike regulations with the force of law, the content, purpose, and scope of administrative guidelines need not be laid out in the relevant statutes.[15]

The requirement of Bundesrat approval is of substantial political and policy importance. The upper house sometimes holds hearings and otherwise seeks to influence the result.[16] In the 12th voting period (1990–1994)—with the Social Democratic party controlling the Bundesrat and a Christian Democratic-Free Democratic coalition controlling the Bundesregierung—this check on the executive gave Germany a watered-down version of divided government.[17]

"Bundestag vetoes" are also constitutional under German law,[18] and they are included in several environmental statutes. For example, under the environmental impact assessment statute, regulations implementing the act must be submitted to the Bundestag, which has several weeks to veto the proposal or to approve it by inaction.[19] The air pollution statute permits the government to implement European Union decisions through regulations, so long as such regulations are submitted to the Bundestag for possible veto.[20] The Environmental Liability Law of 1991 requires its implementing regulations to be submitted to the Bundestag before being considered by the Bundesrat.[21]

Bundesrat and Bundestag vetoes limit the federal bureaucracy's operation. But these constraints are not necessarily conducive to good policy-making. Bundestag vetoes cannot effectively check executive policy-making without a growth in the staff resources of the parliament. Vetoes are a poor tool for controlling the application of technical knowledge to policy. Bundesrat approval depends upon the support of elected Länder politicians. Whatever the political configuration of the federal and state governments, these politicians are likely to be most concerned with the ease and convenience of implementation, not the policy's overall impact.[22] The need for their approval means that they are often deeply involved in the drafting process in federal ministries. Their influence may lead the government to overemphasize administrative convenience and interstate uniformity in situations where neither will produce sensible policy.

THE ADMINISTRATIVE PROCESS

Within the established constitutional and statutory framework, German federal ministries are free to design administrative procedures. Here is where the contrast is sharpest between German and American public law. Although the U.S. Constitution makes no mention of administrative practice, statutory constraints are strong and judicially enforceable. Regulations with the force of law are usually governed by the informal rulemaking provisions of the Administrative Procedures Act, which require broad public notice, the opportunity for a wide range of interests to comment, and a statement of the reasons behind the agency's decision.[23] In contrast, the German Administrative Procedures Act (*Verwaltungsverfahrensgesetz*) governs public agencies only when they are implementing a general policy in a particular case.[24] It does not apply to the writing of legal regulations and administrative guidelines.[25]

The ordinances governing the German federal ministries require them to inform national organizations representing concerned interests and to hold a hearing before a rule or guideline is issued.[26] These ordinances are only internal administrative rules with no legal force. Failure to comply with their provisions does not undermine the legality of a rule.[27] There is no judicial review of the adequacy of representation. Notice need not be general; the hearing and the materials presented need not be open to the public. The rule or guideline that results need not be accompanied by a statement of reasons.[28]

German law distinguishes between regulations and administrative guidelines. The government must always publish legally binding regulations, but administrative guidelines are sometimes not made public, much less justified.[29] Because administrative guidelines have no formal, external legal force, a failure to follow statutory procedures cannot be challenged by citizens. Procedural requirements do not enhance the legal status of such guidelines. For example, the air and noise pollution statute requires a hearing before technical guidelines are set, but if the ministry fails to hold a hearing, the statute's procedural strictures do not give outsiders any legally enforceable claims.[30]

Even for legally binding regulations, the status of procedural guarantees is unclear. In principle, a statute that requires the executive to follow certain procedures in promulgating a regulation will be void if these procedures are not followed.[31] Few statutes, however, actually contain such requirements.[32] Those that exist, such as the hearing requirements of the air and noise pollution statute, give the ministry broad discretion.[33]

One constitutional commentator can cite only a single case, dating from 1959, in support of the proposition that a failure to follow procedures would invalidate a rule.[34] This involved a rent control statute requiring governments to hold a hearing of experts before setting rents. The Constitutional Court invalidated a Hamburg ordinance because the only experts consulted were government officials. The Court held that the procedural requirement was not satisfied unless the government also consulted independent experts.[35] The Court was thus willing to go beyond the government's claim of formal compliance to examine its actual behavior.

A case decided twenty years later suggests a narrow interpretation of the doctrine.[36] It concerned a statute regulating the teaching obligations of technical college instructors. The law required the state of Hesse to permit the instructors' unions to participate in the preparation of an ordinance. The Hessian authorities did not consult the unions during preliminary deliberations. When a union challenged this failure, the Court upheld the legislature's effort to control administrative procedures but refused to invalidate the ordinance.[37] The lack of consultation was, the court explained, a political failure that should be regulated by political means.[38] The Court argued that the procedural requirements were only guidelines and thus that violating them would not invalidate the ordinance.[39] The earlier case, involving rent control, was distinguished as an attempt to ensure that a law passed during the Nazi period was made compatible with the postwar constitution.[40]

In spite of constitutional limits on executive action, the policy-making process in the bureaucracy faces few external controls. Even when statutes do specify procedures, the courts have been reluctant to invalidate executive actions on purely procedural grounds. They fear that a more active stance would be viewed as judicial interference in "politics."

ENVIRONMENTAL POLICY-MAKING

Environmental policy-making within the executive relies on a complex structure of technical and political advice. Given the lack of overall structural constraints, the actual pattern differs from subject to subject. Accountability to private groups and to political actors takes various forms, from consultation with advisory committees to delegation of technical questions to outside experts. Technical and policy advice is provided by public and private groups with varying degrees of independence from the government and from interest groups. In many areas of environmental law the basic policy work is performed by working groups of federal and state officials that draft laws and regulations. National guidelines and standards concerning product quality or technical specifications are prepared with heavy input from industry and the scientific community, but environmental groups are sometimes consulted as well. In several cases, however, the regulated industry and the ministry have agreed informally on a method of compliance that avoids setting formal standards.

PUBLIC SECTOR ADVICE

Two organizations with government ties perform broad-based policy studies not necessarily tied to current regulatory priorities. One group is government-funded but operates independently and is without ties to interest groups. The other, in essence, constitutes the expert staff of the ministry. Both respond to particular requests from the government for studies or opinions. A third, more diffuse group, the Working Association for Environmental Questions (*Arbeitsgemeinschaft für Umweltfragen*), was founded in the early seventies to organize discussions between interest groups, technical experts, and environmentalists.[41] It appears to be mainly a forum for advising the ministry by airing a range of opinions on environmental matters.

THE COUNCIL OF ENVIRONMENTAL EXPERTS

The independent Council of Environmental Experts (*Rat von Sachverständigen für Umweltfragen*) is a group of academic authorities serving part-time that sets its own agenda and responds to requests from the Environmental Ministry.[42] It was established by the Ministry and is federally funded. The Council is modeled after the German Council of Economic Experts, which has independent status, unlike the American Council of Economic Advisors.[43] Although both German councils depend on federal budgetary support, they have each successfully maintained an identity separate from the government and from organized interests.

Since its founding in 1971, the Council of Environmental Experts has published reports on such broad topics as energy and the environment, waste disposal, and chemicals in the environment. In addition, the Council provides advice on particular issues to the Environmental Ministry. Such opinions are published only at the minister's discretion. The Council also provides documents and information to parliamentary committees.[44] Its role is limited by its small staff and the part-time nature of membership, but several of its reports have provided background material used in drafting statutes and regulations, and its specific advice on current legislative and regulatory issues is often influential.[45] For example, the Council contributed to the implementation of the 1983 regulation governing sulfur dioxide emissions from large plants. In November 1983 it issued a proposed sulfur dioxide standard that was viewed as extremely stringent. The regulation issued by the government in 1984 was a political compromise that took into account the concerns of the Länder by providing more leeway for older plants.[46]

THE FEDERAL ENVIRONMENTAL AGENCY

Founded in 1974, the Federal Environmental Agency (Umweltbundesamt) operates as the ministry's expert staff. The agency's agenda is largely set by the environmental minister, but it issues reports under its own name, and its president does not always adopt the minister's positions. The agency gains a certain independence from the fact that its president, Heinrich von Lersner, has been in office since the agency's founding. The staff of more than four hundred professionals consists mostly of engineers and scientists. The agency performs scientific research and data gathering that assist in ministry policy-making, and it frequently contracts with outside experts.[47] Economists and other social scientists play a marginal role, however. Policy analysis is a peripheral activity, although it may be gaining importance. Between 1990 and 1991 the number of professional employees with university degrees in economics (*Wirtschaftswissenschaft*) increased from three to fifteen.[48] Furthermore, the agency's annual reports reflect an interest in economically efficient methods of pollution control, and the organization has recently completed ten studies of the costs and benefits of reducing environmental pollution.[49]

The agency collects information on environmental conditions and publishes a compendium of data every other year. Its research on environmental impacts seeks to link causes and effects, and it represents Germany in international environmental bodies. Much of its work, however, is the preparation of technical background material for specific policy initiatives. For example, in the field of air pollution the agency in 1991 worked on the production and amendment of regulations in such areas as licensing sources, regulating hazardous accidents, refueling motor vehicles, transporting motor fuels, prohibiting CFC Halon production, and reducing smog.[50]

ADVICE FROM PRIVATE GROUPS

The Council of Environmental Experts and the Umweltbundesamt are only two of the many organizations that provide advice and technical assistance on specific issues. Several hundred groups exist. The activities of these disparate institutions demonstrate the difficulty of neatly separating technical and policy concerns or public and private institutions. Their advice ranges from purely technical opinions to the outright setting of legal norms.[51]

PRIVATE NORM-SETTING ORGANIZATIONS

Private norm-setting organizations play a key role in the self-regulation of economic activity outside the environmental area. There are 170 such bodies in Germany that act as industrial standard-setters.[52] Regulators routinely consult these private associations of technical experts, and these groups now help set standards in the environmental field.[53] Most important are the German Institute for Norms (Deutsches Institut für Normung [DIN])[54] and the Association of German Engineers (Verein Deutscher Ingenieure [VDI]).[55] The DIN has a committee for nuclear engineering, and in 1990 the DIN and the VDI established a Commission on Air Pollution Prevention with financial support from the federal government.[56]

Environmental authorities sometimes use the standards of private groups as guides for implementing statutes. Even though these standards are not formal administrative guidelines, they influence statutory implementation in individual cases. The administrative courts refuse to defer automatically to guidelines that have simply been lifted from the professional societies,[57] but the judges' lack of expertise means that the private engineering norms will have almost the same binding effect as regulations and guidelines.[58] German judges can call on their own experts if they are uncertain about how to interpret a technical rule, but they are likely to consult the same people who wrote the guideline in the first place.[59] In other cases the standards are incorporated with little or no change into formal administrative guidelines.[60] The Technical Instructions for Air Pollution Control (*Technische Anleitung zur Reinhaltung der Luft* [TA Luft]) contains several sections that explicitly incorporate DIN and VDI norms.[61] Judicial deference, though not absolute, is strong when these norms are included in guidelines issued by the government.[62]

The norms generated by private technical groups may introduce biases into the policy process. The newly established VDI-DIN Commission on Air Pollution Prevention provides a useful focus because it could, in principle, consider fundamental policy questions. The Commission established a committee to review environmental meteorology, another to measure the damages caused by air pollution, two committees to evaluate techniques for reducing emissions through prevention and treatment, and a fifth committee to deal with measurement technology.[63] Each committee aims to establish uniform standards without much concern for whether the pieces fit together reasonably. The structure appears flawed. There is no mechanism to connect means and ends and evaluate the overall impact of the recommendations.[64]

The basic structure of the VDI-DIN process raises other questions. The Air Pollution Prevention Commission follows the general practice of the DIN in setting standards. Each committee consists of technically competent people charged with negotiating consensus standards. Committees consist of experts employed by industry—engineers and natural scientists—with some representatives from government and a smattering of social scientists.[65] Environmental groups are not represented.[66] Committee members are "volunteers," but the members' employers, rather than the individuals, bear the participation cost. The committees meet privately, but their preliminary proposals are open to review by anyone, including environmental groups.[67] Such groups, however, rarely provide effective review. Draft standards are often costly and difficult to obtain, and the groups are small and lack financial and technical resources.[68] They are usually incapable of understanding and criticizing the details of most engineering standards within allowed time limits.

The DIN has taken one action that may help incorporate environmental concerns into ordinary standards. It is unlikely, however, to play a significant role in developing overall environmental policy. With 75 percent of its funding coming from the Federal Environmental Ministry, the Institute has established a small Coordination Office for Environmental Protection. The office has three professional staff members and an advisory council. It is charged with monitoring all standard-setting processes with environmental implications and providing "honorary experts" to take part in the meetings. This new office is a step in the right direction, but its small budget and limited power will assign it a marginal role.[69]

The role of private societies in the regulatory process has been criticized on the ground that industrial interests are overrepresented.[70] Defenders respond that professional scientific and engineering norms dominate the standard-setting process.[71] Critics and defenders could both be right, but the balance is impossible to determine, given statutes with little focus on means/end rationality and with no possibility for external review of the groups' methods. Several German administrative law scholars have recognized this problem and have urged more transparent processes within the private groups and less reliance on their recommendations in setting standards.[72] Nevertheless, these suggestions have had little effect.

The influence of the private norm-setting organizations goes beyond concerns for objectivity. The problem is not just that the engineering standards may be biased but that the policy problem should not be framed in terms of engineering standards. Even highly competent engineers acting according to professional norms are unlikely to be sensitive to the broader social implications of their technical recommendations. Although they purport to be making purely technical judgments, they will in fact often balance costs and benefits. The nature of many environmental problems makes a neat separation into technical and political or policy issues impossible.[73] Engineers do not necessarily make good policy analysts. Asking engineers to resolve mixed issues invites a bias toward standard-setting rather than toward a more nuanced view of the link between means and ends.[74]

ADVISORY COMMITTEES

Although private standard-setting organizations frequently recommend technical standards, these groups have no formal decision-making authority. The ministry or the cabinet holds ultimate responsibility for promulgating legal regulations and administrative guidelines, subject to Bundesrat approval. Several statutes require the ministry to seek outside advice from advisory committees that include representatives of industry, labor, science, and occasionally environmental or consumer groups. The composition of the committee may be specified by law, but the ministry selects the members. Although technical considerations are important, the advice sought is political, as well as technical.

A few examples will suggest the range of committee types. The federal government has established sixty water pollution task forces—one for each polluting activity. In addition to federal and state officials, the committees include industry representatives and outside technical experts. The task forces have set minimum standards that were incorporated into administrative rules approved by the Bundesrat.[75] Three committees with heavy industry representation play an important role in regulating chemicals.[76] For example, the Committee on Hazardous Substances in the Workplace has thirty-eight members. Nine are from industry, six from state government, seven from unions, four from insurers, three are scientists, and nine represent a range of other public and private organizations (including one from a consumer group).[77] The members of the industry-financed Committee for Environmentally Relevant Old Substances are one-third from industry, one-third from the public sector, and one-third from science. The committee reviews hazard reports that have been prepared by the chemical industry with oversight provided by the Umweltbundesamt.[78]

In the field of nuclear power, three advisory committees are of central importance. Both the Nuclear Reactor Safety Commission and the Radiation Protection Commission are dominated by industry and by scientists with a commitment to nuclear power.[79] The Nuclear Technology Committee (*Kerntechnische Ausschuß* [KTA]) has fifty members. Ten represent producers and builders of nuclear equipment and plants; ten represent purchasers of nuclear technology (that is, power companies); ten represent state and federal agencies responsible for regulating the industry; ten represent bodies with expertise in the field; and the remaining ten represent other federal ministries (5), insurance companies (2), labor unions (1), the DIN (1), and the Atomic Research Institute (1). The committee votes using a five-sixths rule so that any of the five groups can form a blocking coalition if its members cooperate.[80]

These committees are subject to the same criticisms as those leveled against the DIN and the VDI. They seem to be overly susceptible to the influence of the regulated industry and of scientists whose livelihood depends on the industry's continued viability.[81] The composition of these committees, given the vague wording of statutes and the deference of the courts, raises questions about the democratic legitimacy of regulatory decisions that depend heavily on their recommendations.[82]

One student of German nuclear power regulation, however, argues that the system has found a reasonable balance. The advisory committees are dominated by industry, and day-to-day implementation is carried out by self-regulatory bodies. Nevertheless, the industry as a whole is concerned with safety because of the potential for political action by concerned citizens associated with the Green party or other environmental organizations. A major accident would have severe political costs for producers of nuclear power and so should be avoided.[83] This sanguine view of the current situation raises an important question. Can environmental concerns be best incorporated into the regulatory process by statutes giving organized groups direct access to decision-making institutions or by political protests that act as a background constraint?[84] The former route, more typical of the United States, is, I believe, ultimately more conducive to good policy and is more democratically legitimate. The German public law tradition, however, upholds the view that outside protest, rather than inside participation, is the better course. For technically complex issues, this seems a doubtful claim.

BUND-LÄNDER WORKING GROUPS
AND MINISTRY HEARINGS

In some regulatory areas, the federal government can simply announce a regulation or guideline after consultation with public and private experts, advisory committees, and other interested parties. In environmental policy, such a centralized process is usually insufficient because the Länder implement the laws. Standards must be approved by the Bundesrat, and they must be drafted so that the Land administrations are willing to enforce them. Federal-state cooperation is so important that it has been institutionalized in the form of a Conference of Environmental Ministers and through permanent Bund-Länder Arbeitskreise (literally, federal-state work-circles). Work-circles exist in all areas of environmental protection, and they contain Länder technical experts as well as federal officials. Although they have no statutory basis and their meetings are not open to the public, they exert a strong influence on the content of both laws and regulations.[85]

Public and private institutions with technical expertise provide support for these committees. The Umweltbundesamt is often asked to provide technical background, and guidelines developed by the private norm-setting groups influence committee deliberations. The Bund-Länder committees are not structured to produce objective scientific advice. Even when most of their members are technical experts, they are making political decisions. Nevertheless, they are involved in highly technical decisions, such as setting water quality targets on the basis of biological effects.[86] Committee recommendations and reports often provide the background for draft federal government regulations and statutes. Their work mixes technical and political criteria.

With these draft documents in hand, the federal government can move to promulgate formal regulations or guidelines. At this point, several statutes require a hearing of those concerned. Others, however, such as the Federal Water Act, impose no constraints.[87] The air and noise pollution act states that the ministry "shall hear" representatives of those directly affected as well as representatives of the scientific community, the trade, industry and traffic sectors, and the responsible Land authorities.[88] Environmental organizations are not included in the list, although the ministry can consult with them if it wishes. The chemical and waste laws also require the ministry to consult with those concerned before issuing regulations. The waste act's language is similar to that of the air and noise pollution statute, and the chemical act includes several types of public interest groups in the list.[89]

Unlike hearings under the American Administrative Procedures Act, these processes are entirely under the ministry's control. The hearings are not usually open to the public, and they do not produce a public record. If independent experts testify, they are selected by the ministry, and their testimony is not generally made public.[90] Even though the minister has no obligation to include environmental groups, they are frequently invited to testify and may also be informally consulted during the drafting process.[91] The Environmental Ministry routinely consults such moderate public interest organizations as the German Association of Citizens Groups (Bundesverband Bürgerinitiativen Umweltschutz [BBU]), and the Bund für Umwelt und Naturschutz Deutschland (BUND).[92]

Draft regulations (*Arbeitsentwürfe*) are made available to those invited to attend the hearings, but they are not published as public documents. Even when the minister has approved a draft (*Referentenentwurf*), the text is not published although it is, in practice, likely to be available to interested individuals and groups. The next step is cabinet approval, after which the government submits the draft to the Bundesrat for final approval.[93] The Bundesrat requires the executive to justify its proposed rules and guidelines. These documents are not public defenses but are viewed as part of the internal operation of government.[94] The final regulation or guideline is published.[95]

This drafting process blends the concerns of state governments that implement the statute with those of technical experts, most of whom are engineers working for state governments and industry. The process can be relatively insulated from the arguments of social scientists and environmentalists, although in practice both groups are often consulted.

INFORMAL AGREEMENTS

The end result of the processes of consultation and analysis outlined above is either a legally enforceable rule or a standard that is given a good deal of presumptive legal force by the courts. The process may be informal and hard to specify, but the outcome is relatively well defined. Seeking to avoid such clear-cut results, industry groups have sometimes agreed informally to meet certain standards without giving them any legal status and occasionally without their being made public.[96] A press release announces an agreement between the ministry and the industry, with the details in a private letter to the ministry from the affected firms. Such actions are possible because the acts permit, but do not require, regulations or guidelines and set no deadlines for issuing formal standards. Such informal agreements make outside review—of both the process and the substantive standards—impossible.

For example, the law dealing with detergents empowers the government to issue regulations that govern the content of detergents.[97] Instead of issuing a legally binding regulation, the minister approved the measures laid down in a letter from the producers. This letter has no formal legal status and was not approved by the Bundesrat. It was published in an official journal only after career officials in the ministry applied pressure.[98] In its published form, it can be distinguished from a regular legal ordinance only by the lack of section symbols in the text.[99]

Similar informal agreements have been used in regulating chemicals. In 1987 the chemical industry voluntarily agreed to stop using volatile chlorinated hydrocarbons and to decrease the use of chlorofluorocarbons (CFCs) in spray cans.[100] More recently, asbestos was regulated with an informal letter. This time the letter has not been made public.[101] The use of informal, unaccountable actions raises the possibility that ministerial actions will not comport with statutory purposes. Even if the informal agreements are in fact reasonable compromises, they require the check of outside constraints to preserve democratic legitimacy.[102]

CONCLUSION

German environmental policy processes are complex and unstandardized. Research organizations, standard-setting groups, advisory committees, and federal-state working groups interact with one another both formally and informally. The Umweltbundesamt provides backup information to working groups, and it contracts with the DIN and with university scientists for technical advice.[103] Advisory committees use background reports prepared by the Council of Environmental Experts, the Umweltbundesamt, or private expert bodies. Members of the DIN serve on advisory committees. Further, because of the size of the country and the small pool of experts, the same people may serve in several capacities. The same scientist may be part of a DIN committee, serve on an Advisory Committee, and participate in a working group.

The complexity of the links between technical and policy-making bodies, however, disguises a simple basic structure. The German system focuses on producing ambient environmental quality guidelines and emission standards that can be enforced through the licensing activities of lower-level governments. The initial steps are designed to give precedence to technical, scientific concerns. This stage is followed by a weighing process that considers political and administrative aspects. This framework, constructed under the assumption that a sharp distinction between science and politics is possible, fails to accommodate reality. In practice, science, politics, and economic feasibility are intertwined at all stages.[104]

Consider the way standards are set for air pollution. The law requires standards for both emissions and immissions (ambient conditions). In setting ambient standards, the goal is to avoid "dangers, considerable disadvantages, or considerable nuisance to the general public or the neighborhood."[105] The statutory language obviously leaves much to the discretion of the executive. The process proceeds in five stages. The first stage involves calculation of a dose-response relation between the pollutant and harm to humans or aspects of the natural environment. Second, scientists perform a risk assessment; given alternative ambient standards, they calculate the range of possible effects. The Umweltbundesamt and the scientific community are heavily involved at this stage. Third, alternative ambient standards are evaluated. Fourth, decision makers estimate the possibilities of avoiding or mitigating the pollution. A final weighing process (*Abwägung*) produces a standard. The last three steps require balancing in the light of the scientific evidence.[106] Advisory committees, Bund-Länder working groups, and cabinet ministers all participate in this process, depending upon the particular issue involved. The balance struck at one stage may be overturned at another.

Standard-setting procedures for emissions follow a similar pattern. Control measures must be appropriate given the "state of the art."[107] The first step is to discover which measures are technically feasible and effective in reducing discharges. The costs of the alternatives must then be calculated; the private standard-setting organizations have the most influence at this part of the process. Third, some type of benefit measure is calculated, and fourth, a weighing process produces a decision.[108]

These standard-setting processes have a surface logic and plausibility, but they are fundamentally misconceived. It makes no sense to view the setting of emissions standards and ambient levels as distinct bureaucratic enterprises. The appropriate ambient standard is a function of the costs of alternatives and the benefits at particular geographic locations. The public health and ecological impact of a standard cannot be determined in the abstract with no reference to where the emissions are produced. Emissions rules should not be viewed as engineering exercises. Engineers can contribute by specifying technical options, but physical possibility and economic feasibility are insufficient guides to policy. One also needs to know the relation between costs and benefits. In the current process, the balancing that produces the final ambient or emission standard is a function of the economic importance and political power of various groups, not a sober evaluation of the impact of alternative policies on the environment. A weighing process is needed, but it should be one that takes better account of the overall impact of the policy alternatives.

These flaws in the basic structure are exacerbated by the lack of procedural constraints on bureaucratic policy-making. Even when a standard-setting framework is appropriate, the decision is not made in a way that is transparent to citizens and open to their participation. The close link between the legislature and the executive in the German parliamentary system provides insufficient protection for the public. Even in a parliamentary system, the party coalition in power may prefer to issue regulations and guidelines without public discussion, if that will cement political deals. The strength of party discipline and the lack of separation between executive and legislature may result in quiet acquiescence from elected representatives rather than active oversight.

The federal government's actual weighing process may be even less democratically legitimate than the procedures of some private groups.[109] The DIN and the VDI have ordinances governing their procedures. They make draft standards public and invite comments. In contrast, the setting of federal guidelines is not governed by similar laws or legal regulations. Advisory committees are selected by the ministry and biased toward the regulated industry. Hearing requirements are not legally enforceable, and the hearings are usually not public and are entirely under ministry control. No statement of reasons need be produced.

Länder governments do impose constraints on the federal executive. The requirement of Bundesrat approval and Länder implementation give federal officials a strong incentive to involve state officials early in the policy-making process. Although such intergovernmental cooperation is surely valuable, it is not a good substitute for broader, more open participation. The states are likely to be more concerned with interjurisdictional fairness and the cost and trouble of implementation than with good national policy. They are unlikely to focus either on the technical competence of federal proposals or on the impact of policies on groups or individuals not well represented in state politics. In regulatory areas, such as environmental protection, the interested public cuts across state boundaries; therefore, democratic legitimacy requires additional checks.

Private environmental groups have only limited participation possibilities. They are generally excluded from advisory committees and play only a marginal role within the private norm-setting organizations. Public officials may consult with them, but only at the discretion of the officials themselves. The structure of the administrative process encourages these groups to adopt a confrontational style.

German procedures suffer from two deep-seated weaknesses. The first is the structural failure to match procedures to the nature of the environmental problems being regulated. The second is a set of institutions and processes that lack openness and accountability. Neither legislative oversight nor the German model of consensual decision-making is sufficient to provide legitimacy in the technically complex but democratically salient field of environmental policy-making.

5

JUDICIAL REVIEW IN GERMANY

Under the Grundgesetz, judicial review of administrative actions emphasizes the protection of individual rights against the arbitrary exercise of state power. According to article 19(*4*), "Should any person's rights be violated by public authority, recourse to the court shall be open to him."[1] The Administrative Courts' caseload mainly consists of such individualistic complaints.[2] In contrast to the broad protection of individual rights, judicial review under administrative law plays only a limited role in monitoring the political and policy-making activities of government.[3] Individuals and organizations can challenge regulations only if their rights have been violated.[4]

German administrative law does not provide pre-enforcement review of federal rules or guidelines. Organized groups and individuals cannot challenge a general administrative action in the courts before it has been applied in a particular case. Federal *Normenkontrolle* actions, challenging the constitutionality of a federal law, cannot be used to review legal regulations and are not open to private individuals and groups.[5] No one can challenge administrative guidelines, because they are government actions without formal, external legal force.[6]

The deferential position of Germany's courts in the face of executive policy-making is especially important for environmental law. Although all statutes have areas of ambiguity, environmental statutes are particularly likely to be under-determined. The need for substantial technical, scientific, and economic data, along with rapidly changing conditions, argue in favor of laws that delegate considerable authority to administrative agencies. Rather than leave the development of the law to the exigencies of case-by-case application, the law will be more effective and fair if the minister sets standards or policies centrally.

German statutes, however, contain gaps. Neither constitutional nor administrative law does much to regulate the government's policy-making activities. In the face of this legal vacuum, the judiciary has found a number of creative ways to acknowledge modern bureaucratic realities without doing too much damage to traditional legal concepts. The courts have taken some tentative steps to encourage more rational, open, pluralistic administrative processes, although this cannot be said to be a clear trend.[7] Both the Constitutional Court and the Administrative Courts have participated in these acts of creative re-definition.

PROCEDURAL GUARANTEES AND THE REGULATION OF RISKS

The Constitutional Court has held that constitutional principles can constrain administrative procedures in particular cases. It has found the regulation of risks constitutional and has accepted delegation to the executive.[8] The justices have not, however, reviewed the constitutionality of federal administrative procedures that set environmental or safety standards. In three cases dealing with nuclear power, the court dealt with either higher-level or lower-level issues. In one case, it upheld the constitutionality of a regulatory statute that left many important issues open for interpretation by the implementing authorities. In the second, the court reviewed the appropriateness of a power plant licensing decision. In the third, it upheld an atomic power plant licensing regulation that limited the types of complaints that could be brought to court.

The first case, Kalkar, dealt with the construction of a fast breeder reactor under the Atomic Power Act.[9] The court found the act constitutional, and held that the Grundgesetz required passage of a law governing the "fatal" risk of atomic power. Bundestag inaction would have been unconstitutional.[10] The Court then legitimated delegation to administrative officials for technical matters. It found that the administration had not exceeded its statutory authority in interpreting the vague language concerning the technical standards used in licensing nuclear power plants. Keeping within the individual rights framework, the judges found that "good reasons support the use of undefined legal terms in [the Atomic Energy Act]. The wording of . . . [the Act], which is open to future developments, serves as a dynamic protection of fundamental rights. . . . To fix a safety standard by establishing rigid rules, if that is even possible, would impede rather than promote technical developments and adequate safeguards for fundamental rights. . . . In the interest of flexible protection of life and property, the executive must assess and constantly adjust safety measures—a task which it is better equipped to perform than the legislature."[11]

This decision legitimates a regulatory strategy in which the statute articulates the basic legislative goals and empowers the bureaucracy to give these goals specific technical content.[12] It says nothing, however, about what procedures the bureaucracy should follow in carrying out its delegated responsibilities.

The second case, Mülheim-Kärlich, involved procedures, but only in the context of a *particular* power plant license.[13] The decision suggests that administrators can use participatory procedures to justify substantive decisions. It held "the peaceful use of nuclear energy to be constitutional in the face of an objection that nuclear power threatens constitutional rights to life and bodily inviolability [GG art. 2(2)]." The court "cautioned that certain kinds of formalities, such as public participation in nuclear power licensing procedures, may be necessary to protect basic rights and liberties," but the justices found that existing participatory provisions were adequate.[14] Because the case involved review of a single power plant license, not a federal regulation, it can be read narrowly to apply only to statutory implementation in particular cases where the rights of individuals may be violated. Nonetheless, it articulates principles that could be developed in the context of more general policy-making exercises.

The third case, Sasbach, upheld the constitutionality of a procedure for licensing nuclear power plants.[15] Sasbach is important because the Constitutional Court stepped outside the individual rights framework and upheld a procedure on policy-making grounds. A regulation had imposed a time limit of one month after publication of a plan for registering objections.[16] The Court upheld the rule, arguing that it facilitated high-quality administrative decision-making by permitting officials to balance all aspects of the project. The justices conclude with the claim that "the courts review such [administrative] evaluations only to ascertain their legality. They do not substitute their own evaluation of the merits in place of the officials'."[17] For the courts to take on this evaluative task would violate German notions of the separation of powers and undermine the fundamental role of the bureaucracy.[18] The justices reviewed licensing procedures, not substance, and found the procedures adequate.

A recent case, far from the nuclear power field, deserves mention. It concerned a statute restricting the promotion and marketing of books that might be morally harmful to youth.[19] A committee promulgates a list of harmful publications. The Court found that the statute establishing the committee was unconstitutional because it insufficiently regulated the selection of members. Committee decisions should reflect public, not private, interests. The selection process lacked democratic legitimacy because it was not directed at achieving that result. The Court did not impose substantive standards of literary merit, but instead required that the Bundestag modify the procedural aspects of the law in the light of the Court's decision. The case is noteworthy not only because it suggests that the Court will examine mandated procedures to determine a statute's constitutionality, but also because it found existing procedures inadequate on public interest grounds.

One German commentator, Erhard Denninger, argues that the Grundgesetz requires certain procedures to be followed when the government sets technical regulations and guidelines.[20] Citing the Mülheim-Kärlich case, he argues that procedural justice is required not only in individual cases but also when environmental and technical norms are set by a ministry. The more discretion that has been allotted to the executive, the more necessary are transparent and

accountable procedures.[21] Denninger does not spell out the procedural requirements in detail, but they include an obligation to consult with concerned
groups. For him, consultation is a constitutional requirement that holds even in
the absence of statutory language. The range of those consulted should include
environmental and public interest groups, as well as nearby and distant "neighbors."[22] Those consulted should be able to present both factual information and
opinions. The participants would not only present information about claimed
violations of rights but could critique the substance of the proposed rules and
guidelines.[23]

Rudolf Steinberg takes a similar view of the standard-setting process for
atomic power.[24] He argues that the Grundgesetz requires the legislature to provide formal legal grounding both for the committees that set safety standards
and for the standards themselves.[25] Legislation should specify the composition
of committees and the procedures they should follow. Committee membership
should be broader than at present, and procedures should involve hearings and a
decision that is published and accompanied by a statement of reasons.

Neither Denninger's nor Steinberg's proposals have yet been accepted by the
Constitutional Court. Nevertheless, the case law outlined above indicates that
these constitutional interpretations are not inconsistent with recent judicial
pronouncements. The Court has begun to recognize the necessity of delegation
as well as the value of controlling it through procedural rather than substantive
constraints.

THE PROPORTIONALITY PRINCIPLE

The Constitutional Court has been much less reluctant to set forth
substantive principles of judicial review. The most basic of these is the proportionality principle (*Verhältnismäßigkeitsprinzip im weiteren Sinn*), or the requirement that a policy be carried out by the least restrictive means (*Übermaßverbot*).
This broad principle is based on the Rechtsstaat principle, or the principle of a
state ruled by law. It is said by the courts to derive from fundamental rights
protected by the German Constitution.[26] The principle has four parts. First,
the end of the law must be legitimate (*Legitimität des Zieles*); second, the means
must be in proportion to the ends (*Verhältnismäßigkeitsprinzip im engeren Sinn*);
third, the means must be an effective way of reaching the end (*Geeignetheit des
Mittels*); and fourth, the means must be the ones entailing the least intrusion
into individual rights (*Erforderlichkeit des Mittels*).[27] The proportionality principle governs regulations as well as statutes.[28] However, the Court has infre-
quently applied it to invalidate administrative decisions. In a case challenging
the implementation of a statute, the Constitutional Court implied that it would
intervene only in extreme cases.[29]

PROPORTIONALITY AND COST-BENEFIT TESTS

The protection of individual rights is the basis of judicial applications of the proportionality principle.[30] However, the principle need not be viewed so narrowly. It is grounded in the basic democratic structure of the German state and can serve a broader function. The principle invites the Constitutional Court to judge the merits of statutes and regulations by evaluating the relation between statutory means and ends. It permits the Court to ask if a statute is a well-thought-out response to a public problem or if a regulation is a least-cost solution to a legal mandate. The doctrine of proportionality could permit a high standard of review of the substance of administrative decisions—one based on principles similar to the economist's cost-benefit test.

This interpretation is not as farfetched as it might seem. German courts presently weigh benefits and harms in applying the principle. As an example, consider the following case from the Administrative Court in Baden-Württemberg.[31] The court reviewed a nature protection ordinance that restricted diving in two lakes. The complainant argued that the ordinance interfered with the constitutional right to free development of one's personality.[32] The court found that the public interest in nature protection was a legitimate justification for regulation. However, it held that the diving regulations were in general an unsuitable and unnecessary means of protection. Hundreds of people swam in the lakes daily, so regulating diving would have a minimal impact on nature.[33] A prohibition on night diving was, however, upheld. Unlike night swimming, night diving involved the use of underwater floodlights and would thus be very disruptive to wildlife. The court viewed the prohibition as a reasonable restraint on divers because it restricted them only between eleven at night and the early morning. Though it is not a formal cost-benefit analysis, the opinion represents a reasonable balancing of gains and losses.

The Constitutional Court has also articulated a "cost-covering" principle that applies to monetary payments by citizens or firms in return for specific benefits. The principle requires that the financial burdens imposed by statute should not exceed the benefits.[34] The principle is an attempt to limit government to cost-justified activities. The Court has not, however, applied this doctrine in regulatory areas where the costs to regulated entities do not show up as payments to public authorities. Nevertheless, the basic idea, which appears to be a special case of the proportionality principle, could be extended beyond the payment of fees without violating its fundamental rationale.

Within this constitutional law framework, the highest administrative court has accepted the use of cost-benefit or risk-benefit analysis if it is consistent with the regulatory statute. A case arose under the pesticides law when a manufacturer and shipper of a hazardous pesticide complained about being denied a shipping permit.[35] The law requires that a permit be granted only if there will be no harmful effects on the health of humans and animals and on groundwater, and if there will be no "other effects" that are unjustified, given the level of scientific knowledge.[36] The court supported the public authorities' effort to calculate these "other effects" by weighing the probability of their occurrence, the level of potential harm, the availability of substitutes, and the disadvantages of not using the pesticide. This exercise, although not a cost-benefit analysis, represents a sophisticated understanding of the notion of "opportunity cost." The court itself did not apply this version of the proportionality principle, but insisted that the executive do so. The decision falls far short of a general requirement that costs be balanced against benefits, but it does suggest the High Administrative Court's willingness to accept such techniques within the executive.

VORSORGE AND PROPORTIONALITY

The proportionality principle could be given a broad application in environmental law.[37] Although it obviously applies to those environmental statutes that mention the term in the text,[38] it can be invoked independently of explicit statutory language.[39] When the air and noise pollution law speaks about the "state of the art" (*Stand der Technik*), some commentators take that to mean a standard that satisfies the proportionality principle.[40]

The elasticity of the concept of proportionality is illustrated by the judicial conflation of the principle with the *Vorsorge* or precautionary principle of environmental protection. Vorsorge is a buzzword of German environmental policy, and it has a multitude of meanings.[41] At its core, it implies a presumption in favor of regulation even if the data base is weak. The link with proportionality was made in a case dealing with the regulation of air pollution from large power plants.[42] The Federal Administrative Court upheld a stringent federal regulation against a challenge based on a violation of proportionality.[43] Quoting a study performed by the Council of Environmental Experts, the court pointed to the long-distance transport of substances that pollute the air, the time lag between causes and effects, and the difficulty of associating particular harms with the discharges of individual plants. Under such conditions, the court held that the government could use general regulations as long as a risk is suspected and the measures are proportional to the probable risk.[44] The Vorsorge principle has been used to uphold federal regulations and guidelines, but it does not give individuals greater rights to challenge the application of these standards in particular cases. A case dealing with atomic power suggests the limits. The risks of an accident at a licensed nuclear power plant did not give nearby residents a legal claim.[45]

DE NOVO REVIEW AND JUDICIAL RESTRAINT

The judicial tendency to uphold federal regulations and guidelines stems in part from the nature of the administrative process that produced them. The lack of a record means that the courts have no principled way to restrict judicial scrutiny. Even when a hearing is a part of the administrative process, the ministry does not prepare a public record of the proceedings or of the information it used to generate the planned regulation or guideline. Furthermore, it is not required to issue a statement of reasons justifying its decision.[46] Thus if a court did become involved, it could not limit itself to deciding if the agency had competently reviewed the evidence or had followed proper procedures. Instead, it would have to begin from the beginning and generate the evidence itself with the help of expert witnesses and affected groups and individuals.

This would be a problematic procedure for both regulations and guidelines. Given the quasi-legislative nature of regulations, courts would substitute their judgments for those of political actors. Given the status of administrative guidelines as internal bureaucratic instructions, de novo court review would interfere with executive prerogatives. The standards of review employed in ordinary German administrative law cases thus limit the types of cases heard by the courts. If review of regulations and guidelines, once granted, cannot be limited but requires a de novo examination of the entire issue, German judges will obviously balk at taking such cases. The competence and democratic accountability of the policy-making process can be constrained by the courts only if they themselves are constrained. An expanded role for the judiciary would need to go hand in hand with a reform of the Administrative Procedures Act to cover the procedures used by the federal ministries when they issue regulations and guidelines.

REVIEW OF ADMINISTRATIVE GUIDELINES

The failure of the German courts to deal straightforwardly with policy-making in the modern regulatory state is especially evident when they confront administrative guidelines (*Verwaltungsvorschriften*). Technical standards are ubiquitous within the German administrative system. These standards are broadly accepted as a necessary feature of statutory implementation, but they do not fit into conventional legal categories unless they take the form of legal regulations (*Rechtsverordnungen*).

Courts give regulations, promulgated under a constitutional grant of authority, the same legal status as statutes. As long as the delegation doctrine is satisfied, and the regulation is within the scope of the authority conferred, the rule has legal force.[47] Challenges to the application of regulations in particular cases are seldom successful, and the rules are treated as binding laws.[48]

In contrast, administrative guidelines have given the administrative courts considerable conceptual difficulties. Although they do not have the "force of law," they are central to the implementation of many statutes. Courts review guidelines only when they are applied to particular cases. The administrative courts have been creative in upholding administrative guidelines, but further work is required to give them a democratically legitimate basis.[49]

The administrative courts refuse to review guidelines that simply govern the internal operation of a ministry. When a nominally internal guideline has an external effect, however, the courts have trouble absorbing such documents within the existing legal framework. The tortured and artificial language they use to justify the use of administrative guidelines points to the need to re-think the relation between the administrative courts and the state and federal executives.

Environmental policy guidelines direct and rationalize bureaucratic action. German scholars distinguish among three types of guidelines: those that inter-pret norms, those that control administrative discretion in individual cases, and those that make laws concrete and specific.[50] In the first, norm-interpreting, case, the courts evaluate the decisions in individual cases to assure their legality. The courts will be deferential, however, if the guideline helps assure equal treatment of individuals in their dealings with the state.[51] The second type standardizes the exercise of discretion by the bureaucracy. Here, the admin-istrative courts examine individual administrative decisions to be sure that officials have not ignored the peculiarities of the case at hand.[52]

The third type is of central importance in environmental law. The character-ization of these guidelines as ones "making norms concrete" is a recent judicial innovation. Such guidelines existed before the courts found a label to apply. In regulating pollution, expert advice helps determine the complex relation between ambient conditions and discharges into the environment by firms, individuals, and communities. Decision-making requires information on the technical possibilities for control and on their relative costs. The federal gov-ernment, with Bundesrat approval, has issued guidelines for air and noise pollu-tion and for waste disposal.[53] The courts have sought to determine whether federal ministries are permitted to issue such standards. When the courts decide that guidelines are acceptable, that is the end of the matter. The justices do not consider either their contents or the procedures used to produce them.

Given the difficulty of deciding whether a guideline is interpreting a norm (type one) or making a norm concrete (type three), it is hardly surprising that German law is not a model of clarity. The administrative courts have resorted to a series of labels to justify the use of administrative guidelines that set technical standards.[54] A case in 1978 challenged the legality of the *Technische Anleitung zur Reinhaltung der Luft* (TA Luft), the administrative guideline providing technical standards for air pollution control.[55] TA Luft contains a host of spe-cific technical standards and seems to violate the principle of deciding individ-ual cases on their merits. Nevertheless, the Federal Administrative Court up-held the guidelines, calling them "anticipatory" expert opinions.[56] The Court held that the ministry could anticipate that expert advice would be needed in a series of individual cases. Rather than assembling experts each time the need arose, it could save resources and speed up the process by issuing a document that reflected expert, technical judgments. The Court judged the guideline acceptable because the federal government had consulted a large number of experts.[57] The distinctive feature of the opinion is the term *anticipated*. Rather than straightforwardly permitting the ministry to admit that it was making general policy with the help of expert advice, the court held to the individual rights framework and justified the use of technical guidelines as a way of resolving individual cases. In truth, of course, TA Luft's standards are not "anticipated" advice at all. They are a set of policy choices informed by the advice of experts.

The idea that such guidelines are not only expert opinions but also make norms "concrete" arose in cases dealing with nuclear power.[58] This second, judicially generated doctrine recognizes that legal guidelines do not simply articulate technical possibilities; they represent a political or policy choice. Under this approach the administrative courts adopted the new label *normkonkretisierende Verwaltungsvorschriften*, which recognizes that legal guidelines are not entirely based on objective scientific evidence. The courts will approve such guidelines if the agency has independently evaluated the expert opinions and made its own choice. The agency, however, need not state the reasons for its choice. Instead, elected politicians and political parties in the governing coalition or in the opposition must monitor the outcome for conformity with law. Judges accept the validity of guidelines but give them less deference than laws or legal regulations when applied to individual cases.[59] In other words, the courts will review claims that a guideline should not apply in a particular case.[60]

The change in labels for the third type of guideline from anticipatory expert opinions to "norm-concretizing" standards represents a more sophisticated understanding of the relation between science and regulatory policy. Seldom can science resolve legal ambiguities. It must be combined with policy judgments about the economic, political, and social costs and benefits of alternative levels of pollution control.

The administrative courts have accepted the existence of legal guidelines. So long as the guidelines accord with the goals of the authorizing act, however, the courts have not monitored the democratic accountability of the process used to produce them.[61] In fact, the very recognition of the political nature of guidelines leads German judges to conclude that the courts should not monitor such executive branch activity. The result is paradoxical. The courts accept administrative procedures that can be easily justified only if executive decisions really are essentially technocratic exercises that scientific experts can answer far from public scrutiny. Truly accountable political decisions would require a different set of procedures—ones that emphasize openness to outside groups and public justification.[62]

JUDICIAL DEFERENCE AND JUDICIAL REVIEW

The substantive constitutional principle of proportionality requires a rational connection between means and ends. In technical areas, such as environmental protection, however, the courts will generally be unable to judge if the proportionality principle has been satisfied when a ministry issues rules and guidelines. In spite of this failure, the obvious benefits of such technical standards suggest that German judges will continue to find a way to accommodate this type of ministry policy-making. One solution is a more procedurally based jurisprudence applicable to the review of the policy process—one that focuses not on the protection of individual rights but on democratic accountability and means/end rationality. A legitimate procedure would combine less reliance on private standard-setting groups with more emphasis on public participation in administrative processes.[63] But given the absence of a record to review or a statement of reasons from the executive, such a legal development is unlikely under current conditions. The courts are unable to judge whether high-level administrative processes are satisfactory. If the courts are to review procedure, they must have both a standard of evaluation and the materials needed to judge bureaucratic compliance. Both are lacking.

Although the courts could take some steps on their own consistent with the constitution, a better approach would be a statute that systematically sets out the procedural requirements and permits judicial review of the adequacy of the bureaucracy's response.[64] In the final chapter, I suggest a possible model of reform. The model draws on American practice while acknowledging the criticisms of rulemaking under American law and recognizing the difficulties of importing another country's practices into the German context.[65]

Although reference to American models may seem an unwarranted exercise in cultural imperialism, I demonstrate in the next chapter that the accountability required by more democratic administrative processes is not as foreign to modern German thinking as might at first appear. Finding such cross-national echoes does not, of course, demonstrate that Germany should adopt American practice. It merely indicates that debate is possible and that comparative work can contribute to the discussion.

6

GERMAN PLANNING
AND LICENSING PROCESSES:
ACCOUNTABILITY AND JUDICIAL REVIEW

The basic outlines of a responsible administrative process exist in German law. But the procedures apply only to the approval of individual licenses and large-scale projects. These projects may be locally important, but they are geographically self-contained. States and localities use planning and licensing processes when an airport or a nuclear power plant seeks a license, when a local government proposes a nature reserve, when a public authority plans a new autobahn or railway, or when a new source of air pollution seeks to begin operation. The procedures do not apply when the Environmental Ministry issues guidelines for sulfur dioxide pollution or noise, or when it designs a regulation on the recycling of packaging waste.

German licensing and planning actions require public notice, a hearing in which objections from interested persons must be accommodated, and a final decision accompanied by a statement of reasons. Limited judicial review is available. The most general statement is the German Administrative Procedures Act's planning process, which requires public notice, a hearing, and a reasoned opinion.[1] Licensing under the air and noise pollution law follows a similar pattern—one that other environmental statutes have copied. Judicial review has focused not only on the protection of individual rights but also on the balancing of conflicting public interests.[2] Review of the administrative process is limited, however, and does not provide a model for a reformed judicial role in overseeing high-level administrative behavior.[3]

These planning and licensing processes are remarkable in that individuals or groups of individuals are not limited to explaining how they will suffer individualized harm. They can discuss the project's impact on society in general. The law recognizes that such processes can also help produce better-informed public decisions.

One statute, the Nature Protection Law, goes further. It contains an exception to the usual German opposition to formal participation of organized environmental groups. The law requires that nature protection groups be consulted in some types of planning processes, and several Länder provide groups limited access to the administrative courts.[4]

In spite of the apparently greater accountability of these planning and licensing processes, Germans may be surprised to see them used as a model for reform. Few view them as successful attempts to encourage effective public participation. In controversial cases, both administrative processes and subsequent court challenges have involved huge numbers of people. The image of fifty thousand individuals petitioning the Environmental Ministry is enough to deter even a sympathetic observer from recommending a direct importation of planning and licensing processes into the higher levels of the administration. Nevertheless, if modified to take realistic account of the problems of implementation, existing planning procedures could be generalized by statute to the writing of regulations and administrative guidelines at both federal and Land levels.

The possibility of such a transfer of institutional form depends on the basic function of these processes. Under either of two contrasting views, the connection is strained. A third conception, however, could permit generalization of this procedural framework.

Under the first view, one begins with the license—the basic tool of German regulatory law. Administrative attention focuses on whether the public authority should grant a license. Because the state is granting permission to a specific person or firm, licensing is inconsistent with a policy-analytic focus on large-scale means/end rationality. The process emphasizes the technical attributes of a particular project seen in isolation. A licensing law fits well with technical standards based solely on engineering criteria. Law and engineering are in alliance against the prescriptions of social science.

From this point of view, a planning process is useful when a project requires a large number of licenses that would be cumbersome to grant one at a time. The German focus is thus not on "planning," as that word is used in English, but on the administratively efficient consolidation of a multitude of licenses. The process helps accomplish the traditional goals of administrative law. The work of the federal ministries is a wholly different kind of activity, akin to legislation, not licensing. If this were the only way to view German planning processes, these processes could not provide much guidance to policy-oriented reformers.

A second view sees planning procedures as "mere" planning exercises, rather than generalized licensing processes. The resulting plans are akin to U.S. regional or city plans. They have no legal force, but they express the goals of the authorities who made them.[5] Alternatively, the analogy might be with local American zoning laws. Zoning maps set legal limits to development in various parts of a city, but municipalities commonly grant exceptions. The maps provide a background within which negotiations can proceed between local governments and developers. This view emphasizes the local nature of the process and resists generalization to the state and national levels.

Although both views help explain the origin of the German planning process, a third perspective accords with part of the function these processes actually play. Under this view the procedure is designed to produce a publicly accountable, technocratic policy choice. It requires administrators to be open to the range of scientific and technical opinion and to develop a sensitivity to the interests of various groups. The aim is a policy that can and must be publicly defended on both technical and political grounds.[6] It is a substitute for the more secret, consensual processes characteristic of policy-making in other areas of German law.

The goals reflected in this third view of the planning process are equivalent to those of policy-making within the federal and state ministries. If consultation with public interest organizations is justified in terms of improved policy decisions, the extension of participation rights to higher-level policy choices is straightforward. The transfer is especially easy to justify in such areas as environmental protection, where decisions based on complex scientific and economic factors have an impact on ordinary citizens.[7]

PLANNING PROCESSES AND POLLUTION LICENSES

Planning procedures and licensing under some environmental statutes require notice, a hearing, and a written statement of reasons. The planning process detailed in the German Administrative Procedures Act contemplates a concrete "project" with a limited geographical impact.[8] The organization responsible for the project prepares a plan.[9] This plan must be available to the public in the affected jurisdictions. These governments must notify the public that the plan is available for inspection.

Only those "whose interests are affected by the project" can express opposition, but the law does not regulate the nature of their objections.[10] Individuals have six weeks to object after the plan has been made available.[11] The public authority must hold a hearing. The date of the hearing must be publicly announced and must occur "in good time." The authorities regulate the hearing and can establish time limits and other procedures. After the hearing, the officials in charge issue a statement that, together with the remaining objections, is sent to the planning authorities for a final decision.[12]

The planners' decision must be in writing and must contain a statement of grounds. If the decision is inconsistent with some of the data, the planning officials must explain why they have not given much weight to this material. Restrictions imposed on the project must be "necessary for the general good" or needed "to avoid detrimental effects on the rights of others."[13] For large-scale proceedings (those with more than three hundred objections), public notice of the decision is permissible, and those affected by it can obtain a copy.[14]

In the environmental field, licensing of large projects serves much the same function as planning processes. It helps inform the authorities about the costs and benefits of projects. The Air and Noise Pollution Statute includes elaborate procedural requirements, similar to those of the general German planning process.[15] Analogous procedures are included in the atomic power and genetic engineering statutes.[16] A firm seeking a license must submit a written application.[17] The authorities must give public notice of the project and make the application available minus any trade secrets. The notice tells people where and when the application can be examined and sets the date of the public discussion (*Erörterung*).[18] The time periods for inspecting the plan and recording objections are the same as under the Administrative Procedures Act.[19] In the subsequent public discussion, "the licensing authority shall discuss the arguments against the project with the applicant and those having raised them."[20] The wording suggests an informal bureaucrat-directed process of balancing pros and cons.[21] The public authority must issue a written decision that includes a statement of reasons.[22] The decision need not be published, but it must be delivered to the parties involved.[23] Anyone who lodges objections during the hearing process may write for a copy of the decision and the statement of reasons.[24]

For some major projects, technically oriented procedures occur before the planning process begins. In general, "factual" issues resolved at the preliminary stage cannot be reexamined later.[25] In the atomic power field, such hybrid processes reveal tensions among the goals of protecting individual rights, making a competent technical evaluation, and accounting for a broad range of interests.[26] Citizens who raise objections during the second stage complain that the most important decisions were made at the first stage in the guise of resolving purely technical questions.[27] Even when no formal preliminary process is mandated, considerable informal negotiation occurs before the public portion of a planning or licensing process begins, making the entire process something of a sham.[28] Some claim that the real decision has often been made before the hearing begins, thus undermining the effectiveness of public participation.[29] Nevertheless, hearing requirements may still be influential if officials write their plan in anticipation of submitting it to a public hearing.

Even a licensing process with effective public participation would be inadequate for the control of air and water pollution. Such procedures focus too heavily on individual cases and not enough on the way discharges interact over long distances to produce ambient air and water quality. An appropriate planning process should consider the regional and interregional effects of pollution. Licensing procedures are too limited in scope. Most statutes require supplementary planning processes, but their actual importance is variable. Planning appears to be most important in water and nature protection, which are largely the responsibility of low-level governments operating under federal framework laws.[30] In the air and noise pollution law, where such plans ought to have the most legal force, they are relatively unimportant exercises with no legal bite.[31]

My aim is not merely to criticize current environmental practice but to point out that, properly understood, these procedures can provide the underpinnings of reform. In spite of their weaknesses and limited applicability, planning and licensing processes can generate information about the costs and benefits of a project that might not be available through official channels. The goal is not simply to air the complaints of injured individuals but to modify the plan in the light of the political and technocratic information presented.[32] Of course, these processes do not always fulfill this ideal, and opponents of proposed projects complain that the deck has been stacked against them,[33] but at least the principle of a process open to public participation and influence has been recognized by courts and officials. The generalization of this process to broader policy-making contexts does not seem beyond the conceptual horizon of German public law.

MASS OBJECTIONS AND ORGANIZED GROUPS

Mass objections have delayed public projects and made them more costly. This has made many Germans skeptical of extending participation rights to new areas of law. The most controversial issues have been the licensing of nuclear power plants and the building of airports, railways, canals, and highways.[34] Such projects raised difficult policy issues broader than the scope of the projects themselves. Planning and licensing processes have attracted hundreds or even thousands of individuals. For important projects, tens of thousands of objectors are common.[35]

Germany had special problems dealing with such outpourings of public concern because it was slow to recognize public interest groups as valid participants in the administrative process.[36] Nevertheless, it obviously needed some way to accommodate these numbers without collapse. The Administrative Procedures Act, passed in 1976 at the height of public concern, regulates cases in which more than fifty people make identical submissions. When this happens, the group members must designate a representative—an individual, not an organization—or risk having their individual submissions disregarded.[37] Other features of the planning and licensing processes may limit participation. For example, a six-week comment period must elapse after the issuance of the preliminary plan or proposed license. This period may be too short for opponents to prepare a reasoned response.[38] Others may be put off by a hearing process that limits the time available to objectors and that might not permit them to question project supporters.

These procedural limitations have not, however, choked off mass opposition. Where large numbers object, they may be represented through local citizens' initiatives (*Bürgerinitiativen*). These organizations originated as loose associations of neighbors who came together to oppose a project or to demand its modification.[39] Over time some have taken on a more permanent character. A national umbrella organization deals with issues of common concern. Germans now recognize the existence of "altruistic" Verbände, in contrast to "egoistical" Verbände which represent economic interests. Although citizens groups are not formally incorporated organizations and generally have no research capabilities or paid staff, they may in some respects play the same role as formal environmental organizations.[40] In fact, as collections of individuals, they have a greater impact than formal organizations in many administrative law disputes, given the German emphasis on individualized harm. Here the paradox of German notions of public participation is clear: groups claiming to represent the public interest may thereby lose their legitimacy. But groups may intervene so long as they assert that they are merely collections of individuals. The elected representatives of the people and the bureaucrats to whom they delegate power are seen as the legitimate interpreters of the public interest. Private groups that make such claims may be viewed with suspicion.[41]

The activity of Bürgerinitiativen varies by statute. Under the Air and Noise Pollution Act and the Atomic Energy Act, citizens groups can participate as members of the general public. In a study of the Air and Noise Pollution Act, 88 percent of the officials questioned said that citizens groups were active in the area, and officials generally viewed the groups with favor.[42] In contrast, formal group participation is not permitted when emission licenses are issued under the water laws. Only individuals who are directly affected can lodge complaints.[43] As a consequence, citizens groups are less active and less accepted in water pollution regulation.[44]

The Nature Protection Law of 1976 is the only environmental statute that requires organized groups to participate in some decisions.[45] The statute recognizes that certain environmental interests cannot be effectively represented by individuals or even by associations of neighbors. State governments determine which groups to consult from among those whose primary mission is nature protection and landscape conservation. These groups are not Bürgerinitiativen but include middle-of-the-road environmental groups and conservative nature protection organizations.[46] The information they submit is meant to help structure the plan itself rather than just handle individual problems.[47] The principles of participation recognized under the Nature Protection Statute could be extended to participation at the federal level.

JUDICIAL REVIEW

After the administrative process is complete and a plan has been announced or a license issued, appeal to the administrative courts is possible.[48] Judicial challenges can impose delays, raise public concern, and serve as part of a strategy of opposition politics. In the seventies and early eighties, court challenges to nuclear power projects appear to have contributed to the almost complete halt in new plant construction.[49] Petitioners were seldom successful on the merits, however.[50]

OBSTACLES TO EFFECTIVE REVIEW

There are serious obstacles to using the German courts to improve the quality of the administrative process. Four problems appear to be most salient: the focus on subjective rights, the link to individual licensing decisions, the payment of lawyers, and the large number of complaints.

First, petitioners must claim that their subjective rights have been violated.[51] Access to the court is generally limited to neighbors of the planned facility or to residents of the community where the plan will be implemented or the plant built.[52] Yet some projects, such as coal-fired or atomic power plants, have far-reaching geographical impacts. Others, such as projects that destroy rural landscapes, harm lovers of nature living far from the site and benefit near neighbors. Obtaining standing to bring a case to the administrative courts is all but impossible for those who live far from the project.[53] They must show that injury is likely, and the presumption is against being able to demonstrate harm.[54] The "mere" risk of developing cancer or other health problems will not confer standing. The administrative courts have not completely ruled out claims of long-distance harm, although the damage one might suffer in a possible nuclear power plant accident is not sufficient to get one into court.[55]

Once granted standing, individuals can defend only their own subjective interests, not public interests.[56] Subjective rights do not include a general right to attack the project as a whole. The successful plaintiff must generally be satisfied with either specific protective measures or the payment of compensation.[57] If both neighbors and distant citizens object to a project's impact, a solution crafted to help the neighbor may be opposed by those seeking to preserve the natural environment. Construction of highway embankments to limit noise or compensation for the purchase of soundproof windows will hardly satisfy those concerned with the encroachments of modern civilization on the landscape.[58] The Federal Administrative Court, however, has permitted one exception. Neighbors of a project can argue that a planning decision infringes public interest norms. The infringement, however, must be linked to injury to the plaintiff's property rights.[59]

Second, because cases arise in the context of individual planning and licensing decisions, the courts cannot consider the general pattern of implementation. The overall impact of approving scores of licenses and plans does not come before the courts. To the extent that they consider costs and benefits at all, it will only be in the narrow context of an individual project, and even then the judiciary may not consider all the long-range and synergistic impacts.

The third limitation concerns the payment of lawyers and court costs. In

German courts the loser is responsible for court costs and for both parties' legal fees.[60] This rule discourages risky cases that, if won, might affect future administrative proceedings and people not involved in the case. In practice, the judiciary contains the risk by issuing a schedule of costs and fees tied to the amount at stake in individual cases, rather than the lawyers' actual hours of work. In many administrative law cases the "amount at stake" is essentially a fiction, but it does result in relatively low lawyers' fees for individual plaintiffs.[61] Even so, if a losing plaintiff cannot pay, he or she can petition to have these fees waived or reduced with the state paying the court costs and the balance of the victor's legal fees.[62] The plaintiff's own lawyer is not paid, thus introducing a de facto contingent fee arrangement into administrative law cases. Furthermore, lawyers are not required in the lowest administrative courts (*Verwaltungsgerichte*) and the appellate courts (*Oberverwaltungsgerichte*).

The very effort to keep costs manageable for individuals, however, introduces another problem. The earnings of lawyers in the typical administrative law case may be too low to give them much incentive to take the case. The fee is tied to the dollar amount at stake for the individual, but many administrative law cases have importance far beyond these stakes. As a result, the level of representation may be incommensurate with the importance of the case.[63] This problem can be reduced by raising the legal fees, but then individuals will bring fewer cases with external benefits in clarifying the law.

Fourth, when courts review large projects, they face the same multitude of complaints as do administrators. In the absence of class actions, it is hard to manage the large number of petitioners. In practice, this problem may not be as severe as it seems. The judiciary has developed ways of managing cases with thousands of claimants. They can require that plaintiffs select a representative case as a way of reducing the caseload. The judges themselves may determine that only a few issues have been raised by the thousands of cases and decide five to ten cases rather than ten thousand. Similarly, the court can require individuals to use the same lawyer to argue similar cases as a unit.[64]

The German courts have rejected the American solution that permits groups themselves to have standing. In general, neither organized environmental groups nor Bürgerinitiativen can be plaintiffs, because they cannot claim that their rights have been violated.[65] To overcome this difficulty, Bürgerinitiativen have purchased land in the neighborhood of projects. The Federal Administrative Court has ruled that standing should be granted in such cases even if the site is small and the group has not paid the market price. Mere purchase is sufficient to claim violation of ownership rights. The Constitutional Court has affirmed this decision. Nevertheless, the highest administrative court has ruled that if a plaintiff's property interest was created solely for the purpose of getting into court, then it can be given less weight than the interests of other parties in the case.[66]

Again nature protection is an exception, but only a limited one. Environmental groups sought a federal statute that gave them a right to challenge decisions in court, not just participate in the administrative process. The federal lawmakers refused to enact such a statute.[67] The Nature Protection Law is, however, a framework statute under which the federal government provides the outline of a policy to be filled in by the Länder. Several Länder have enacted subsidiary laws that give nature protection organizations standing in court. Even when standing is granted, however, the issues that organizations can raise are restricted, and the number of cases has been small.[68] The Federal Administrative Court upheld the constitutionality of organizational plaintiffs under such circumstances.[69] Recently it went further and permitted nature protection groups to bring a case to court even when no explicit Land statute granted them standing. The organizations, however, could only challenge their exclusion from the administrative process, not the substantive outcome.[70] This case is a landmark because it holds that organized groups can challenge procedural failures in court, at least when their own rights of participation have been violated.

Organizational plaintiffs are, however, limited to suits against Land authorities. A case decided in 1993 held that nature protection groups operating under Land law cannot challenge decisions of federal officials.[71] One important federal responsibility is the construction and operation of the railroads. Thus public interest groups cannot challenge in court the federal government's compliance with the nature protection statute.[72] Overall, one recent review of environmental group actions in Germany concluded that, limited as such actions are, their impact has been positive. The possibility of an association lawsuit "safeguards to a certain degree the growth of environmental consciousness in the planning authorities, it ensures the respect for participation rights of conservation groups, and gives them at least legally an equal footing with the proponents of economic interests."[73]

THE NATURE OF REVIEW

When plaintiffs challenge a licensing or planning decision, they can generally object only to those portions of the decision that may violate their rights. The Law on Administrative Courts and the Administrative Procedures Act limit plaintiffs' ability to challenge procedures.[74] Nevertheless, when technical matters are before the courts, substance and procedure blur. Because German judges are not competent to evaluate the scientific evidence, their review of administrative actions has a decidedly procedural air.[75]

The administrative courts have held that on technical matters the government must consult recognized experts. The executive should take account of professional technical standards, but it can apply them as it wishes. It need not, for example, use optimistic or pessimistic assumptions when evaluating risks. It does not need to do its own research, but it must make its reliance on experts known. In reviewing technocratic decisions, the administrative courts can call in their own experts and can refuse to accept the information used by public officials if that information is not "professional." In practice, however, the courts seldom take this course. Most major planning processes take eight to ten years before they even reach the court, and the authorities will usually have consulted the relevant experts at some point.[76]

In an important early case, the Federal Administrative Court established standards for review of planning processes.[77] The constitutional principle of proportionality is behind these guidelines. Whatever their justification in terms of "subjective rights," they nevertheless support a policy-analytic approach to judicial review. If followed, these standards could help push public authorities to engage in competent policy-making. The guidelines have five parts. First, the public officials must recognize that they are engaged in a balancing of interests. Second, they must accumulate information and investigate the issue. Third, they must hold a hearing in which all those who wish to present information are in the same room and can confront each other. Fourth, the authorities must play an active role in assessing the evidence and balancing the interests. They cannot passively accept expert advice. Finally, the officials must accompany their decision with a statement of reasons. If they reject the arguments made by some participants, they must explain why.

Within this framework, suppose that the administrative courts do determine that a procedural or other error has been committed. How do they proceed? The first question is one of materiality. Would the outcome have been the same if the error had not been made? If the answer is incontrovertibly "yes," they will permit the decision to stand.[78] If the error was material, they void the decision and remand the case to the public authorities. The authorities must then decide whether to drop the issue or to reopen the proceedings with the aim of correcting previous errors.[79] Alternatively, for planning decisions, if the error only affects the rights of a few individuals, the courts can require a substantive change in the plan to remedy the problem. They will ask whether the cost of satisfying the plaintiff's claim could tip the scales against the entire project. If not, the court will simply order the project managers to avoid violating the individual's rights. If an individual complains of the noise from a highway project, the court may resolve the case by ordering the builders either to buy out the homeowner or to construct a soundproof wall next to the property. The key variable is not the size of the extra investment involved but whether the entire project is marginally acceptable. The courts are more likely to require that a marginal project be reconsidered than one whose benefits far exceed its costs.[80]

CONCLUSION

Deep-seated German attitudes make reform of high-level executive policy-making difficult. German lawyers should reexamine their conventional views of bureaucratic information, interest group activity, and lawsuits involving large numbers of plaintiffs. The sheer volume of complaints in some licensing and planning processes makes it seem that the public has very strong rights of appeal. The courts appear, if anything, too active in reviewing administrative proceedings. People flood the public hearings and then file a large number of practically identical claims asserting that their rights have been violated. This perception of an overactive judiciary is based on a misconception. Critics focus only on the planning and licensing of important projects where a window for public participation exists. The thinking of public lawyers has been traumatized by the wealth of legal complaints accompanying proposals for large public projects, such as airport runways or nuclear power plants. Reformers have therefore focused on pragmatic responses to this multitude of complaints—responses that would permit agencies and courts to manage the process without having to rethink the nature of administrative action and judicial review.[81]

A superficial view might indicate that the problem is not an absence of public participation but an excess, and not too little judicial review but too much. My argument, in contrast, is that the problem is not too much public participation and judicial involvement but the wrong kind. Many of the objections to nuclear power plants and airport runways came from people with policy preferences opposed to those of the decision makers. Opposition came from environmentalists and other concerned citizens who put a lower weight on inexpensive electric power and economic growth than members of the government did. Their voices could be heard through the election of Green party members to state and federal parliaments, the lobbying of members of the governing coalition, and civil disobedience. In addition, these individuals could attend hearings, make legal challenges, and engage in more informal methods of persuasion. The opening up of the planning and licensing processes has channeled the activities of environmental groups and others with policy objections into the relatively limited framework of individual cases. Though many cases are critical to the regions involved and though the procedures have broadened the range of information and opinion available to decision makers, the opportunities available risk focusing democratic participation on sideshows. Access to the courts is limited to review of the particular process in which the plaintiffs participated. Organized groups are admitted to hearings and as plaintiffs in lawsuits in only a few situations. The result is thousands of participants. The approval of individual projects takes an inordinate amount of time. In contrast, general policies are established by federal ministries with no legally enforceable participation and are subject to approval only by the cabinet and by the Länder politicians sitting in the Bundesrat.

The system's weaknesses have not escaped the notice of German legal scholars and policy analysts. Heinrich von Lersner, head of the Federal Environmental Agency (*Umweltbundesamt*), has proposed using the planning procedures in the Administrative Procedures Act as a model for reforming the standard-setting process.[82] First, an expert group, such as a DIN committee, would propose a standard accompanied by a statement of reasons. The statement would clarify the standard's empirical basis and explain how uncertainties were resolved. For example, if animal studies are used to predict human responses, the proposal must explain how the translation was made. In addition, a list of those involved in the process and those who provided assistance must be made public. The list would include the affiliations of all participants, including the research contracts of those in educational or research institutions. An easily accessible journal would publish the plan as well as the time limit and place for registering objections. Von Lersner argues that a public hearing is "advisable" except for minor matters where no objections are anticipated.[83] The hearing would be overseen by people independent of those who prepared the standard. Anyone filing an objection could participate. The process would thus be more open to outsiders than under the provisions of the Immission Control and Waste Prevention Acts.[84] The discussion at the hearing would be recorded and published. The hearing officers would evaluate the objections and forward a recommendation to the ministry charged with setting the standard.

Von Lersner's proposal is a thoughtful attempt to merge the procedures described here with the existing pattern of expert advice. It aims to encourage neutrality and objectivity by requiring participants to disclose their affiliations. At the same time, it broadens public participation and requires more formal accountability. Surprisingly, however, the proposal makes no mention of judicial review. Of course, judicial review of planning and licensing processes cannot be uncritically extended to setting standards. If the courts ordered the ministries to rewrite their regulations in particular ways, concerns would be raised about judicial interference with political choices. Instead, review should focus on the legitimacy of the administrative procedures.

PART III REFORM

7

GERMAN REFORM EFFORTS

Many German scholars are dissatisfied with the present system, particularly as it operates in the environmental area. They observe contentious, time-consuming administrative procedures followed by multiple lawsuits against the location of such public facilities as airports, power plants, and hazardous waste dumps. They criticize the overlapping and inconsistent jurisdiction of the multitude of environmental laws. They decry the weak remedies of public law. They argue that environmental problems should be viewed as part of the larger problems of economic and social development on an interdependent globe. In spite of the breadth of these critiques, the solutions at the center of reform discussions do not confront the underlying structural problems of German law and may delay recognition of these difficulties. Three of these partial efforts nevertheless deserve discussion. They are the creation of an environmental law code, the expanded use of environmental tort actions, and the advocacy of regulatory negotiation.

THE ENVIRONMENTAL LAW CODE

The *Bürgerliches Gesetzbuch,* or Civil Code, is a powerful model for German law reformers. Predating the Grundgesetz by almost half a century, the code provides a model of systematic and organized legal norms. German public lawyers look to this respected body of law for guidance. For example, in 1987 a *Baugesetzbuch,* or Town and Country Planning Code, went into effect that codified two previous statutes dealing with planning and building law.

Following this model, a group of legal scholars is drafting an Environmental Law Code (*Umweltgesetzbuch* [UGB]). At present, twenty statutes specifically govern environmental matters, and several others apply in part. The drafting group, working under a government contract, is seeking to codify environmental law and to avoid inconsistencies and overlaps. The code aims to streamline administration practices, not to reform substantive law. A draft of the general section has been completed by an academic group;[1] it is under review by a second committee that is to propose a draft law. This second committee includes one of the professors on the original committee (Michael Kloepfer) and is chaired by Horst Sendler, the former chief judge of the administrative court. The special section, dealing with substantive environmental issues, was completed in the fall of 1993.[2] Despite this activity, the project is not high on the government's agenda. Participants doubt that a statute will be enacted before the end of the century.

In spite of the essentially conservative nature of the codification enterprise, it includes a number of positive features that respond to some of the problems and concerns raised in previous chapters. Even when the language of the draft code is inconclusive or vague, the background material sometimes goes further to raise questions about the legitimacy of existing practices. The general section of the code recognizes the value of enhanced public participation and administrative transparency.

The proposed code gives the public access to environmental information held by the government. In spite of numerous exceptions to protect rights of privacy and commercial secrets and to protect the authorities' decision-making processes, the presumption is shifted in favor of public access. Similar language is included in the recently passed Environmental Information Law, implementing a European Union directive.[3]

Under these proposals, organized groups would participate more in the policy-making process than they do now. The authorities, however, would make the ultimate decision about which groups to consult. Using the Nature Protection Law as a model,[4] the draft lists the types of groups that should be recognized. The groups must have environmental protection as their basic goal. They should not merely be local groups but must have an area of interest at least as large as a Land.[5] These groups have a right to be heard in processes where an environmental impact assessment is required,[6] in local planning processes, and most important for my purposes, in federal-level processes with policy or regulatory impact. The groups must be given a hearing not only in federal environmental planning and program development activities but also in the development of legal regulations and administrative guidelines.[7] The code does not make these rights legally enforceable, but the Länder may permit organizations to bring court cases to enforce their rights.[8] The special section of the draft code, moreover, gives nature protection groups limited access to the courts.[9]

The UGB requires the government to provide a statement of reasons when it issues a regulation or guideline.[10] It also establishes a process for the periodic review of existing standards. An administrative guideline (but not a regulation) would become void unless it had been reviewed and renewed after eight years.[11]

Technical standards have presumptive force in environmental law under the UGB, but the code constrains the processes used to produce them. In addition to the obvious requirement that standards comply with the law, they must be produced by a committee of experts that is "balanced" (*ausgewogen*), and the standards must be published.[12] The bureaucracy can also set technical standards to bind itself.[13] When it does this, it must either hold a hearing of the concerned parties, including recognized environmental groups, or consult a committee of experts. The authorities must publicly justify their choices.[14] The discussion makes clear that the aim of this section is to strike a balance between the value of expertise and the need for democratic accountability.[15]

The procedural reforms proposed for legal regulations and administrative guidelines are relatively modest. The UGB remains within the German legal norm-setting framework. The code accepts the constraints of current administrative law and does not explore the fundamental tensions between German administrative law and the substance of environmental problems. For example, although market-like reforms and flexible instruments are permitted,[16] the proposal makes no explicit attempt to restructure environmental law with incentive-based reforms in mind. The drafters themselves point out that they have not changed the traditional emphasis on licensing as the principal tool of environmental regulation.[17] Nevertheless, the proposed code demonstrates acceptance of the need for reform. It is a first step toward recognition of the importance of accountable policy-making procedures. If, however, it is viewed as an adequate response to the weaknesses of the existing system, it may derail more comprehensive proposals.

ENVIRONMENTAL TORTS

Tort law can be used both to encourage efficient risk-reducing activities and to compensate victims. In the standard law and economics account, the liability system holds firms responsible for the harm caused by their products and processes. As a consequence, firm managers take efficient precautions to avoid the imposition of liability. Unfortunately, this simple characterization of the tort system has only limited applicability to environmental problems.[18]

Tort judgments cannot influence those who are not threatened with suit. Many important environmental problems involve large numbers of affected individuals and multiple, complex, and interrelated causes. They cannot be characterized as one-on-one disputes suitable for resolution by courts. Single individuals often have no incentive to bring suits, either because the harm they suffer is small or because they do not even know that a problem exists. They notice noises and smells, but they might not be aware of invisible yet harmful contamination of air, water, and soil.[19]

In many cases, even sophisticated science cannot determine who is responsible for a particular, individual harm. For such problems, the liability law's effort to divide the world into self-contained disputes between named plaintiffs and defendants is both difficult and unnecessary. Instead, systemic approaches should model the links between discharges and harms without, for example, trying to identify which smokestack "caused" which cancer. The government must regulate dischargers directly, perhaps through fees or tradable licenses. If compensation is thought desirable, it should be provided by the government. Taxes on dischargers who have contributed to the risk could finance the compensation fund.[20]

Furthermore, even when the environmental harm can be parceled into lawsuit-sized bits, the insurance system may drive a wedge between compensation and deterrence goals. If insurance rates are not calibrated to reflect differences in caretaking, dischargers face a moral problem. If the harm they cause is fully covered by insurance and if insurance companies have difficulty monitoring their customers, high tort judgments may simply raise everyone's rates without affecting risk prevention.

Both the nature of many environmental problems and the operation of the insurance market suggest that environmental liability law can be of only marginal importance. For diffuse and complex problems, tort judgments can act as supplemental fines in the enforcement of statutory requirements. They cannot serve as the primary enforcement device or as the major source of compensation. Tort suits could help deter localized accidents and restrain nuisances, such as noise or waste dumps, but liability law cannot play a central role in policy.[21]

Given this assessment, Germany's recent effort to strengthen its statute that governs environmental tort actions is unlikely to have important policy consequences. Several distinctive features of German private law will further limit the relevance of environmental tort actions.

The German law was amended in 1990 to ease the burden on plaintiffs.[22] The act, however, falls well short of a general mandate for cancer victims to sue profitable companies that discharge toxic substances into the environment.[23] A tort claim will not be accepted without strong evidence of causation.

A source of pollution can be held liable if it is "inherently suited" (*geeignet*) to cause the damage claimed. However, this presumption does not apply if the facility was properly operated. Proper operation can be inferred if the plant complies with regulations and passes government inspections.[24] In other words, a plaintiff suing a plant that complies with pollution control statutes cannot claim that the source was inherently capable of causing the damage, but must prove that it actually did do so, a more difficult task. The burden of proving causation is shifted back to the plaintiff.[25]

German law, like American law, has not accepted the notion of probabilistic causation for toxic torts. Thus if several sources are inherently capable of causing the damage, none of them may be presumed to have caused the harm. Even a single identified polluter can avoid a presumption of liability if other causal factors exist.[26] This language could well imply that health claims based on air and water pollution will be all but impossible to bring successfully when multiple causes exist.

If the court accepts the causal link, liability is strict. However, if multiple defendants exist, commentators disagree on whether the defendants are jointly and severally liable.[27] The act lists the ninety-six types of facilities to which it applies. The list is extensive and "includes certain toxic waste disposal and burning facilities not previously subject to major environmental legislation."[28] Pollutants include not only substances that have effects on soil, air, and water, but also noise, vibration, and pressure.[29] The act gives both defendants and claimants rights to obtain information from each other and from government regulatory agencies. The rights are, however, subject to other laws, such as those protecting trade secrets and personal data.[30] Given these liability rules and information rights, the impact of the law will depend on the ease of establishing causation and the courts' interpretation of the burden-shifting terms "inherently suited" and "properly operated."

Even if these terms are interpreted in favor of plaintiffs, the German legal system will limit the statute's reach. Class actions are not allowed, contingency fees are viewed as unethical, rights of discovery are limited, and two-sided fee shifting increases the risk of suits.[31] Discharges that cause a small amount of harm to many people are unlikely to produce lawsuits, and any uncertainty in the outcome will discourage risk-averse plaintiffs.

Liability claims will also be stymied by the law's failure to extend causation back to an identifiable, solvent party. The act does not apply to damages caused before the law entered into force on January 1, 1991.[32] Take the example of waste sites. If "caused" is read narrowly, the law will not cover damages from old sites. The new law does cover damages from sites currently in use, but German law is unlikely to recognize a causal chain long enough to make suits worthwhile. Generators of waste, as opposed to operators of waste facilities, will apparently be able to escape liability just as they have in the past.[33]

The law's force will also depend on the interaction between insurance and liability. If most firms are covered by insurance, the law may succeed in compensating some injured individuals without providing much incentive to prevent harm. Under the statute, many facilities must obtain insurance coverage.[34] The casualty insurance industry has produced a model policy that covers most forms of pollution but limits coverage.[35] The reinsurance industry has expressed concern about the potentially open-ended nature of its exposure.[36]

Given the fundamental limitations of tort law as a method of controlling pollution, the amended statute and its insurance provisions will make a marginal contribution at best. It is far from obvious, however, that a strengthening of tort law would represent a worthwhile development in environmental law. Even a liability law that reduces the cost of individual suits by lowering the standard or shifting the burden of proof can play only a supplementary role.[37]

REGULATORY NEGOTIATION

Regulatory negotiation has recently become the watchword of German reformers.[38] Picking up the American fascination with consensual decision-making, some German legal scholars are advocating negotiated solutions to environmental problems.[39]

Regulatory negotiation must be distinguished from other methods of decision-making involving outside groups and individuals. Instead of simply presenting their views to officials, citizens and group representatives are themselves involved in reaching the decision. It may be an intermediate decision that must ultimately be approved by a government body, but it is a choice nonetheless. The issues on the table must be suitable for a consensual negotiated solution. The problem must be structured so that all groups will gain from participating in the process and from the final decision.

APPLICATIONS TO ENVIRONMENTAL PROBLEMS

Regulatory negotiation comes in a variety of forms, and its application to the environmental field requires care. Several basic issues must be resolved before a negotiation can be recommended.

First, the bureaucracy must identify those affected by the decision. They must all be represented by organized groups that can operate effectively. Thus the groups must not be deeply divided within themselves, and they must all have competent and well-informed advocates. Diffuse, unorganized groups, like consumers or those who breath polluted air, will be hard to represent. Groups that profess to speak for such individuals will have difficulty demonstrating their claim. Even groups that make a legitimate effort to mirror the interests of a broad public will face a resource constraint. Many people will not contribute funds to the group because they know they can benefit from its efforts without contributing. In contrast, labor unions and industrial associations face fewer free rider problems and may face none at all if members are required to join and pay a fee. For such groups the main problem is the competence of those selected to represent their interests.

Because representation is problematic, negotiation is not useful for environmental harms that are diffuse, causally complex, and affect millions of people.[40] In contrast, regulatory negotiation may succeed in bringing together those affected by specific government choices that have determinate local environmental effects. Alternatively, a consensus of technical experts can be a preliminary step in a decision eventually made by public officials after consultation with a broader, more representative group of participants.[41]

Second, if the representation problem can be solved, the authorities must clarify exactly which decisions the group is to make and which will be left to the bureaucracy. Public officials must explain how they will reach a decision if negotiation fails. This is a key strategic step that affects both the probability of a successful result and the acceptability of the outcome. If the decision is made by consensus, all groups must be better off with the choice than with the fallback position. Inconsistent and overly optimistic perceptions about the reversion point can make agreement impossible.[42] If there is no alternative mechanism for decision, anyone who benefits from the status quo has a veto. The bureaucracy must also set time limits so that those who gain from delay will not have a bargaining advantage.

Third, the authorities must determine the ground rules. Regulatory negotiation is predicated on reaching a consensus. It is an alternative both to the majoritarian choices of elected representatives and to the bureaucratic choices of civil servants. The consensus of those concerned is the justification for implementing the negotiated choice.

But consensus can be sought by many methods. Considerable controversy has centered around the form of the negotiation. Should government officials participate, should meetings be open or private, should a mediator guide the process, should the authorities supply experts to evaluate the technical aspects of the problem?[43] If the system of representation is satisfactory, government officials need not attend, and meetings can be private. If it is not satisfactory, adding bureaucrats and opening the process are unlikely to compensate for this failure. Instead, the state should either use an open process led by bureaucrats or return the issue to the legislature for resolution by majoritarian processes. Help from neutral mediators and technical experts, in contrast, could facilitate negotiation. There is no conflict between their use and the basic structure of a negotiated outcome.[44]

The United States has recently passed a statute that sets standards for the use of regulatory negotiation as part of the rule-making process.[45] The procedure is undertaken not in the context of a particular application of the law but in the setting of general regulations. Representatives of the affected interests convene under agency auspices and attempt to reach a compromise before the informal rule-making process begins. That second process must still be carried out under requirements of the Administrative Procedures Act, and judicial review is still possible, but a successful negotiation will limit the range of disputes and save time. The American law is still too new to be evaluated with confidence.[46] Nevertheless, experience under older laws suggests that success requires careful issue selection and process design.[47] I am skeptical that the negotiation model is the right one for complex environmental policy-making. Even if the individual participants agree, the risk remains that they are poor representatives of those who bear the social costs and benefits of a program.

GERMAN EXPERIMENTS

The German interest in American models of regulatory negotiation arose in response to criticisms of the procedures used to approve large projects and to grant licenses. The procedures described in the previous chapter often involve huge numbers of people who both register complaints in the administrative process and bring lawsuits challenging the decision. Delays of a decade or more are common.[48] Court injunctions often halt work on projects for many years. If no injunction is issued, construction of the project presents litigants with a fait accompli for which damages are the only remedy.[49] The proposals for negotiated solutions are an alternative that seeks to make the process less confrontational and to avoid judicial review.[50]

Negotiations must be carried out by representatives of organized groups. In Germany a move to negotiations implies more than just a shift from public hearings and judicial review to closed-door consensus. It also implies a shift from procedures based on the protection of individual rights to procedures analogous to the consensual processes common elsewhere in German law. Instead of struggling to accommodate groups within a legal framework designed to give individuals a hearing, the process allows only group representatives to participate. One of the advantages of regulatory negotiation is that it permits officials to face the problem of representation straightforwardly, rather than treat it as a nonissue. A regulatory negotiation is explicitly political, not formally legal. Nevertheless, expanding the role of organizations in public hearings and in court is always an alternative and one that is less dependent on finding groups that truly represent the public interest.

Negotiations that substitute for or precede formal planning and licensing procedures involve local projects, not federal policy-making. This is appropriate. Some local problems, such as the siting of waste dumps, have mainly localized effects, and local citizens groups can be effective advocates for neighbors. When the project raises broader policy issues that can affect the health and safety of distant households or the viability of an ecosystem, however, the problem of representation is likely to be severe.

Those interested in the possibilities for regulatory negotiation in Germany have reviewed past experience and set up model experiments. Most examples involve the siting of waste disposal facilities, a problem that has proved difficult to solve, especially for hazardous materials. During the 1980s all efforts to site hazardous waste facilities failed, at least in part because of opposition from local residents, the Green party, and national environmental groups.[51]

A wide variety of participatory processes has been used, and the results are decidedly mixed.[52] On the positive side, a federal government grant is supporting a mediation project managed by the Berlin Science Center (*Wissenschafts- zentrum Berlin*). The two projects under its jurisdiction are the only ones using neutral mediators to facilitate the negotiation process. In the first, a member of the Evangelical Academy of Loccum helped defuse conflict over the rehabilitation of a toxic waste dump in Lower Saxony. He brought experts and concerned groups together and was able to clarify which issues had been settled and which remained in dispute.[53] The process did not, however, resolve the issue. It was an input into the next stage of decision-making.[54]

The second project, begun in 1991, concerns a planned waste incinerator in the district of Neuss. The first mediation session in March 1992 included more than sixty people from about thirty organizations and groups, too large a number for effective negotiation. Smaller groups will apparently do most of the actual drafting work. In 1992, in the midst of the process, participants had generally positive views of the mediator. Nevertheless, only half of the participants thought that a mutually satisfactory solution was even conceivable. The rest were unsure or skeptical. A report on the project is upbeat but cautious.[55]

A study of citizen participation in the planning and siting of several hazardous waste facilities suggests the difficulties of achieving negotiated solutions. The study, performed by researchers interested in high-risk, technically complex policy problems, examined four cases in which innovative processes were used.[56] The participants included the waste disposal industry, public administrators, citizens groups, political party representatives, residents, national environmental groups, experts, and counter-experts (*Gegengutachter*).

The authors demonstrate that participatory consensus-building processes are not easy to organize successfully and do not necessarily produce outcomes that are better than those of public authorities. As one indication of the problem, they asked participants in the processes to describe themselves and then to describe representatives of other interests. Representatives of citizens groups and national environmental organizations saw themselves as powerless defenders of nature who warned others of dangers. Nearby residents saw themselves as disadvantaged victims. Other participants viewed both neighbors and members of citizens groups as hysterics who raised fears and hindered pragmatic solutions. Waste disposal industry representatives saw themselves as weak but reasonable pragmatists seeking a competent solution. Others viewed them as powerful, profit-oriented degraders of the environment. Experts saw themselves as independent. Others viewed them as taking orders.[57] Such expressions of hostility were compounded by the fact that communication was hindered by the technical and economic terminology used by experts and industry representatives.[58] Furthermore, "win-win" solutions were not available for the subjects under negotiation, for example, the location of a hazardous waste facility. Because of the parties' opposing goals, much of the interchange was based on strategic considerations rather than a desire to communicate information. This made it difficult or impossible for a consensus to evolve.[59]

The authors conclude their rather negative assessment of participatory processes with an affirmative proposal. They recommend a process managed by the bureaucracy in which participation by a group of outsiders occurs at specific points in the process. The *Streitparteien* (literally, "quarreling parties") are consulted frequently but cannot hold up the process and do not have ultimate decision-making authority.

REGULATORY NEGOTIATION AND POLICY-MAKING

Recent German experience with regulatory negotiation focuses on implementing statutes in particular cases. The experiments involve projects that would otherwise fall under the licensing and planning procedures of the German Administrative Procedures Act. They do not deal with the promulgation of general regulations and guidelines. The "regulatory negotiation" label is, however, a late twentieth-century variant of the Germans' long-standing use of consensual methods. When such techniques are used, representatives of the affected groups sit around a table in a closed-door negotiation designed to produce a consensus. This model is central to labor-management relations in Germany and has been extended to some aspects of workplace health and safety.[60] As previously discussed, applications of this model exist in the advisory committees and private standard-setting institutes that help set regulatory standards and in the federal-state committees that draft regulations and guidelines.

The German processes do not, however, fulfill the conditions required to produce a legitimate policy choice. For most important issues of environmental policy, the model of well-established groups negotiating a mutual accommodation does not describe the neocorporatist processes actually in use. The committees are unrepresentative. Some groups who will be affected by the deliberations are not at the table. Furthermore, even the admission of environmental groups or citizens organizations as parties to such negotiations would not solve the problem. Such groups cannot make strong claims to represent the general public. Once one admits this difficulty, the decisions lack legitimacy. Regulatory negotiation is not the best way to assure the accountability of broadscale environmental policy choices. Tinkering with the proceedings by adding environmental groups, government officials, or mediators will not overcome the fundamental mismatch between technique and policy problems.[61] For such environmental problems, it is difficult to be sure that organized environmental groups represent the public. Yet their expertise and interest in the subject can provide an important source of information about both technical and political matters not available elsewhere. The process needs to be constrained by statute, as in the United States, or limited to local problems, where the concerned citizens can have a direct impact on their representatives.

CONCLUSION

All of the reforms under consideration in Germany have value, but none of them is a sufficient response to the fundamental weaknesses of substantive law and of administrative procedure. At least to an outside observer, the existing policy-making process is deficient on both scientific and democratic grounds. Yet Germany has succeeded in removing the worst environmental threats, at least in the old Länder, and is on its way to cleaning up East Germany's legacy of environmental degradation. Given this successful record, why seek reform? The answer is straightforward. In the future it will not be sufficient to remove the worst threats. We are approaching the stage in environmental policy in the developed world where conflicts between economic growth and the environment have become salient. Symbolic victories will not be enough. Defenders of strong environmental measures will need to show that their preferred policies will be, on balance, beneficial before the political mainstream will accept them. Although the German citizenry does not seem especially concerned with the consensual and technocratic nature of environmental policy-making, a democratic deficit exists. In a future in which policy-making becomes more controversial, this deficit will need to be overcome if government policy initiatives are to be politically acceptable.

8

EXTERNAL CONTROL:
THE ROLE OF THE EUROPEAN UNION

The European Union is a weak environmental regulator.[1] It has no independent monitoring and inspection authority; it cannot impose penalties; its budget is small; and its bureaucracy is inadequate for its regulatory tasks. Nevertheless, it has the potential to mount a challenge to conventional German administrative law and practice. This challenge takes two forms: directives that cut across the grain of German bureaucratic and federal traditions, and objections to German methods of incorporating EU law into the German system. The conflicts between Germany and the EU are grounded in tensions between German legal doctrines and the exigencies of policy-making in a democratic state.

The European Union's solutions take two forms: those that can play a constructive legitimating role and those that make implementation of environmental policy excessively legalistic. The EU has had contrasting effects on German administrative and environmental law. On the one hand, beneficial results are possible from two sources. Reform may flow from procedural directives that challenge the bureaucracy-centered focus of German law, or it may flow from judicial opinions that question the organization of German federalism. On the other hand, the European Court of Justice's (ECJ) focus on the formal legal incorporation of EU directives into national law may simply reinforce German legal traditions most in conflict with the development of sensible environmental policy.

EUROPEAN UNION ENVIRONMENTAL POLICY

The Treaty of Rome made no provision for a common environmental policy. Nevertheless, the European Community used other powers to justify numerous environmental regulations and directives.[2] In the early years, the emphasis was on harmonizing laws to avoid trade barriers. Even in the seventies, when the EC became more active, most directives referred to the nontariff barriers created by differing environmental policies.[3] The Single European Act of 1987, which amended the Treaty of Rome, explicitly addressed environmental protection.[4] Most important, the amended treaty stated "that preventive action should be taken, that environmental damage should as a priority be rectified at source, and that the polluter should pay."[5] The Treaty of Maastricht goes further, adding "sustainable and non-inflationary growth respecting the environment" and "the raising of . . . the quality of life" to the list of EU tasks.[6] The substantive provisions have also been strengthened. The EU treaty now includes as goals the promotion of international measures "to deal with regional or worldwide environmental problems," the protection of the environment and human health, and the "prudent and rational" use of natural resources. The principles of EU action have been expanded to include "the precautionary principle."[7]

When environmental protection was included as an EC goal in the Single European Act, it was subject to the condition that "the Community shall take action relating to the environment to the extent to which the [Community environmental] objectives . . . can be attained better at Community level than at the level of the individual Member States."[8] The Maastricht Treaty removes this paragraph from the environmental section and replaces it with a broad-based endorsement of the subsidiarity principle for all European Union activities.[9] The burden of proof is on the EU to justify its actions.

PROCEDURES

Before 1987, all important legislation required unanimous support of the Council of Ministers, the law-making body of the EC. As a consequence, the EC failed to make policy in many controversial areas.[10] Moreover, the need for consensus generated either vague and general directives or ones that accommodated the differing practices of member states.[11] The Treaty of Rome's emphasis on unanimity was attenuated by the Single European Act. The act permitted the Council to use qualified majority voting for legislation designed to establish the internal market. Such legislation required parliamentary review but fell short of giving the Parliament an outright veto.[12] The legislative process thus became more democratic—both in permitting Council decisions to be made over the opposition of some countries and in giving the Parliament a stronger role.[13]

The Single European Act procedures did not apply to most environmental issues, which still required unanimity unless the Council decided otherwise.[14] Not all issues with environmental consequences, however, are "environmental issues" under the Treaty of Rome. Uniform product standards, for example, can be described as measures designed to further the development of the internal market. Hence they could be approved by a qualified majority.[15] Indeed, just as the new voting rules went into effect in July 1987, the EC adopted regulations on automobile exhaust over the opposition of Denmark, which wanted even stronger measures.[16]

The Treaty of Maastricht further increases the range of environmental issues that can be decided by a qualified majority, and it strengthens Parliament's role.[17] The exceptions, for which unanimity will still be required, are both broadly and vaguely defined.[18] In principle, however, the Council can enact strong legislation over the opposition of some member states.[19]

ENFORCEMENT

The passage of legislation is only the first step. Most EU environmental laws are directives, which are not legally effective in their own right. They are merely binding as to the result to be achieved. Although some directives contain specific environmental goals, others are open-ended and leave considerable discretion to national legislatures. It is up to the individual member states to pass laws or take other measures to put directives into effect.[20] In practice, members frequently ignore environmental directives or delay passage of the necessary statutes.[21]

Even when a member state has a law on the books, its provisions may not be enforced. The EU must rely on voluntary compliance by individual member countries because it has no independent authority to monitor pollution dischargers' compliance with EU law, and it cannot levy fines or otherwise punish recalcitrant dischargers or governments.[22] Its information about environmental quality is a compilation of member state reports. Adverse judgments of the ECJ are frequently ignored because the court has no enforcement power and can issue only declaratory judgments or, in emergencies, declaratory interim injunctions.[23]

Lacking inspection and enforcement authority, the EU Commission (the EU's administrative arm) can do little more than check that directives have been properly incorporated into national law.[24] Even if its formal authority were increased, the change would not mean much without a vast increase in EU staff and budget.[25] One member of the Commission has a portfolio that includes the environment, but the legal department of the Environmental Directorate contains only a handful of officials to oversee fifty-one environmental directives.[26]

Individuals cannot challenge directives or regulations in the ECJ.[27] The Commission can, however, respond to citizen complaints, and at the end of the 1960s it established a system by which private citizens could lodge complaints concerning implementation failures.[28] Beginning in the mid-eighties, the Environmental Directorate responded to its own lack of resources and monitoring authority by explicitly encouraging individuals and environmental organizations to bring complaints to the Commission.[29] The number of complaints received increased from 10 per year in the early eighties to 480 in 1990.[30] According to a 1991 report, the Commission is considering a directive that permits individuals to lodge complaints directly with member states and perhaps also allows them to take action in the courts.[31]

The complaint process has led to an increase in enforcement efforts. The Commission first tries to resolve a problem by sending a letter to the member government concerning the alleged violation. If it cannot obtain a promise of compliance, it initiates a more formal process that results in a "reasoned opinion."[32] These preliminary stages are secret, marked only by a notation when the problem has been resolved.[33] The number of complaint letters that concerned environmental matters increased from an average of 23 per year between 1978 and 1983 to 116 per year between 1984 and 1991. The number of reasoned opinions increased from 5 per year to 35 in the same periods. Only a small number of unresolved cases are finally appealed to the European Court of Justice.[34] Court referrals show considerable variation from year to year, but the average has increased from 2 per year between 1978 and 1983 to 11 between 1984 and 1991.[35] Germany has not been a particular focus of Commission activity. Only 2 of the 39 reasoned opinions in 1990 concerned Germany, as did 2 of the 14 court referrals.[36] Nevertheless, the Commission's need to rely on complaints by outsiders probably produces a relative overemphasis on Germany, which has better organized environmental groups and broader public concern for environmental matters than some other member states.[37]

Given the relative weakness of enforcement through EU institutions, a recent decision of the ECJ is of potential importance. In 1988 the court held that if a directive has a direct effect on individuals, then they can sue in their national courts to protect their rights.[38] Environmental groups are beginning to take advantage of this possibility. Friends of the Earth is suing Great Britain, for example, alleging that water supplied by the Thames Water Utilities does not comply with the EU directive on the quality of drinking water.[39] This development in EU law may force German jurists to rethink the role of environmental groups as plaintiffs. Although Germany seldom gives standing to organized groups and takes a narrow view of subjective rights violations, EU law may eventually encourage the courts to consider more permissive options.

When an EU law does not have a direct effect on individuals, legal action in national courts may still be possible. In a recent case involving a labor issue, the ECJ held that even though an unimplemented directive did not have direct effect, it still created an enforceable EU right. If rights have been violated as a result of a state's failure to apply a directive, the affected individual can sue for damages in the member state's courts. Damages are available to the same extent that compensation would be available under national law.[40] In Germany such suits could be powerful enforcement tools for those environmental policy failures that constitute violations of the "subjective" rights of individuals.

CONSTRUCTIVE EUROPEAN UNION POLICY

The environmental policy of the EU could further two constructive goals. First, it could support more rational substantive policies, encouraging member governments to link means and ends and to consider the broader impact of pollution generated within their borders. Second, the EU could support government processes that are more democratic and open to public participation. These objectives may conflict in particular cases, but they can help delineate a principled role for EU legislative and enforcement efforts.

Both goals form the nominal basis of EU policy. The European Union has incorporated the first, substantive goal into general statements on environmental policy and into some specific directives. Many directives, however, are of a familiar standard-setting type that does not require a strong link between means and ends.[41] The European Environmental Agency, devoted to research and information gathering, could provide the background for more rational policy-making. The agency, however, is not yet a force in EU policy-making. Disputes over its location and fears that it might eventually play such a policy-making role delayed its establishment.[42] Although authorized in 1990, the agency was not assigned a location in Copenhagen until the fall of 1993.[43]

The second, procedural goal has been of particular interest to Commission lawyers charged with reviewing the implementation of directives.[44] It is reflected in two recent directives modeled on American statutory precedents. These directives concern environmental impact assessments and access to environmental information. Clashes between the EU and Germany over the status of the Länder in the German federal system may also encourage procedural reform.

ENVIRONMENTAL IMPACT ASSESSMENTS

An EU directive, recently incorporated into statute in Germany, requires assessments of the environmental effects of many public and private projects.[45] Under its terms, applicants must supply information about their project's environmental impact and describe the abatement measures it will take.[46] "The public" and government authorities with environmental responsibilities must have access to this information. The body charged with approving the project must consult both environmental officials and "the public concerned."[47] When a decision has been made, the authorities must inform the concerned public of the decision and provide a statement of reasons.[48]

The directive envisages a process similar in many ways to German licensing and planning processes. The statute that implements the directive incorporates the environmental impact assessment processes into existing procedures. The new law will have little impact on the implementation of environmental statutes beyond forcing a somewhat greater emphasis on cross-media effects. In contrast, land developers have a new responsibility to submit written environmental impact statements and make them available for public inspection.[49]

The German law appears to be a narrow response to the European Union directive. It goes beyond the directive's list of required projects, but it is not the comprehensive approach that some commentators recommend. These critics find the participation of third parties too limited, especially at the initial "scoping" stage, where the German law says only that such people "could" be consulted.[50] The process is likely to have limited impact for several reasons. The agency need not make public the document it prepares in response to a developer's statement of environmental impacts and the comments of the public.[51] Concrete alternatives need not be presented by either the applicant or the authorities, and there is no follow-up monitoring of the results. The law creates no separate group of expert officials to oversee the process. Critics would give the environmental impact assessment process independent status. They recommend that the officials overseeing it be different from those presiding over general licensing or planning activities.[52]

The critics are right to view the statute skeptically. Nonetheless, even this weak and vaguely worded statute is controversial in Germany. Enactment occurred one and a half years after the European Union's deadline.[53]

The German law must be given an expansive interpretation if it is to comply with the directive. The directive requires two types of openness and accountability. First, it contains a broader right to information than is usual in German law. In particular, authorities must make information gathered in the assessment process available to the public in general.[54] The German statute states, however, that existing legal guidelines concerning secrecy and data protection are not affected.[55] The breadth of these exceptions will determine the limits of the right to information.

Second, the directive requires authorities to consult with and inform those who are "concerned" about their decision.[56] Environmental activists argue that "the concerned public" should include a broader range of people and groups than those permitted to participate under existing law. This interpretation would be a more fundamental challenge to familiar German licensing and planning processes, especially if these groups can use the courts to enforce their rights.[57] If the directive opens up planning and licensing processes to environmental groups and to people affected by pollution but living at a long distance from a facility, it could have a major impact on the nature of the processes themselves. Environmental assessments could then provide ammunition to nongovernmental groups and individuals seeking to cancel or modify projects. This would be a positive development if it could be managed to avoid excessive delays.

A decision in 1992 by the Federal Administrative Court suggests, however, that the statute will be narrowly interpreted by the courts. The statute itself does not mention judicial review, and existing limits on review and on the participation of third parties and environmental groups were applied by the court.[58]

PUBLIC ACCESS TO INFORMATION
ABOUT THE ENVIRONMENT

A second directive requires public access to environmental information held by governments and was supposed to be implemented by member state statutes by the end of 1992.[59] The directive permits anyone to request environmental information held by the government without demonstrating an individual interest. Although it contains numerous exceptions which may blunt its impact, the directive is a clear move in the direction of using EU law to affect administrative process as well as substantive policy.[60]

The directive runs directly counter to German bureaucratic traditions. The Administrative Procedures Act permits access to files by individuals only when they are personally affected, and even then the authorities can deny permission for a range of open-ended reasons.[61] Access to government files by members of the public with an interest in policy but no personal stake in the outcome is a novel idea in German public law.

Two and a half years after the EU deadline the Bundestag approved a statute to implement the directive on July 8, 1994.[62] The law, which reproduces much of the directive's language, was drafted by the Environmental Ministry after consultation with a committee of Länder representatives.[63] To persuade skeptics that the law represents no threat, the drafters pointed to the more general freedom-of-information acts in the United States, Scandinavia, and several EU countries. They also pointed out that Germany already permits limited access to some kinds of government information.[64] The ministry sees the statute—along with environmental impact assessments and the newly amended Environmental Liability Law—as a building block in the future rationalization of environmental law.[65]

The impact of the new law is unclear. The law includes a list of exceptions in the EU directive without providing specifics.[66] The law's importance will depend on subsequent federal and state implementing regulations and on whether or not officials interpret the exceptions narrowly in individual cases.[67]

The statute contains no explicit language permitting judicial review of denied requests. This is the case despite the directive's requirement that each member state provide for some type of appeal consistent with its own law.[68] The omission is important because under German administrative law, appeal to the administrative courts is not automatic unless individual rights have been violated. Nevertheless, judicial review will be available in some instances. The act gives everyone who applies a claim to publicly held environmental information, subject to various conditions. This language appears to grant rights to individuals.[69]

The implementing statute could enhance environmental organizations' effectiveness in the environmental impact assessment process and under the Nature Protection Law, where recognized groups already have a right to participate in planning. The law could improve the quality of public and organizational participation by assuring access to most of the information available to the authorities. The freedom-of-information act could be part of a more general reform of the administrative process in a technocratic world.[70] Although the law does not go this far, at least the EU directive is forcing German administrators to reconsider some of the premises of their day-to-day practice.

The directive has had an impact on the constitutions written by the new Länder. Several Länder have included public rights to environmental information in their constitutions, and the State of Brandenburg includes a more general right to information similar to that provided in the Freedom of Information Act in the United States.[71]

One commentator discusses the possible interaction between the freedom-of-information directive and the EU's proposed environmental liability directive. He suggests that, in principle, an environmental group in the Netherlands should be able to obtain information from Great Britain about British pollution of the North Sea. The group could then use that information to bring proceedings in Dutch courts.[72] The German Environmental Liability Law may permit such suits. Potential plaintiffs could use the German environmental information law to obtain government data needed to pursue a claim under the liability law. Defendants might also use public data on compliance and environmental quality in their defense. These possibilities may improve the ability of the Environmental Liability Law to function as a supplementary enforcement tool.

FEDERALISM

The federal structure of Germany gives authority to the Länder to implement federal laws on the environment. It also gives the Länder legislative authority that is either concurrent with or subject to federal framework laws. This structure means that some EU directives must be implemented by both federal and Länder legislation. The ECJ has made it clear that Germany will be held in violation of directives if the Länder have not passed conforming legislation—a ruling that has led to a debate between Germany and the European Union. There are two questions in this debate. First, can the EU require the Länder to pass legislation, and second, does EU law give the federal government an enhanced responsibility to monitor the Länder? These issues have particular salience in nature conservation and water quality control, where the Grundgesetz provides that the federal government can enact only framework or skeleton laws.[73] The European Court of Justice has not permitted Germany to appeal to its own constitutional structure as a legal justification for failing to incorporate directives into law. The ECJ is thus implicitly asking whether the division of authority between federal and state governments is adequate in an environmentally interdependent world.

For example, in cases dealing with implementation of directives concerning ambient levels of sulfur dioxide and lead, the court notes that two Länder have no "anti-smog" plans and finds similar holes in Länder plans to control airborne lead.[74] Plans that the Länder have drawn up have no legal force. Individuals or groups have no legal right to bring a court or administrative action against a Land for failing either to promulgate a plan or to abide by the terms of an existing document. In light of these weaknesses, the court did not accept the German argument that EU standards with respect to sulfur dioxide and lead are in fact generally met within the western part of Germany.

Court decisions finding that Germany failed to implement properly the drinking-water and wild-bird directives are based on similar difficulties with the federal structure of administration.[75] These opinions also conclude that Länder implementation is inadequate. The cases suggest that the constitutional assignment of water pollution and nature protection to the framework category may be incompatible with EU law. The opinions suggest that a stronger federal hand is necessary to carry out EU purposes.[76]

The German constitution's assignment of environmental tasks does not make policy sense. In chapter 3 I argued that there is little reason for greater federal authority over waste disposal, air purification, and noise abatement than over nature conservation and water pollution. The fundamental question is whether the problem is actually a local one with the costs and benefits concentrated in one political jurisdiction or whether the costs and benefits cross Länder or national borders. A modern approach to these issues would look at the interjurisdictional transport of water and air pollution and at the general interest in preserving endangered species and preventing the dispersal of harmful substances into the environment. Further justifications for centralized policy are the poor information available to citizens and the political pressure from businesses at the state level as they threaten to relocate if not given environmental concessions. Certain aspects of conservation and planning policy should be entirely local or regional; others, such as the control of discharges into the air and water, should be national or EU responsibilities. The enforcement of EU directives brings to the forefront the problems of a decentralized approach to many environmental problems and could provide the impetus for constitutional restructuring in the environmental area.

The current emphasis on subsidiarity, however, could work at cross-purposes if subsidiarity is used to narrow the scope for federal or EU action. Beginning with a presumption in favor of devolution creates risks in the environmental area, where the opposite presumption is warranted. Some of the rhetoric surrounding the concept of subsidiarity suggests an unreflective endorsement of devolution. Nevertheless, that is not the only way to interpret the principle. As stated in the Treaty of Maastricht, subsidiarity could be understood in the light of the economic theory of federalism outlined in chapter 3. Under that view, the principle requires strong EU-level policies when problems cross jurisdictional lines. Such cross-border external effects are the essence of many environmental problems. A sophisticated understanding of the subsidiarity principle thus supports an active EU environmental policy-making.[77]

FORMAL INCORPORATION OF DIRECTIVES INTO LAW

The Commission has a stellar record of winning cases in the European Court of Justice. This is not surprising because in many cases the Commission essentially points out the discrepancies between the language of a country's statutes and the language of the directive.[78] No complex problems of proof or means/end rationality are involved. Few cases concern implementation failures.[79] The one recent environmental case against Germany in which a substantive government action was subject to review was the one case that the Commission lost.[80] Although the nature of the cases brought by the Commission against member states is understandable given its limited resources, the focus on the formal incorporation of directives may ultimately have a detrimental effect on the development of environmental law in Germany and perhaps elsewhere.[81]

The Commission and the ECJ object to the German implementation of directives through administrative guidelines (*Verwaltungsvorschriften*) that do not have the external legal force.[82] A case concerning implementation of the groundwater directive set the stage.[83] Germany argued that the EU should consider substantive outcomes rather than legal forms.[84] In contrast, the court held that in the case of groundwater, full implementation required a specific legal framework. Existing law and administrative practices were not sufficient even if the safety of groundwater was not in doubt.[85] Some of the procedures used to implement the directive were based on the general federal law on administrative procedure supplemented by unpublished guidelines.[86] Monitoring by the Länder was also governed by administrative guidelines, which, according to the court, were not adequately publicized.[87] Using language similar to that used in earlier cases, the court held that "mere administrative practices, which are alterable at the will of the administration and are not given adequate publicity, cannot be regarded as constituting compliance with the obligation imposed on Member States to whom a directive is addressed."[88]

The court did not disapprove of all administrative guidelines. Instead, it condemned unpublished standards promulgated by procedures entirely under the bureaucracy's control.[89] The ECJ thus followed a line quite consistent with my own critique of German administrative procedures. The justices focused on the democratically illegitimate nature of the administrative process.

Two cases dealing with air pollution further limit the use of administrative guidelines. They involve the implementation of directives concerning ambient levels of sulfur dioxide and suspended particulates[90] and of lead.[91] The *Technische Anleitung zur Reinhaltung der Luft*—TA Luft, the administrative guideline governing air pollution, contains sections on ambient air quality ("immissions" in EU terminology). The Commission's objections, which were accepted by the court, focus not on the substance of these guidelines but on the formal method by which the directives have been implemented in Germany.[92] TA Luft explicitly incorporates EU standards, but it does not have the force of law reserved for statutes and legal regulations.[93] Just as in the groundwater case, the court objected to the use of such guidelines as the method of implementation. It did this despite the fact that TA Luft is a widely circulated public document and was adopted under special procedures involving consultation with outside interests.[94] The court objected that the legal guidelines do not implement the directive in a clear and precise manner sufficient to permit individuals to know their rights under the law. It refused to accept German legal precedents in atomic power law as evidence of the binding effect of the air pollution guidelines.[95]

There is, of course, some contradiction between the idea that each member state can implement directives in a way that takes account of conditions specific to that country and the inclusion of specific quantitative requirements in the texts of directives. This tension is reflected in the recent cases and exemplifies the deficiencies of both German and EU policy. EU lawyers run the risk that, in seeking examples of foot dragging, they will wipe out justifiable delegations of authority to bureaucracies and Länder governments.

At a time when Germany needs to recognize and control the delegation of policy-making authority to federal ministries, ECJ decisions of this kind can easily push the process in the other direction—toward the writing of overly detailed statutes. This would be unfortunate. The Commission and the ECJ are right to be concerned about the democratic legitimacy of administrative guide-lines produced through unaccountable informal processes, but the solution is not to outlaw such guidelines.

Instead, the administrative process should be open to public input and sub-ject to outside review. Because guidelines are often at least as influential in practice as the underlying statutes,[96] the answer may be to give such guidelines more legal force while at the same time reforming the processes that produce them. There is a trade-off between the specificity of statutes and the political accountability of the regulatory process. Detailed statutes can be implemented by a bureaucracy without further controls simply because the statutes limit the range of discretion. In contrast, laws that establish legislative goals require constraints on executive procedures. These constraints should assure that spe-cial interest groups do not have too much influence at the implementation level, and they should avoid policies that simply make life easy for public officials. The ECJ's opinions on air pollution rely instead on legal formalisms and are not particularly nuanced.

Although EU efforts to restrict the use of legal guidelines are, I believe, a mistake, its legal efforts are necessarily constrained by the possibilities pre-sented by the member states. Even though EU lawyers at the Commission accept the trade-off outlined above, they are in no position to reform the pro-cedural basis of German administrative law.[97] Germany's fledgling efforts to acknowledge the realities of policy-making in a modern regulatory state should not, however, be undermined by excessive legalism on the EU level. Commis-sion lawyers should urge the ECJ to recognize that democratically open and accountable procedures can legitimate executive branch policy-making.

CONCLUSION

The European Union has the potential to encourage constructive developments in German administrative law and environmental policy. Currently, however, the results are mixed. EU enforcement efforts have usefully highlighted the anomalies of German federalism. Recent ECJ cases should encourage Germany to rethink the constitutional assignment of environmental protection tasks. Directives on environmental assessment and access to information can have a beneficial impact if subject to creative implementation. The directives, however, leave room for exceptions and interpretations that could limit the jolt they can deliver to existing practice.

Other developments in EU law are not so helpful. The delegitimizing of technical guidelines reflects an overly mechanical, legalistic interpretation of German practice. Germany needs more accountable bureaucratic processes. It should not freeze the technological and scientific learning of one generation into hard statutory form. The Commission should focus on the accomplishment of environmental goals instead of on the niceties of legal forms. It should concentrate its efforts where they make the most sense: on concrete environmental achievements. Paradoxically, Germany, with its relatively good environmental record, would be better off with a powerful, rather than a weak, EU environmental mandate.

If the EU were given stronger implementation authority the nature of EU directives might also change—away from setting technical standards, and toward setting goals in terms of the benefits to human beings and the environment. Public policy arguments suggest that the EU should have a mandate to monitor and enforce environmental protection measures. So far, however, it has not had this authority. The Treaty of Maastricht does not remedy the basic weakness of EU monitoring and enforcement tools. Although the gains would be unequally distributed, the citizens of Europe would benefit from an environmental policy for the whole of Europe supported by strong bureaucratic and legal capabilities.

Under current conditions, however, the European Union is unlikely to be a potent source of constructive law reform within Germany. The Germans themselves need to rethink their existing patterns of policy-making and public participation in the light of the substantive imperatives of environmental policy.

9

ENVIRONMENTAL LAW
AND ADMINISTRATIVE PROCESS:
GERMANY AND THE UNITED STATES

Environmental policy illustrates the difficulties that democracies experience in reconciling technocratic knowledge with the concerns of ordinary citizens. In spite of the status of Germany and the United States as policy leaders, both countries have seriously deficient substantive laws and both need to improve the operation of their political systems to take account of present-day realities.

Modern states should develop principles of administrative practice that match substance with procedure. After outlining such principles, I argue that the political nature of environmental problems should govern the design of bureaucratic structures. Reliance on scientific canons or judicialized models will not do; consensual processes have only limited applicability.

On the basis of this outline, I criticize German practice. Some students of comparative politics argue that political structure determines policies. The German case appears to demonstrate this proposition. In spite of the similar policy pathologies of German and American environmental law, the different political structures have affected the way public concerns are translated into specific policy initiatives. Even if one can explain the existing pattern through references to history and tradition, however, Germans need not be the prisoners of the current legal and political order. Environmental law has raised new legal problems that conventional German public law cannot solve.

The Federal Republic should consider reforming its administrative process and strengthening court review. My comparative study suggests that the American model is better adapted to the distinctive problems involved in accountable environmental policy-making. Procedural reform would not be a panacea, however. Germany and by extension the European Union should also consider substantive environmental law reform.

The German experience has lessons for the United States. Although some features could be usefully borrowed by the United States, Germany is most interesting as an example of a public law system based primarily on individual rights and consent. The German case highlights the risks of moving the U.S. system in such directions.

LEGITIMACY AND COMPETENCE

The central tension is between competence and legitimacy. If we are not content to define competence as providing legitimacy, or legitimacy as meaning competence, policymakers must face the potential for conflict. Much past discussion has, however, exaggerated the conflict. Fundamental difficulties arise, not so much from the democracy-technocracy trade-off itself as from a mismatch of techniques and tasks. Table 9.1 provides a simple schematic representation of good matchups.

The upper left-hand side of the table matches purely scientific or technical questions (row A) with evaluation methods using the canons of the relevant science (col. A). The goal is to establish scientific validity, not to promote fairness or democratic legitimacy. Peer review is the evaluative method accepted within the scientific community. Bias is limited by such devices as using independent reviewers, giving greater credence to replicated results, and preparing written evaluations.[1] The reviewers' identities may be kept secret from the researchers so that they can respond only to the criticisms and not the critics. Judicialized procedures are not used.

Of course, such conventional processes may overlook truly innovative or unusual approaches, but that is the price of assuring a basic level of competence. The aim of the administrative process is not to advance science but to provide a sound background for regulation.[2] The ideal is a balanced assessment of existing research that points to strengths and weaknesses in theory and in empirical testing and that isolates those areas of uncertainty most relevant to the ultimate policy choice. Nevertheless, although scientific norms guide the evaluative process, the choice of topics remains a policy question that must be determined by politically responsible authorities.

The protection of individual rights (row B) requires a quite different procedural framework (col. B.1). The aim of the courtlike process is a fair decision that permits individuals to defend themselves against arbitrary state authority. Under one familiar view of such procedures, individuals have a right to a hearing and must be able to discover the basis of the bureaucracy's decision. They must be able to challenge the state's decisions as unfair or illegal before independent bodies, such as courts. Although the content of rights and the details of the required procedures are controversial issues, the basically individualized nature of the proceeding is not in doubt. Procedures derived from civil and criminal trials frequently form the basis for such proceedings within the executive. Their purpose is to protect individual rights; they are poorly designed for resolving policy issues.

Environmental statutes frequently delegate political tasks to the bureaucracy. A bureaucracy cannot use majority voting; it must find other means to make choices. Neither scientific nor judicialized procedures are appropriate. The bureaucracy's job is to balance conflicting interests, not to discover scien-

TABLE 9.1   Matching Substance and Process

	Process				
	A	B Bureaucrat-Led			C
		1	2	3	
Substance	Peer Review	Court-like	Quasi-legislative	Administrative balancing	Consensual
A. Technical	X				
B. Individual rights		X			
C. Political					
1. Distributive			X		
2. Net benefits possible					
a. All interests not well-represented				X	
b. All interests well-represented					X

tific truths or to preserve rights. Science and technology provide a background to many political disputes, and the preservation of individual rights is always a constraint on policy. Nevertheless, neither peer review nor judicial procedures provides a helpful framework for policy decisions that involve conflicts of values and interests.

Table 9.1 distinguishes three types of political choices faced by bureaucratic policymakers. In the easy case (row C.2.b), everyone can come out ahead, and all interests have strong and equally balanced representation. In such win-win cases, consensual or "participant-led" processes (col. C) seem appropriate.[3] The participants will disagree about the division of the gains, but a negotiation designed to produce a unanimous decision is, in principle, possible. The bureaucracy can play the role of facilitator. It can structure the process, clarify the consequences of failure, and select the participants.[4] Given these background conditions, the state could simply accept the policy agreed on by the participants and promulgate it as a rule or guideline. Although the range of outcomes is determined by the statutory framework, the actual outcome is the result of negotiation. Publicity and reasoned decision-making are unimportant. If everyone agrees, the outcome is, by definition, legitimate.

The easy case seldom describes the reality of political choices delegated to the bureaucracy. When it does not, the process must be "bureaucrat-led," with public officials trading off interests and values. There are no objectively right answers. A decision's acceptability is a function of an individual's political philosophy and personal stake in the issue. For distributive choices (row C.1), bargaining will never produce consensus. Instead, bureaucrats should make the choice in a self-conscious way that balances the conflicting interests but does not require everyone to approve of the outcome (col. B.2). The administration should articulate the mixture of principle and political expediency that produced the choice. Politically expedient choices are not, by that fact, illegitimate, but they should be acknowledged as such.

In many situations, mutually beneficial solutions exist, but they cannot be reached through negotiation (row C.2.a). Most environmental problems arise from failures of the market system and so could be solved with net gains for all. Nevertheless, most are not suitable for regulatory negotiation. The problems of group representation are intractable because some of those concerned are members of extremely diffuse groups, such as consumers of manufactured goods or breathers of the air. Thus the public authorities must make the ultimate decision. They must hear representatives of those affected and then apply policy analytic tools to reach a decision. I label this approach "administrative balancing" (col. B.3).

Even if each group prefers the new policy to the status quo, everyone may be unhappy with his or her share of the gains. Further, although ordinary citizens may prefer policies that impose costs on polluters, dischargers will support subsidies and tax concessions. Because of conflicts over the distribution of gains, the government must justify its decision to the public and the business community. The aim is not to make everyone happy—democratic government implies the existence of minority parties and defeated politicians. Instead, the authorities must show that the outcome is consistent with the legislative purpose. For example, a policy designed to correct a market failure could be carried out using principles of cost-benefit analysis. A policy designed to aid the homeless could be implemented under egalitarian principles of distributive justice. The explanation must both articulate the goals behind the policy and clarify the link between the available information and the outcome.

Because direct oversight by the legislature is generally insufficient, the authorities must use legitimate procedures to produce a decision. In particular, administrative procedures should permit experts, ordinary people, and organized groups to present their information and views. This implies broad public notice, an openness to information and opinions from diverse sources, and a willingness to share this material with those interested in the outcome. But openness is not sufficient. I have postulated that groups are not equally well represented, which means that the bureaucracy must gather data and opinions itself.

Bureaucrats have incentives to avoid the bother of publicly accountable processes and may favor organized groups with a high stake in the outcome. Thus judicial review should be available. This review would recognize the superior expertise of agencies vis-à-vis the courts as well as acknowledge agencies' incentives to deviate from competent and democratically legitimate procedures. The courts would review procedures by requiring officials to listen to a wide range of facts and opinions and to explain their decisions. Bureaucratic choices are acceptable not because they satisfy everyone but because the process assures that no major bodies of knowledge and opinion have been ignored.[5]

FALSE DICHOTOMIES

My outline of the ideal matches of procedure and substance is too simple. Not all cases fit cleanly into one box or another. The hard cases involve both science and politics, where hybrid procedures are sometimes possible. Negotiations that resolve preliminary issues could be followed by a bureaucratic choice, or conversely, preliminary technocratic fact-finding could be followed by negotiation in the light of this information.[6] Scientists, engineers, and social scientists would assess the quality of research and technical information. This material could then form the basis for policymakers to ascertain "the state of the art," locate thresholds where human health is "protected," or trade off human lives against economic prosperity. Such choices are not scientific, or even social-scientific, judgments. They are at the heart of the policy-making enterprise.

Often, however, it is impossible to evaluate the technical data first and then use it to make a policy decision. When this happens, how should the administration proceed? Should it emphasize competence through the use of scientifically acceptable methods, or should it develop a politically legitimate procedure? For bureaucrat-led processes there is often no need to make a choice. Procedures can be designed to further both goals. If hearings provide information, there is no inconsistency between them and the subsequent technocratic exercise used to generate a final rule or standard. If democratic legitimacy requires a statement of reasons, so, too, do scientific canons.

Conflicts will continue to exist, but they are disputes over values and administrative competence, not over process. Suppose, for example, that officials, operating under an open-ended statute, believe that cost-benefit or risk-assessment techniques are the best way to balance interests. In public hearings, individuals provide information and explain how they will be affected by the policy. Some individuals, however, question the agency's methodology and go on to challenge the ultimate decision in court. Such disputes indicate the lack of a political consensus over how to make competent policy. Challengers may don the mantle of democratic legitimacy in criticizing the agency's decision, but their fundamental complaint is over policy, not procedure. If everyone agreed on a single balancing technique, it is hard to see how anyone could object in principle to an open and accountable process.

The remaining conflicts would be prudential ones over the cost in time and money of extensive procedures and over bureaucratic capacity. Outsiders may claim that the agency is failing because of laziness, stupidity, or venality. The issue for judicial review would be the agency's failure to live up to legislatively mandated standards. Such cases can produce sharp conflicts between public agencies and outside groups, but they are not conflicts between technocratic decision-making and democracy.

In short, for bureaucrat-led processes, the conflicts between competence and democratic legitimacy appear to be less prevalent than some commentators would have us believe. The apparent conflicts that we observe are frequently the result of disputes over substantive standards and over the way public officials fulfill their duties *given* a view of proper behavior. If the democratic legitimacy of the administrative process can be improved with no major sacrifice in terms of substantive policy, we can focus on reforms that further these joint goals. We can concentrate on the design of administrative procedures that match the problem to be solved. With this background, I consider how well the German system has tailored its techniques to substantive problems.

CONTROL OF THE EXECUTIVE IN GERMANY

In Germany, expert bodies operating under scientific principles resolve purely scientific issues. The state generally protects individual rights through appropriate procedures. The widespread acceptability of the scientific method and of judicialized procedures makes it natural to extend the reach of both to problems where they do not fit. In general, German administrative law does a poor job of matching process to substance for political issues. The failure of public law to acknowledge the political and policy-making role of the executive has produced an inadequate legal structure.

Germany constrains executive discretion through statutory commands, parliamentary oversight, and Länder independence. These constitutional methods are inadequate. The first risks the production of rigid, overly detailed statutes. The second is too intermittent and ineffective, given the Bundestag's lack of both independence and technocratic competence. The third is too limited to deal with the inter-Land and cross-border effects of environmental pollution. The Länder are likely to be most concerned with administrative issues, not the achievement of overall policy goals. German principles of a state based on law or *Rechtsstaat* need to take account of the special nature of environmental problems.

The preferred German solution to complex political-technical issues is a negotiated solution, produced away from the public eye by representatives of those concerned—a solution that is then given legal or presumptive force (col. C). This model is used in labor-management relations, where it fits quite well. For environmental issues the match is generally poor, and, as a consequence, German environmental policy-making is not entirely based on consensual processes. Instead, regulations and guidelines are approved by both the regime and the Bundesrat. Nevertheless, approval by political actors sometimes has a pro forma quality.

Rules and guidelines are often based on standards negotiated by groups of experts. The goal is to evaluate technical evidence through a process similar to scientific peer review. Some of these groups are dominated by those employed by or dependent on the industries being regulated. Not all interests are well represented. Nevertheless, such groups are asked to make policy judgments by, for example, deciding on a feasible technical standard.[7] These judgments are important because technical norms appear to be the real engine of German environmental regulation. In principle, the ministry engages in an independent assessment before issuing a rule or guideline. In practice, it tends to rely on outside experts. When this happens, the experts act as policy-making advisory bodies, and their procedures should reflect this fact. Those included on the committees may well be the most competent scientists, but the policy content of their work needs to be reviewed in an open and accountable manner.[8]

Even these relatively unstructured processes are sometimes too formal for German environmental policymakers. Instead, in a few situations, the regulated industry and the ministry have negotiated informal agreements. These agreements are not always made public and are not subject to Germany's admittedly weak constraints on the policy-making process.[9] This is a troubling development, but as yet it seems confined to limited areas of law.

AMERICAN MODELS

INFORMAL RULEMAKING AND JUDICIAL REVIEW

Germany can learn from the United States when the substance is political and the process should be bureaucrat-led (rows C.1 and C.2.a). The informal rulemaking and judicial-review clauses of the American Administrative Procedures Act (APA) of 1946 provide an outline. The basic principles are public notice, a rulemaking process open to a broad range of interests, and a statement of reasons accompanying the publication of the rule.[10] When the bureaucracy is charged with making a political decision and when consensual processes are inappropriate, these conditions provide a minimum of legitimacy.

The administrative process is not overly judicialized. This is appropriate because informal rulemaking procedures do not fundamentally concern individual rights. American law places few constraints on the use of scientific or technical information. The decision is not a formal one, made "on the record." Rather, the agency can consult whomever it wishes and can request the advice of both in-house and outside experts. Conversely, if anyone comes forward with information, the agency must be willing to accommodate responsible petitioners. Officials need not follow the recommendations of public participants, and they can manage the process in the interest of administrative efficiency.

A rule produced under these procedures has legal force under the implementing statute. It can be challenged in court, however, on the ground that procedures were inadequate or that the final decision was "arbitrary and capricious" or in violation of the Constitution or the implementing statute.[11] If the agency ignores relevant information, it runs the risk that a court will overturn the regulation. Review emphasizes the process by which the bureaucracy makes policy and at the same time limits the scope of the judicial inquiry. The possibility of court challenges gives the agency an incentive to follow the law's strictures. The executive is not only constrained by the possibility of political backlash at the next election. In addition, those affected by the rule can raise objections even if they are not supported by a legislative majority.

The American Administrative Procedures Act has left gaps that substantive statutes and judicial opinions have had to fill, but the resulting jurisprudence permits a measure of popular control of the bureaucracy that supplements the control provided by elected officials. Although judicial review is criticized in the United States as time-consuming and ineffective, especially in highly technical fields,[12] it has the advantage of explicitly requiring that the political and policy decisions of agencies should be accountable to citizens, whatever their party affiliation. It acknowledges that the constraints imposed by elected officials may be inadequate.

Germany should consider amending its Administrative Procedures Act to apply to the political decisions of the federal administration when it issues rules and guidelines. The basic principles expressed in the American Administrative Procedures Act provide a minimal standard of accountability. Establishing similar requirements would open up the German administrative process and set limited constraints on executive-branch behavior. Because judicial review focuses on process rather than substance, a cautious judiciary could avoid embroiling itself in political squabbles.[13]

In both Germany and the United States, some commentators criticize requirements for formal hearings as irrelevant. In the United States, informal negotiation precedes the publication of proposed rules in the Federal Register, and groups with good access to the bureaucracy can be influential at that stage. German critics claim that most important policy decisions are made in closed-door sessions of powerful interests.[14] Even assuming this criticism is correct, it does not follow that notice and comment procedures have no impact. If agency procedures can be subject to judicial review, the government will be less likely to ignore the information or concerns of an outside group capable of both submitting a comment and mounting a court challenge.

ADAPTING AMERICAN MODELS TO
GERMAN REALITIES

Obviously, the American administrative law structure cannot simply be imported, as is, into the German system. A number of specific issues of administrative law and judicial review must be resolved.

German law distinguishes between regulations with the force of law and administrative guidelines with external effects. American administrative law distinguishes between rules that are subject to the APA and policy statements or internal organizational guidelines that are not.[15] The line between rules and policy statements in American law differs from the line between regulations and administrative guidelines in Germany. Many guidelines and informal agreements in Germany would require APA informal rulemaking procedures in the United States. For example, the German technical standards for air pollution are in the form of administrative guidelines, but similar American standards are regulations with the force of law. Procedural reform should apply to both types of executive action. It seems unnecessary, however, to change established labels. The new law could preserve the differing constitutional status of regulations and guidelines and provide across-the-board procedural guarantees as well.

Both systems permit agencies to issue intermediate guidance documents without formal legal force. Interpretive rules, policy statements, manuals, and guidelines influence the implementation of many regulatory statutes, especially in the environmental area.[16] Some claim that the expansive use of such documents violates principles of American administrative law and makes the system less open and accountable.[17] Others view the documents as practical expedients that make implementation more effective.[18] If the German policy-making system were reformed to mirror the American model, the Germans, too, would have to resolve these issues. The current American answer seems applicable to Germany. A federal appellate court has held that the administration cannot treat a policy statement like a binding rule unless it has complied with APA procedures.[19] In Germany, where Länder implementation is the rule, this doctrine would hold for state-level actions as well.

Reforms in the administrative process will not be effective unless plaintiffs can learn the basis of the administration's decision. German public-administration traditions stress the closed, expert nature of officialdom. The new statute on public access to information could be expanded to cover all types of information.[20] Public accountability will be furthered by mandating that a statement of reasons accompany each rule and by making compliance with this requirement reviewable by the courts. Further, Germany should critically examine the use of private organizations in setting public standards. If such organizations have de facto decision-making authority, they should be subject to the same procedural guarantees as public agencies.[21] Otherwise they should be subject only to the canons of scientific peer review.

JUDICIAL REVIEW: TIMING, STANDING, AND POLITICS

Administrative court practice should be modified to facilitate review of the administrative process. Both pre-enforcement review and organizational standing should be included in a general reform that incorporates aspects of American procedures. Clear limits on the scope of review can counter the danger of an overly political judiciary.

The timing of judicial review should reflect the nature of the administrative action before the court. If the German courts are to monitor federal policy-making procedures, oversight should occur, as it does in the United States, soon after the government has acted. Because of substantial delays introduced by judicial review, it may be desirable to modify the American model by imposing time limits. Some delay is, however, inevitable, especially given the property rights of license holders under German law. If enforcement were not suspended, the courts would have to resolve difficult compensation claims. A firm granted a license under a disputed standard might demand compensation for subsequently required modifications.

When the German courts review a rulemaking process, they should be generous in giving standing to groups whose members will be affected. If administrative procedures are modified to be open to public interest groups, these groups should also be granted access to the courts. The usual German objections to such plaintiffs would not apply, because these cases are not meant to protect rights but to preserve participatory values.

One issue should be faced squarely. Many organized groups in Germany are creatures of political parties. The Green party in particular is closely linked to environmental groups.[22] Germany does not currently have the range of relatively well-funded, independent public-interest law firms that exist in the United States. Electoral politics can easily become mixed with legal challenges. Although this connection cannot be avoided, the nature of review can blunt its impact. If the courts limit themselves to bureaucratic procedures and the administration's conformity to statute, they can avoid cases in which a minority party asks the courts to rule on the validity of policies promulgated by the majority coalition. Substance and procedure cannot be neatly separated, but the courts should struggle to make the distinction.

LEGAL FEES

In German law the loser generally pays the legal fees and court costs of the winner under a court-determined schedule that is usually calculated as a fraction of the amount at stake. Because there is no straightforward way of calculating these sums in cases that challenge procedures, the administrative court system should issue a fee schedule, just as it already does in other areas of administrative law.[23] The fee schedule would try to strike a delicate and difficult balance between rewarding lawyers who take such cases and discouraging the use of suits as a delaying tactic.

But more fundamental changes in the method of paying lawyers should be considered. Two-sided fee shifting reduces the number of frivolous suits, but it also discourages individuals and groups from filing suits to further the public interest. Judicial review of the administrative process seeks to defend public values, making the common American practice of one-sided fee shifting seem appropriate. Under this system, the state pays the victorious plaintiffs' legal fees, and losers must absorb their own legal costs. Such rules are used in the United States in the area of civil rights and under the citizen suit provisions of several environmental laws.[24]

One-sided fee shifting could be combined with contingency fees, with lawyers donating their time if the case is not successful. Such arrangements are common in the United States, but the German legal community views such fee arrangements as unethical. This position should be rethought for public interest lawsuits. A mixed system of one-sided fee shifting and contingent fees could strike a balance between subsidizing the prosecution of meritorious public-regarding claims and discouraging the merely disgruntled.[25]

BEYOND THE APA

The American Administrative Procedures Act cannot resolve all of the problems of German administrative law. The APA is designed neither to defuse conflicts over the meaning of competence nor to improve the analytic capabilities of officials. It does nothing to encourage the legislature to write clear and logical statutes. Yet in both Germany and the United States, environmental laws frequently fail to resolve fundamental policy trade-offs.

Judicial review could, however, be a tool for encouraging competence in both countries. Courts could respond to the legislature's tendency to write vague and unclear standards by establishing a set of background norms for agencies that the legislature must explicitly override. Such review aims to improve the transparency and consistency of legislative enactments by imposing costs on the legislature if it fails to articulate its goals. For example, for regulations designed to correct market failures, the courts could apply a cost-benefit test as a background norm.[26] The idea is to get away from technical feasibility and move toward means/end rationality. The legislature could explicitly draft statutes to prevent such a standard from being applied, but in the absence of clear language, courts would examine regulations for conformity with cost-benefit criteria. Offending regulations would not be redesigned by the courts, but would instead be sent back to the executive for reissue.

This proposal may sound either utopian or dangerous applied to the German context, yet it may actually fit better with German than with American legal doctrine. German constitutional law already acknowledges a "proportionality principle" for the review of statutes and regulations. This principle implies that the means must be proportional to the ends.[27] One could interpret the principle to imply that administrators should balance benefits against costs. The courts would then check the adequacy of these efforts.

Expanding the German courts' role would necessitate confronting questions of judicial capacity and respect for the courts. If the courts carried out their new tasks poorly, they would jeopardize the viability of the reforms I am suggesting.

Unfortunately, this is a real possibility. Few German lawyers have been exposed to science or social science beyond high school, and German legal education, even in the best law schools, is much less interdisciplinary than in the United States. The notion that law, even administrative or public law, is a self-contained body of knowledge is prevalent.

Yet an institutional structure exists in Germany that would make reform simpler than in the United States. Germany already has a specialized system of administrative courts, and within the higher courts judges are divided into permanent Senates that specialize in particular substantive topics. It seems quite compatible with past practice, therefore, to designate a subset of judges who would become expert in policy analysis so as to decide regulatory cases competently. The only new element is the subject matter in which they would need to become expert. Further, the law clerks for high-level German judges usually are not recent graduates but are more mature lawyers who may spend several years in their positions. Once again, though innovative, it would be possible to expand the corps of aides to include social scientists. At present, judges on the state and federal administrative courts can consult "representatives of the public interest." These are lawyers charged with representing the interests of the state and federal governments to the courts.[28] These bodies are not much used by the judges, at least at the federal level. These groups could be reconstituted and given a more general public interest mandate; they could be charged not with conveying political judgments but with helping judges understand the complexities of modern regulatory problems.

SUBSTANTIVE LAW REFORM: GERMANY AND THE EUROPEAN UNION

Process is only part of the problem. Substantive reform requires amending German statutes and recasting European Union policy. Statutes generally ignore the connection between means and ends. The laws give prominence to technical norms. In the air and noise pollution statute, for example, the core regulatory process is the licensing of individual sources, and licensing standards are determined by the state of technology. The setting of norms guides statutory implementation. Planning is largely an enterprise left to state and local governments. More comprehensive efforts to link discharges into the air and water with ambient air and water quality are academic exercises with little policy bite. The possible efficiency benefits of market-like incentives play little role in the debate over environmental policy because policy-making is not viewed in causal terms. The proximate goal of limiting the discharges from individual plants has become the ultimate goal of public administration. If public authorities think they know what engineering measures they want a firm to adopt, market incentives look needlessly indirect.

Only in individual licensing processes can balancing be carried out, but at that level, broad policy tradeoffs are impossible. The major German statutes should be refocused—away from reducing emissions and toward reducing the real-world harms caused by environmental pollution. Germany should recast its laws to emphasize saving lives and preserving nature. Goals should be calibrated in terms of cancers avoided, respiratory disease prevented, trees saved, and wildlife preserved. In determining these levels, the federal government needs to specify the links between fundamental benefits and ambient levels of environmental quality, between ambient levels and the discharges of pollutants, and between discharges and economic costs. Of course, the data are imprecise, and most of the benefits are difficult to measure in monetary terms. Even so, politicians and top officials need to know the basic parameters in order to decide what problems to emphasize and what political considerations to recognize. Licenses, if required, would be the result of an analytical process rather than an end in themselves. Further, licensing is only one of many methods that can be used to implement statutory goals. Incentive-based systems that permit the trade of pollution rights or that charge for the production of pollution are alternatives.[29]

Because many of Germany's environmental problems have cross-border consequences, a strengthened role for the European Union would be desirable not only for Germans but also for all Europeans. A stronger mandate, however, would be worthwhile only if the EU shifted its focus away from technical standards toward the achievement of goals. After the EU sets goals, directives could then set maximum levels of discharge for each pollutant on a country-by-country basis. The standards would be minimal ones that countries could exceedif they could do so by controlling their own pollution sources.

In accord with the principle of subsidiarity, directives would not distinguish between types of sources and would include nothing about technical standards or methods of compliance. However, general principles would apply that forbid members from favoring their own industries over industries in other states. Each member could then decide what type and level of regulation would best achieve EU goals. Directives would, in short, specify both ambient pollution levels and permitted emissions. They would not specify the technology or the raw materials.

European Union enforcement efforts should be limited to determining that a statute has been enacted and to monitoring ambient air and water quality. For global problems, such as ozone depletion and global warming, the EU would have to monitor discharges, but within the EU discharges would become relevant only if the ambient quality standards were violated and several states' polluters might have been the cause. The burden would be on the individual member states to demonstrate that their dischargers were not to blame. An institution with independent authority to monitor environmental quality is therefore central to the recasting of EU law. The EU would not, however, need to have authority to enter the premises of dischargers to inspect their pollution control activities, so some of the objections to creating an intrusive European police force would not apply in this case.

There are two exceptions to this goal-oriented approach. The first concerns the basic structure of property rights. The EU principle that polluters should pay for harm they cause must be uniformly applied.[30] Otherwise intercountry differences in implementation will affect decisions about business locations. If the polluter-pay principle were well enforced, however, a country could sell pollution rights to dischargers even if other countries were using other enforcement methods. In general, EU-level policymakers should encourage the use of systems based on charges or subsidies to give incentives to industries, consumers, and member states to take account of the environmental costs they impose on society.[31]

The second caveat applies to standards for products, like automobiles and gasoline, sold throughout the EU and to the regulation of packaging waste.[32] In both cases, uniform specifications are appropriate, given the efficiencies of mass production and the cost to individual countries of monitoring products. This last area of regulation is in fact where the European Union has had the greatest success.

At present, however, a thoroughgoing reform of EU environmental policy appears unrealistic. The past head of the Environmental Directorate, who resigned in the summer of 1992 to become the Italian environmental minister, left office making sharply critical remarks about the Commission's lack of commitment to strong environmental measures.[33] The Treaty of Maastricht strengthens the Council's hand by permitting it to pass more legislation by a qualified majority, but the treaty does not give the Commission monitoring and inspection authority and does not require a rethinking of environmental policy. Germany cannot simply put off reform of its own system in deference to the newly constituted European Union.

LESSONS FOR AMERICA

German administrative law echoes the reform agendas of two different groups of American legal scholars and judges. One group deplores the contested nature of the administrative process and urges the adoption of consensus-building procedures. The second group of critics argues that judicial review of the administrative process should focus on the preservation of individual rights in the face of state power.[34]

CONSENSUAL PROCESSES

Some American commentators argue that rulemaking, done in the shadow of judicial review, has become unnecessarily adversarial and time consuming.[35] The widespread availability of court review has overly judicialized the policy-making process. In spite of the lack of specificity in the Administrative Procedures Act, the actual process has, according to these observers, become more like a trial than an administrative fact-finding and policy-making exercise.[36] Cooperation is discouraged because participants are busy making a record for courts to review, and that record is overly detailed and massive.

These critics recommend downplaying judicial review and moving toward negotiated solutions. They recommend regulatory negotiation, business–government cooperation, and advisory committee structures. The aim is to streamline and accelerate the regulatory process by fostering an atmosphere of trust and cooperation among the affected groups. The German experience counsels caution. Advisory committees, federal-state working groups, and quasi-private committees of technical experts all help generate German technical standards and public policies. The system is accountable to the scientific community, business, and lower-level governments. It is only indirectly accountable to the public and the environmental community through the cabinet's responsibility to the Parliament and through the voluntary efforts of the ministry and its advisors. The result is a process close to what American critics would find ideal, but it is poorly matched to the nature of many of the problems facing the administration. Consensual decision-making is appropriate only for a narrow range of issues in environmental law.

JUDICIAL REVIEW

In the United States, criticisms of judicial review of agency actions have increased in recent years.[37] Studies demonstrate the impact of judicial decisions on agency behavior and priority setting.[38] For example, judicial decisions have required the Environmental Protection Agency to emphasize narrow issues that may not have the highest policy importance and to give power to lawyers at the expense of scientists. Nevertheless, some court orders have had positive effects on agency morale and performance.[39]

Some critics claim that judges have a model of the administrative process in their heads that does not conform to reality.[40] They see the process as a technical exercise that consists of accumulating the relevant data and making an expert judgment.[41] Even when this view is correct, judges err in supposing that court-like procedures are an effective way for agencies to resolve scientific questions. But in many cases the technocratic model is a poor description of reality. Although some of the issues to be resolved are scientific, others are political problems that require a balancing of interests.[42]

Several commentators argue that judicial scrutiny of rulemaking has induced agencies both to make fewer rules and to seek less accountable ways of making policy.[43] John Mendeloff's studies of the Occupational Health and Safety Administration (OSHA) illustrate the first proposition. He argues that OSHA both overregulates and underregulates. It regulates too few substances, and it excessively restricts those it does control.[44] OSHA responded to this criticism in 1989 with a single massive rulemaking process that established baseline standards for 428 toxic substances.[45] Unfortunately, a federal court of appeals refused to permit the rule to stand because it failed to establish a significant risk for each substance and failed to establish economic and technical feasibility on a substance-by-substance basis.[46]

The shift away from rulemaking is demonstrated by several studies of agency behavior. The National Highway and Traffic Safety Administration and the Consumer Product Safety Commission shifted to product recalls after failing to uphold rules in court.[47] The Federal Energy Regulatory Commission may be less likely to use rules in the future after a series of court reversals in 1989 and 1990.[48] The Environmental Protection Agency uses circulars to communicate enforcement standards to regional offices, state agencies, and pollution sources.[49]

American courts have two ways of going wrong. First, they may mischaracterize the nature of the agency's problem. They may view an issue as a technical one involving the application of scientific or legal knowledge when it is actually a political exercise in balancing interests. Second, they may favor bureaucratic techniques that are poorly fitted to the issue at hand. For example, courts might correctly view an issue as political or technical and then argue that court-like procedures are the best way to resolve such disputes. These are serious problems, but the response of conservative jurists is inadequate. Rather than recasting and reforming the process of judicial review of policy-making, they would abandon it.

Supreme Court Justice Antonin Scalia is the chief judicial advocate of this position—a position very close to conventional German public law doctrine. According to Scalia, the courts should avoid the political issues that arise in overseeing the rulemaking process. Instead, they should give standing only to individuals who have suffered injuries. Agencies freed from intrusive court review would be able to revamp the administrative process for greater efficiency and efficacy. More statutory deadlines could be met, and less agency time would be taken in defending against court challenges.

To demonstrate the close connection between Scalia's position and German law, consider two recent Supreme Court opinions that denied standing to organized wildlife groups seeking to challenge government actions.[50] Although the Court gave various reasons for keeping the groups out of court, the opinions also make clear that the plaintiffs would have lost on the merits.

In *Lujan v. National Wildlife Federation* the wildlife organization challenged the federal government's reclassification of certain lands to open them to mining.[51] Several members of the National Wildlife Federation claimed that they used land in the vicinity of the disputed parcels. In a five-to-four decision the

Court agreed that the individuals' interests in recreational use and aesthetic enjoyment were among those protected by the statutes in question. Nevertheless, it found the claims of injury too tenuous to accept.[52]

The opinion then goes on to argue that, even if the plaintiffs had been injured, they would not have the right to challenge the land classification policy of the Federal Bureau of Land Management. They would have to take a case-by-case approach. To Scalia, pre-enforcement review of regulations is a narrow exception. It applies in two cases. First, the courts can review substantive rules that require a plaintiff to adjust its conduct immediately. Scalia thus avoids overruling cases that others read as permitting widespread pre-enforcement review. Second, he acknowledges that a few specific statutes permit review "even before the concrete effects normally required for APA review are felt." In general, however, Scalia claims that "a regulation is not ordinarily considered 'ripe' for judicial review under the APA until the scope of the controversy has been reduced to more manageable proportions, and its factual components fleshed out, by some concrete action applying the regulation to the claimant's situation in a fashion that harms or threatens to harm him."[53] This language is only dictum[54] since the case does not deal with a regulation but with a more general government policy. Nevertheless, Scalia uses the occasion to criticize attempts to influence agency policy-making through the courts. General acceptance of Scalia's position would make review of high-level policy-making difficult. It would make the challenges mounted by environmental groups especially problematic because they are seldom the addressees of regulations.

The second case goes even further. *Lujan v. Defenders of Wildlife* concerns the extraterritorial reach of the Endangered Species Act.[55] The wildlife group challenged a rule that limited the scope of the act to the United States and the high seas. Two members of the group had traveled to Egypt and Sri Lanka, where they claimed that American aid projects were threatening endangered species. The court found that these people had suffered no injury.[56] A plurality also held that even if the plaintiffs had been injured a favorable decision on the merits would not help them.[57] Thus standing was denied.

Not content to rest there, Scalia goes on to deal with the issue of "procedural injury." The lower court held that the citizen suit provisions of the Endangered Species Act gave the wildlife group standing to seek court review of executive branch consultation procedures. Scalia writes, "This is not a case where plaintiffs are seeking to enforce a procedural requirement the disregard of which could impair a separate concrete interest of theirs. . . . Rather, the court held that the injury-in-fact requirement had been satisfied by congressional conferral upon *all* persons of an abstract, self-contained, noninstrumental 'right' to have the Executive observe the procedures required by law. We reject this view" (footnotes omitted).[58] The Justice recognizes that procedural rights have a special status when concrete interests are at stake. In such cases, requirements of redressibility and immediacy can be waived.[59] In contrast, the opinion rejects in strong terms the notion that courts should vindicate the public interest.[60] That is the function of the Congress and the chief executive. Scalia does not admit that it is legitimate for Congress itself to use the courts to monitor the executive.

Justices Blackmun and O'Connor in dissent question the breadth of the Court's rejection of standing for procedural injuries, criticizing the opinion's "anachronistically formal view of the separation of powers."[61] In the eyes of the dissenters, "acknowledgement of an inextricable link between procedural and substantive harm does not reflect improper appellate factfinding. It reflects nothing more than the proper deference owed to the judgment of a coordinate branch—Congress—that certain procedures are directly tied to protection against a substantive harm.[62]

Justice Scalia's rejection of such procedural review strengthens his argument against judicial review of executive policy-making. If courts are to review high-level policy-making, they must be careful not to substitute their own policy judgments for those of agencies. One alternative is review of procedures to assure democratic legitimacy. A busy legislature might conclude that the courts could perform this function well. Scalia seeks to rule out just the sort of judicial review that the courts are best able to perform without taking on a policy-making role.

Germany already follows Scalia's line. Its administrative law system comes close to the Justice's view of the ideal relationship between the courts and the administration. In Germany, review of high-level actions is difficult because no statute sets the procedural parameters for ministry policy-making. Judicial review is not used to safeguard democratic legitimacy. Even when a rule's legality comes before the court, the judges do not evaluate the procedures used. The courts do not review rules and guidelines before they go into effect in particular cases. With only minor exceptions, organizations have no right to appear before public bodies and cannot obtain standing in court unless they can assert a personal interest by, for example, buying land near a project.

Given the necessity of delegation, such an unconstrained system is risky. The American bureaucracy, lacking Germany's close connection between executive and legislative, would have even more independent power than German authorities if not constrained by procedural limits. Judicial review of process provides a needed check on agencies' attempts to ignore the democratic basis of their power. Even if the current American review process is cumbersome and imperfect, it is responding to a genuine problem. It should be reformed to reflect the democratic and policy analytic nature of many bureaucratic choices. It should not be eliminated.

PROPORTIONALITY, NORM CONTROL, AND ADMINISTRATIVE COURTS

Germany has given explicit constitutional status to the administrative state. The Grundgesetz includes a nondelegation doctrine and requires the

Bundesrat to approve the rules and administrative guidelines administered by the Länder.[63] Given this constitutional basis, German public law is not simply a collection of negative examples for Americans. Several of its features are worth examining more closely. The most relevant are the proportionality principle of statutory interpretation, norm control actions, and the separate system of administrative courts.

The constitutional doctrine of "proportionality" is the creation of the German Constitutional Court.[64] Whatever its ambiguities, the principle gives German judges an underlying standard of evaluation. It is broadly consistent with my argument for using the cost-benefit criterion as a background norm in reviewing regulatory statutes designed to improve economic efficiency.[65] The principle could also permit courts to review statutes for internal consistency.[66] A statute whose statement of purpose bore little relation to the details of the legislative scheme would seem to violate the proportionality principle.

The second feature of German public law worth examining concerns *Normenkontrolle* actions asking the Constitutional Court to rule on the constitutionality of federal or state law.[67] Such requests can be made before a new law goes into effect by federal or Land governments or by one-third of the Bundestag. This type of action is unfamiliar to most Americans. It seems a violation of that most unclear of doctrines, the separation of powers. The American federal courts refuse to evaluate the constitutionality of statutes until a concrete violation of the new law comes before them. Yet structural weaknesses in the legislative process suggest that judicial oversight on the German model might help. Some of the problems of judicial review of the regulatory process stem from the inadequacy of the underlying statutes.

Such actions are not quite so foreign to American legal practice as they might seem. Several American state governments permit courts to rule on the constitutionality of bills and new laws.[68] These opinions sometimes explain how defects might be remedied. In addition, judges in their individual capacity and through the Judicial Conference advise Congress on the content of bills that will affect the court system.[69] Although advisory opinions are not forbidden by the text of the Constitution, their use would have to overcome longstanding judicial practice.[70]

Finally, Germany has a separate administrative court system that is nevertheless independent of the bureaucracy. Given the specialized and technical nature of many administrative law cases, this is an idea worth considering. The United States has something like a federal administrative court in the Court of Appeals for the District of Columbia, but not all of its judges are administrative law experts, and few are trained in science or social science. The United States has accepted the idea of specialized courts by establishing the Federal Circuit and the specialized courts that report to it. There seems to be no strong reason in principle not to consider similar specialization for the administrative law caseload. Such specialization should go beyond the German model to include judges and legal assistants trained in social science and other technical matters. Such courts would not be "science courts" reviewing the adequacy of the evidence, but they would be better able to judge if the agency's techniques were matched to the nature of its policy problems.

CONCLUSION

Germany's piecemeal efforts to accommodate technocratic policy-making within a democratic welfare state are insufficient. Despite the large numbers of complaints filed whenever a government seeks to expand an airport, build a nuclear plant, or establish a waste site, high-level environmental policy-making is remarkably unconstrained and unreviewed. Formal complaints, raised in licensing and planning processes, focus on the violation of individual rights. Complaints about general policy can only be raised indirectly in the context of a particular project.

The German parliamentary system provides an alternative route for those who object to current policies. Individuals can try to put ideological issues on the public agenda through support for the Green party or attempts to influence one of the dominant political parties. Consciousness-raising is not sufficient, however. Germany's heavy reliance on political parties to channel public concern has left too much environmental policy-making to unaccountable technocratic processes.

The European Union could encourage reform of German law, but currently that channel is indirect and not very effective. Direct popular control of the EU legislative process is limited. Further, German citizens can only complain to the Commission about government failure to comply with existing directives or regulations. They cannot bring cases themselves. Finally, the EU's lack of direct enforcement authority means that even successful court judgments rely on the goodwill of the German government.

A model of democracy different from the one pervading German thinking is needed to deal reasonably with environmental problems. Germany should consider adopting the outlines of the American administrative law system. Doing so would require rethinking traditional administrative law concepts, but it would not require a fundamental reorientation of the democratic structure of German government. For environmental issues, Germany needs a policy-making system that operates with constrained openness rather than unconstrained, closed consensus.

The German case can help Americans understand whether they wish to move toward a system that underemphasizes judicial review of agency policy-making. Although I have pointed out several positive features of the German system, it seems doubtful that many American malcontents would rush to embrace it. American critics need to distinguish between relatively superficial problems that represent failures of management and lack of bureaucratic competence, on one hand, and fundamental flaws in the structure of democratic government itself, on the other. Bureaucratic processes that emphasize openness and explanation provide a counterweight to the widespread and necessary delegation of policy-making to the executive. The courts can enhance the democratic legitimacy of the modern American state by assuring that these basic procedural conditions are met.

INTERVIEW LIST

On this list are the names of the people I interviewed during my stay in Germany between October 1991 and July 1992. The interviews were not formally structured and were designed to help direct my research. I have tried, where possible, to substitute references to published material or legal cases and statutes for my interview notes. Where this has proved impossible, I have cited the interviews themselves. Several of the people on this list also generously provided comments on my draft manuscript.

Herr Hermann Bachmaier,
   SPD Member of the Bundestag from
   Baden-Württemberg

Frau Susannah Baer, Esq., Berlin

Dr. Gotthold Alexander Balensiefen,
   Ministry for the Environment,
   State of Brandenburg, Potsdam

Prof. Dr. Jörg Berkemann, Justice,
   Federal Administrative Court, Berlin

Dr. Eberhard Bohne, M.A.,
   Ministerialrat, Ministry for the
   Environment, Nature Protection
   and Nuclear Safety, Bonn

Prof. Dr. Michael Bothe, Faculty of
   Law, Goethe University, Frankfurt

Prof. Dr. Winfried Brohm, Faculty of
   Law, University of Constance

Herr Lutz Eichler, Economist,
   Council of Environmental Experts,
   Wiesbaden

Herr Joschka Fischer,
   Minister for the Environment, State
   of Hesse, Wiesbaden

Dr. Günter Gaentzsch, Justice,
   Federal Administrative Court Berlin

Dr. Rolf Giebeler, Esq.,
   Pünder, Volhard, Weber and Axster,
   Düsseldorf

Prof. Dr. Peter Glotz, SPD Member of
   the Bundestag from Bavaria

Prof. Dr. Dieter Grimm, Justice,
   Federal Constitutional Court,
   Karlsruhe

Prof. Dr. Elke Gurlit, Faculty of Law,
   Free University of Berlin

141

Dr. Günter Halbritter, Secretary General, Council of Environmental Experts, Wiesbaden

Dr. Bernd Holznagel, LL.M., Faculty of Law II, University of Hamburg

Prof. Dr. Gerhard Igl, Faculty of Law II, University of Hamburg

Prof. Dr. Martin Jänicke, Faculty of Political Science, Free University of Berlin

Dr. Otto Keck, Privatdozent, Free University of Berlin

Prof. Dr. Wolfhard Kothe, Faculty of Law, University of Bremen

Dr. Ludwig Krämer, Esq., Head, Legal Affairs Unit, Directorate XI, Commission of the European Communities, Brussels

Dr. Jürgen Kühling, Justice, Constitutional Court, Karlsruhe (interviewed in July 1993)

Prof. Dr. Philip Kunig, Faculty of Law, Free University of Berlin

Dr. Irene Lamb, LL.M., Faculty of Law II, University of Hamburg

Dr. Hans Lindemann, Esq., Umweltbundesamt, Berlin

Herr Eckart Meyer-Rutz, Esq., Ministerialrat, Ministry for the Environment, Nature Protection and Nuclear Safety, Bonn

Dr. Margarete Mühl-Jäckel, LL.M., Esq., Berlin

Dr. Volker von Prittwitz, Privatdozent, Free University of Berlin

Prof. Dr. Eckard Rehbinder, Faculty of Law, Goethe University, Frankfurt

Dr. Dieter Rucht, Wissenschaftszentrum, Berlin

Prof. Dr. Jürgen Salzwedel, Faculty of Law, University of Bonn

Prof. Dr. Fritz Scharpf, Director, Max Planck Institute for Social Research, Cologne

Prof. Dr. Otto Schlichter, Vice President, Federal Administrative Court, Berlin

Herr Frank Schwalba-Hoth, Director, Greenpeace, Brussels

Prof. Dr. Wolfgang Seibel, Faculty of Administrative Science, University of Constance

Prof. Dr. Rudolf Steinberg, Faculty of Law, Goethe University, Frankfurt

Dr. Dieter Weingärtner, Referent for Environmental Affairs, SPD-Bundestagsfraktion, Bonn

Prof. Dr. Gerd Winter, Faculty of Law, University of Bremen

NOTES

1. The document promulgated in 1949 was called a Basic Law (Grundgesetz) rather than a constitution to emphasize the provisional character of the divided German state. I will, however, use the terms *Grundgesetz* and *constitution* interchangeably.

2. The most important general statutes are the Verwaltungsverfahrensgesetz (VwVfG) of May 25, 1976, as amended September 12, 1990, and the Verwaltungsgerichtsordnung (VwGO), newly promulgated on March 19, 1991.

3. Expenditures for pollution abatement and control in the United States totaled $85.9 billion in 1988, of which 21% was spent by governments. Of the 65.71 quadrillion Btu of energy produced in the United States in 1989, 21.23 quadrillion (32.3%) were from coal, 17.53 (26.7%) from natural gas, 18.31 (27.9%) from crude oil and liquid natural gas, 2.74 (4.2%) from hydroelectric power, 5.69 (8.7%) from nuclear power, and 0.24 from other sources. Most American coal is bituminous. Only 9% of 1989 production was lignite. Per capita energy consumption in 1990 was 341 million Btu. (One Btu is 1.055×10^8 joules.) The data are from tables in U.S. President's Council on Environmental Quality (1991).

   Public spending on the environment in Germany totaled DM 17.4 billion (approximately $10 billion) in 1988, of which DM 8.3 billion was for investments, mostly in sewage treatment and waste disposal. Spending by business on both investments and operating costs totaled approximately DM 18 billion, of which about DM 8 billion was investment. Energy consumption was 11,500 PJ in the western Länder in 1989. The proportions were 27% from coal (8% lignite), 17% natural gas, 40% oil, 12% nuclear, and 3% other. In the east consumption was 4,000 PJ, two-thirds from lignite. Umweltbundesamt (1992b) p. 19; PJ $= 10^{15}$ joules.

4. The population of the United States was 250.4 million in 1990, with a population density of 26.7 per square kilometer. Gross domestic product in 1989 was $5,132 billion in current dollars, or $20.6 thousand per capita. Exports and imports are approximately 10 percent of GDP. OECD (1991b) pp. 7, 27; U.S. President's Council on Environmental Quality (1991) p. 263.

   Germany at the end of 1990 had a population of 79.6 million—of which 15.9 million lived in the former German Democratic Republic—and had a population density of 223 per square kilometer. Gross domestic product in the western Länder

143

was $1,189 billion in 1989, or $19.2 thousand per capita. Import and export volumes were about a quarter of the country's GDP. Bauer, Klinke, and Pabst (1992) p. 4, and OECD (1991b) pp. 6, 26.

5. Umweltbundesamt (1992b), pp. 214–219, shows the volume of sulfur and nitrogen oxides transported in and out of the western and eastern parts of Germany. In Europe, countries to the north and west generally export more than they import, and those to the east and south import more than they export.

6. Schwarze (1992) pp. 123–125. According to Schwarze, "interests of a purely moral or economical nature . . . cannot confer *locus standi*" (p. 124). See also Currie (1993) pp. 251–259.

7. German law recognizes the need for accountable procedures when individual rights are at stake. See VwVfG §§28, 29.

8. For example, the use of courts for the objective control of the bureaucracy is controversial [Schäfer (1963), pp. 162–164]. German lawyers are debating the question of how to balance the protection of individual rights against competent administrative performance and have considered the possibility that enhanced participation rights could produce improved substantive decisions [Schwarze (1992) pp. 1177–1178].

9. Jacob (1963); Seibel (1992b); letter from Wolfgang Seibel, August 1993.

10. According to one German commentator, "Administrative practice and theory have been faced with a number of new challenges which the law has not always been capable of meeting adequately. Thus environmental law in particular has been the scene of many far-reaching departures from traditional administrative law theory" (Schwarze [1992] p. 121). See also Brohm (1987); Wahl (1982) p. 52; and Wolf (1987).

11. Katzenstein (1987), especially pp. 31–45, 58–80.

12. See Stewart (1975) for an early articulation of the role of courts in controlling administrative discretion. See also Edley (1990) and Sunstein (1990).

13. The literal-mindedness of the Supreme Court in cases dealing with administrative law and separation of powers issues is shown in such cases as *INS v. Chadha*, 462 U.S. 919 (1983), and *Bowsher v. Synar*, 478 U.S. 714 (1986). More recent decisions— *Morrison v. Olson*, 487 U.S. 654 (1988), and *Mistretta v. U.S.*, 488 U.S. 361 (1989)— suggest a more flexible approach.

14. Edley (1990), Rose-Ackerman (1992b) pp. 33–42.

15. For recent critiques see Edley (1990), Mashaw (1994), McGarity (1992), Rose-Ackerman (1992b), and "Twenty-Third Annual Administrative Law Issue," *Duke Law Journal* 41 (June 1992).

16. Recent cases have sought to avoid review of agency procedures and to limit the standing of organized groups. *Lujan v.National Wildlife Federation*, 497 U.S. 871 (1990); *Lujan v. Defenders of Wildlife*, 112 S.Ct. 2130 (1992). See chapter 9 for a discussion.

ONE DEMOCRATIC GOVERNMENT AND POLICY IMPLEMENTATION

1. For example, the public's apparently greater respect for bureaucrats in Germany than in the United States has deep historical roots. In Germany a professionalized

bureaucracy developed before the institutions of democratic government. In the United States the reverse pattern holds. Compare Jacob (1963) and Seibel (1992b) with Skowronek (1982). Jacob describes the rise of the bureaucracy in Germany beginning with Bismarck. Skowronek demonstrates America's failure to develop a professionalized bureaucracy in the period between the Civil War and World War I. Seibel (1992b) p. 351 notes that at the end of World War I the German state had a strong judiciary and administration with a weak parliament and government. Germany lacked traditions of political competition and procedurally regulated compromise building.

2. Palmer (1994) chapter 7 makes similar observations in comparing the United States and Canada. Canada has a parliamentary system and a plurality electoral system based on the Westminster model.

3. Germany uses a mixed system of representation in which half of the 656 members (662 in the 1990–1994 transitional parliament) represent particular geographical constituencies and others are selected by proportional representation from party lists on a state-by-state-basis. The party affiliations of members representing particular districts are counted as part of the total when seats are assigned. With one minor exception, parties must obtain at least 5% of the national vote to be represented in parliament. Every member must be elected with a party affiliation. The makeup of the Bundestag elected in 1990 was CDU/CSU: 319, SPD: 239, FDP: 79, PDS 17, Bündnis 90/Die Grünen: 8 (Holzapfel 1991, p. 297).

During most of the postwar period the government has consisted of a coalition of one of the major parties (Christian Democrats or Social Democrats) and the small, centrist Free Democrats. Between 1966 and 1969 there was a grand coalition of the SPD and the CDU/CSU. From 1990–1994 a coalition of the CDU/CSU and the FDP controlled the government.

4. See Currie (1994) pp. 174–338 and Kommers (1989), chapters 6–9. GG arts. 1–19 list the fundamental rights.

5. An indication of this view of the public interest is the "representative of the public interest" associated with each administrative court. This individual can intervene in an administrative court proceeding by filing a brief. These officials are government appointees bound by the advice of the government that they represent. For the Federal Administrative Court the chief public attorney (*Oberbundesanwalt*) serves this function (*Verwaltungsgerichtsordnung*—VwGO §§35–37; Singh, 1985, p. 110). In practice, however, those familiar with the operation of the highest administrative court report that these "public interest representatives" are unimportant in the actual work of the court.

6. Maunz and Zippelius (1991) pp. 92–93.

7. In mid-1994 the Greens were included in coalition governments in Bremen and Hesse. On the origin and development of the Greens see Boehmer-Christiansen and Skea (1991), pp. 85–91, Fogt (1989), Kitschelt (1989), Rohrschneider (1993), and Ševčenko (1986).

8. In 1983 the Green party entered the federal parliament with 28 seats, but its political influence began earlier when in 1978 it obtained 3.9% of the vote in Lower Saxony and 4.4% in Hamburg. This was not enough to satisfy the 5% threshold required to

be represented in the state parliaments, but it showed that the party could become an important political force. The popularity of the Greens' positions even for those who voted for established parties pushed the larger parties to take a stronger, public stand in favor of environmental policies (Müller [1989] p. 11, Rohrschneider [1993]).

9. Paterson (1989b) pp. 77–78. For example, the Greens were active in investigating and applying political pressure in connection with accidents at Hoechst AG plants near Frankfurt in February and March 1993 (*Süddeutsche Zeitung* February 24, March 16, 1993). The Greens also promote social welfare and civil rights causes.

10. GG arts. 77, 78, 80(2), 84(2), 85(2). Since the early 1950s more than half of the bills passed by the Bundestag have been sent to the Bundesrat for approval. Katzenstein (1987) p. 17. See also Currie (1994) pp. 61–65 and Kommers (1989), p. 107. Other types of statutes can become law even when a majority of the Bundesrat is opposed.

11. The largest Länder have six votes and the smallest, three. Each state must cast its votes as a bloc so that states with coalition governments cannot split apart and form coalitions with portions of other state delegations (GG arts. 50–53). When the Bundesrat takes up environmental matters, state environmental ministers participate (Jarass and DiMento, 1993, p. 52). In the early nineties the Bundesrat was controlled by a slim SPD majority so that Germany had its own version of divided government.

12. See GG arts. 83–87b and Currie (1994) pp. 66–73. Länder may implement laws either "as matters of their own concern" or "as agents of the federation." While both types of delegation leave some policy discretion to the political coalitions governing each particular Land, the former is less restrictive than the latter. When federal laws are executed by the Länder as matters of their own concern, the states establish their own authorities and finance the regulatory effort. However, the federal government may issue administrative rules and supervise implementation (GG art. 84). In the less common situation where the Länder execute federal laws as agents of the Federation, federation supervision is much closer, and the Federation pays the cost of the execution of the laws (GG arts. 85, 104a[2]).

13. GG, arts. 104a, 106, 107. Jarass and DiMento (1993) pp. 54–55.

14. Lorenz (1980) pp. 563–569. In addition, a formal Petitions Committee, created by a 1968 constitutional amendment, GG art. 45c, can hear complaints of administrative abuses (id.), and Enquete Commissions can investigate areas of special concern. See, for example, Germany, Bundestag, 1994.

15. Linde (1980) p. 605; Greve (1989); Katzenstein (1987) p. 273.

16. "West Germans expect that the exercise of state power will be predictable, inconspicuous and deliberate." Katzenstein (1987) p. 383.

17. According to Steinberg (1989) p. 222: "Die faktische Autorität liegt überwiegend bei der Exekutive." See also Currie (1993) p. 231, and Jarass and DiMento (1993) p. 52. Böhret (1983) p. 37, claims: "Parliament and individual MPs are simply unable to compete with the growing information and manpower resources of the executive (especially of the administration). This leads increasingly to a reduction in detailed control."

18. Brickman, Jasanoff, and Ilgen (1985) pp. 60–61, 64. See also Steinberg (1989) p. 223.

19. Nelkin and Pollak (1981) pp. 38–40.

20. Paterson (1989b) p. 83; Germany, Bundestag (1994).

21. Brohm (1987) pp. 265–266, argues that the vagueness of modern statutes derives both from the technical nature of the subject matter and from the need for political compromise.

22. On the attitude of civil servants and their changing credentials, see Katzenstein (1987) pp. 273, 379–380; and Kvistad (1988) pp. 116–117. During the Second Reich, civil servants almost always studied law. Their education "attempted to inculcate unquestioning loyalty to the State, the Crown, and to bureaucratic superiors." Jacob (1963) p. 63. Although lawyers are no longer so dominant, Weale (1992) points to the continuing importance of lawyers and engineers in the environmental field.

23. A federal law dating from 1970 requires economic efficiency studies for all major public projects. More than one hundred studies have been done in the traffic and water management areas. The obligation to carry out cost-benefit analyses is limited to projects of "considerable importance." Third parties are not entitled to demand that a study be done. In the environmental area few studies have been performed (Schulz and Schulz 1991, pp. 6–7).

24. Of the 417 professionals employed by the Umweltbundesamt in 1991 fifteen were economists and eighteen were political scientists or psychologists, as judged by the subject of their highest university degree. Umweltbundesamt (1992a) p. 6. The independent, government-financed Council of Environmental Experts does include an economist among its members.

25. Germany, Federal Environmental Ministry 1991; Schulz and Schulz 1991.

26. Germany, Federal Environmental Ministry 1991, pp. 55–56.

27. According to one study of the regulation of chemicals (Brickman, Jasanoff, and Ilgen, 1985), the major differences between the United States and the Federal Republic were the much lower level of technical and economic information in the FRG and the lower level of publicly available information and public input in Germany.

28. *Verwaltungsverfahrensgesetz*—VwVfG §29, Gurlit (1989). Access to files depends first on the process being an "administrative process" (*Verwaltungsverfahren*) as defined by the Administrative Procedures Act (VwVfG §9), and second on the personal interest of the individual in obtaining access to his or her files. Administrative acts range from awarding licenses to individuals to practice a profession or build a house to approving or outlawing chemicals under the chemicals law (*Chemikaliengesetz*—ChemG §22[d]) to approving major projects under a licensing (*Bundes-Immissionsschutzgesetz*—BImSchG §10) or planning procedure (VwVfG §§72–78).

    On July 8, 1994, the Bundestag approved a statute to implement a European Union directive providing broader access to environmental information held by the government. For a discussion, see chapter 8.

29. Katzenstein (1987) pp. 58–64, Mayntz and Scharpf (1975) pp. 133–142; Peacock (1984).

30. Brickman, Jasanoff, Ilgen (1985) pp. 82–84; Paterson (1989b).

31. Allen (1989) pp. 174–175 discusses self-regulation in the chemical industry and shows how new social movements have challenged traditional ways of doing business. On nuclear power see Halfman (1989), Linse et al. (1988), and Steinberg (1994).

32. Greve (1989). According to Thiem (1977) p. 366, while "the democratic principle of participation is underlined by some, . . . others see a contradiction between participation and democracy, because the executive may be guided by individual interests rather than by Parliament and the voters."

33. See chapter 6. For examples, see Linse et al. (1988) and Sellers (1994). The only explicit provision for participation of organized groups is in the Nature Protection Law (*Bundesnaturschutzgesetz*—BNatSchG §29), which permits a limited selection of such groups to participate in planning processes.

34. Citizens' groups (*Bürgerinitiativen*), which grew up in the 1970s, were heavily involved in environmental issues. They organized federally in 1972, forming the German Association of Citizens' Initiatives for Environmental Protection (*Bundesverband Bürgerinitiativen Umweltschultz*—BBU). By 1980 there were 130 supraregional and 1100 regional groups (Boehmer-Christiansen and Skea [1991] pp. 85–86).

35. A recent survey of the major groups found that the Environmental Defense Fund had a staff of 85, with 10 attorneys and a budget of $8.5 million. The National Resources Defense Council had 30 attorneys on its payroll and a budget of $11 million. The Sierra Club/Sierra Club Legal Defense Fund had 20 attorneys and a budget of $28 million, and the National Wildlife Federation had 17 attorneys, out of 670 employees, working with a budget of $65 million. Groups with less of a focus on litigation are the Conservation Foundation (50 employees, $5 million), the World Wildlife Fund (100 employees, $30 million), and the National Audubon Society (25 employees, including 2 attorneys). Openchowski (1990) pp. 103–104. See also Russell (1993) for more recent but less comprehensive data.

36. Rucht (1991) p. 354. The Öko-Institut was founded by Siegfried de Witt, a prominent lawyer in anti-nuclear cases. The Institute was designed to link science and legal advice and to aid citizens initiatives. Nelkin and Pollak (1981) p. 93.

37. The data for 1989 are presented in Rucht (1991) p. 354. In 1989 the Green party had 200 professional employees at the federal level and a budget of DM 41.4 million. Greenpeace had ninety professional employees and a budget of about DM 50 million. Paterson (1989a) p. 271 argues that environmental groups have been largely replaced by political parties.

38. For example, after a February 1993 accident at a Hoechst AG plant near Frankfurt, the Association of Citizens' Initiatives announced that it had filed a "report of an offense" (Strafanzeige) against the company for violating the air pollution laws. *Süddeutsche Zeitung* February 25, 1993.

39. In 1992, the year of the Earth Summit in Rio, the Environmental Ministry provided DM 900,000 in public money to environmental *Verbände* ("Umweltverbände ringen um Einfluß," *Das Parlament*, June 5, 1992). Although Germany has a sizable nonprofit sector, private charity is less important than in the United States. Government funding of private organizations is common. Anheier (1990), (1992); Seibel (1992a). Private research institutes, even those concerned with "counter-expertise," are usually publicly funded. Nelkin and Pollak (1981) p. 98 point out how such funding makes the scientists involved vulnerable to shifts in the political landscape.

40. *Verordnung über Großfeuerungsanlagen*–13.BImSchV; Boehmer- Christiansen (1992).

41. Compare Paterson (1989a), who argues that environmental groups were blocked from participating in federal policy-making on nuclear power issues. As a result they focused on implementation at the Land level using both legal and extralegal techniques.

42. GG art. 19(4) states that: "Should any person's rights be violated by public authority, recourse to the court shall be open to him." Rehbinder (1985) p. 6 reports that judicial review of the administration historically included both the protection of individual rights against the state (a southern German legal tradition) and the objective control of the legality of the administration (a Prussian concept). The former concept was given most emphasis in the postwar Grundgesetz.

43. GG art. 19(3). Local governments have constitutionally protected rights against the federal state. GG art. 28(2) guarantees to municipalities [Gemeinde] "the right to regulate on their own responsibility all the affairs of the local community with the limits set by law." The associations of communes have similar rights. GG art. 93(4b), an amendment of 1969, states that the Federal Constitutional Court shall decide on certain complaints of unconstitutionality entered by communes.

44. One partial exception occurs in planning law since the *Baugesetzbuch*—BauGB requires that public and private interests be balanced. "Bei der Aufstellung der Bauleitpläne sind die öffentlichen und privaten Belange gegeneinander und untereinander gerecht abzuwägen" (BauGB §1 [6]). Judicial review of the adequacy of this weighing process is possible. Steinberg (1992b); Brohm (1985) pp. 108–113; and letter from Winfried Brohm, June 7, 1993.

   "Some countries view judicial control of State agencies both as a means of *objective* control and as one of *subjective* legal protection of the individual. The German system is generally regarded only as one of *subjective* control as a means exclusively for the protection of individual rights. One of the consequences of this is that *locus standi* before the administrative courts is given only in those cases where individual *rights* or legally protected interests are infringed. An 'injury in fact' is not sufficient to bring an action against State agencies" (Thiem [1977], p. 368 [notes omitted]). However, as Thiem's cautious language suggests, some commentators do view the courts as a means of objective control of the administration (Schäfer [1963] pp. 162–164). This appears to mean judicial review of the regularity and formal correctness of administrative behavior, not a review of the competence of their policy choices.

45. Greve (1989); Lorenz (1980) p. 577; Van Dijk (1980) p. 194.

46. For an overview of the administrative court system, see Rehbinder (1985). See also Jacob (1963) pp. 51–54, 125–126, 176. An administrative court system was established in Prussia in 1875. The Nazis abolished the administrative court system in 1939, but it was reestablished after World War II with a new federal administrative court. Only cases that raise issues of federal law can be appealed to the highest court. For other cases the final appeal is to the high administrative court in the Land where the case was brought. The administrative courts can refer constitutional issues to the Federal Constitutional Court and Economic Union issues to the European Court of Justice (Hartley [1988] pp. 223–225).

47. *Normenkontrolle* actions are governed by the Administrative Court Statute (VwGO §47). Only those who have suffered or are likely to suffer from the application of the

law or regulation can bring a challenge (VwGO §47 [2]). Challenges to the constitutionality of federal or state laws or claims of incompatibility between federal and state law can be brought in the Constitutional Court by the federal government, a Land government, or a third of the members of the Bundestag (GG art. 93[1]2).

48. Singh (1985), p. 107; see also Greve (1989).

49. According to Seibel (1992b) pp. 356–357, using procedures as a means of legitimating government actions is an underdeveloped area of German legal and political thinking.

50. Currie (1993) pp. 251–252. Rehbinder (1985) p. 2 claims that the appeals courts hardly ever carry out de novo review of the facts. In 1983 judges heard new evidence in only 8% of the cases. The lowest courts not only review the facts presented by the parties but also may call their own experts. For a defense of the use of court-appointed experts in German private law cases, see Langbein (1985) pp. 835–841.

51. Greve (1989); Pakuscher (1976) pp. 97, 101; Singh (1985) pp. 65, 71.

52. VwGO §113 (1) and (5).

53. VwGO §113 (5).

54. Lorenz (1980) p. 575.

55. Jarass and DiMento (1993) p. 53 claim that American environmental laws are more detailed than their German counterparts. Palmer (1994) chapter 8, in his comparison of the United States and Canada, concludes that American laws are less coherent and more specific than Canadian statutes.

56. In the prewar period, statutes tended to be short and administered by "independent" agencies. These agencies, which still predominate in economic regulation, are bipartisan and have members whose terms do not coincide with the president's. The independent agency is another way in which the legislature attempts to reduce the president's authority while allowing delegation. Melnick (1983) discusses the shift in the structure of regulatory statutes.

57. Strauss (1989) pp. 18–23. But see Chief Justice Rehnquist's effort to revive the nondelegation doctrine in *Industrial Union Dept., AFL-CIO v. American Petroleum Inst.*, 448 U.S. 607, 687 (1980) (Rehnquist, J., concurring); and *American Textile Mfrs. Inst. v. Donovan*, 452 U.S. 490, 543 et seq. (1981) (Rehnquist, J., dissenting).

58. *Chevron v. Natural Resources Defense Council*, 467 U.S. 837 (1984), held that agencies can reinterpret statutory language as a result of changes in political as well as technical realities.

59. In 1983, 25.2% of total committee meeting days were spent on oversight. The number of days that congressional committees spent on oversight increased from 146 in 1961 to 587 in 1983 (Aberbach [1990] p. 35). The EPA appeared 198 times before Congress between 1984 and 1986. (National Academy of Public Administration [1988] p. 22). According to Lazarus (1991), pp. 210–218, the EPA was subject to an especially high level of oversight. This was in part because of overlapping committee jurisdictions. At least 11 standing House and 9 standing Senate committees and up to 100 of their subcommittees have some jurisdiction over the EPA (p. 211).

60. Federal Administrative Procedures Act (APA), 5 U.S.C. §§551–706 (1988).

61. APA, 5 U.S.C. §553. The requirements in the Clean Air Act are in CAA §307(d). Public participation is facilitated in some agencies by government subsidies to needy

citizen groups to cover the costs of participation. The Federal Trade Commission, the EPA, the National Highway Traffic Safety Administration, and the Department of Energy began to use "intervenor funding" in the 1970s. Specific statutory authorizations to use funds for this purpose are found in 94 Stat. 376; 90 Stat. 2023 (1976); 94 Stat. 1681 (1980) (Rosen [1989] p. 109).

62. APA, 5 U.S.C. §552. Strauss (1989) pp. 163–164, 195–200.

63. Badaracco (1985). Rosen (1989) pp. 93–94 mentions the attempt by the Johnson administration to encourage "maximum feasible participation" by beneficiaries of programs for low-income people. The idea was to give citizens direct decision-making authority. The difficulties of implementing these programs and the opposition of established politicians led to the demise of these participatory processes. By 1972 the public participation section of the Federal Water Pollution Control Act merely urged state and local governments to consult with citizens, not give them decision-making authority.

64. Negotiated Rulemaking Act of 1990, 5 U.S.C. §§561–570 (Supp. IV 1992).

65. APA, 5 U.S.C. §706.

66. Strauss (1989) pp. 244–249. According to then Judge Scalia in *Ass'n of Data Processing Service Organizations, Inc. v. Board of Governors of the Federal Reserve System*, 745 F. 2d 677 (D.C.Cir. 1984): "In their application to the requirement of factual support the substantial evidence test and the arbitrary and capricious test are one and the same. . . . The 'scope of review' provisions of the APA, 5 U.S.C. §706(2), are cumulative. Thus, an agency action which is supported by the required substantial evidence may in another respect be 'arbitrary, capricious, an abuse of discretion, or otherwise not in accordance with law'—for example, because it is an abrupt and unexplained departure from agency precedent."

67. APA, 5 U.S.C. §706(2)(F) limits de novo review to those cases where the facts are subject to trial de novo by the reviewing court.

68. APA, 5 U.S.C. §704 provides for review of "final agency action." Regulations are included in this category and can be reviewed before being applied in particular cases (*Abbott Laboratories v. Gardner*, 387 U.S. 136 [1967]; Strauss, 1989, pp. 216–217, 233–234). The use of the courts by public interest environmental groups began with challenges to DDT in the mid-sixties. The Environmental Defense Fund emerged out of a Long Island case seeking to restrain the use of DDT. Soon after, the Sierra Club founded a separate legal defense fund, and in the early seventies the Natural Resources Defense Council and Environmental Action were founded specifically to bring lawsuits. In the United States the use of the courts has an advantage over lobbying—the organization can be tax-exempt and accept tax-deductible contributions. Bosso (1987) pp. 135–136.

69. *Vermont Yankee Nuclear Power Corp. v. Natural Resources Defense Council, Inc.*, 435 U.S. 519 (1978), limited the ability of federal courts to impose additional procedural requirements on agencies. *Heckler v. Chaney*, 470 U.S. 821 (1985), affirmed the agency's right to set its own agenda, at least in enforcement matters. *Chevron, U.S.A., Inc., v. Natural Resources Defense Council, Inc.*, 467 U.S. 837 (1984), strengthened the presumption in favor of agency interpretations of ambiguous statutory language. Within these constraints, however, the federal courts continue to

review final regulations before they go into effect in particular cases. Compliance with the basic APA provisions is routine when agencies promulgate rules. Cases, however, continue to occur in which the plaintiffs successfully argue that notice and the opportunity to comment were inadequate. See *Shell Oil Co. v. E.P.A.*, 950 F.2d. 741 (D.C. Cir. 1991), and *Chocolate Mfrs. Ass'n of United States v. Block*, 755 F.2d 1098 (1985). The procedures followed by the agency can be examined for conformity with statutory provisions and constitutional requirements. Courts ask whether the agency has "adequately considered" the relevant alternatives, an open-ended doctrine consistent with various levels of judicial scrutiny (*Motor Vehicles Mfrs. Ass'n v. State Farm Mut. Auto. Ins. Co.*, 463 U.S. 29 [1983]).

70. Sunstein (1992) at p. 165, n. 11; Miller (1987). Clean Air Act (CAA) §707, 42 U.S.C. §7604 (1988 and Supp. II 1990); Resource Conservation and Recovery Act §7002, 42 U.S.C. §6972 (1988); Clean Water Act (CWA), also called the Federal Water Pollution Control Act (FWPCA) §505, 33 U.S.C. §1365 (1988); Comprehensive Environmental Response, Compensation and Liability Act §113, 42 U.S.C. §9659 (1988); Oil Pollution Act §1017, 33 U.S.C. §2717 (Supp. II 1990). All environmental statutes have such provisions except the Federal Insecticide, Fungicide, and Rodenticide Act, 7 U.S.C. §§136–136y (1988).

    No damages are available as a result of such suits (*Middlesex Cty. Sewerage Auth. v. Natl. Sea Clammers Assoc.*, 453 U.S. 1 [1981]). Successful suits, however, result in fines being paid to the EPA or to state environmental agencies. Cases that are settled out of court can produce financial payments divided between governments and environmental organizations. The legality of payments to environmental groups was upheld by the Ninth Circuit in *Sierra Club Inc. v. Electronic Controls Design Inc.*, 909 F. 2d 1350 (9th Cir. 1990).

71. CWA, 33 U.S.C. §§1319(c)(3)(B)(iv)(4), 1365. A challenge to the standing of public interest groups to bring such suits has been turned down. In *Public Int. Research of N. J. v. Powell Duffryn*, 913 F. 2d 64 (3d Cir. 1990), *cert. denied*, 111 S.Ct. 1018 (1991), the third circuit ruled that a public interest group could sue to enforce a water permit without showing that its members had been directly harmed by pollution. The act states that any citizen may bring a suit where "citizen" is defined as "a person or persons having an interest which is or may be adversely affected" (33 U.S.C. §1365[g]).

    Citizen suits have been less common under the Clean Air Act because penalties were not available under that statute. The amendments of 1990, however, authorize penalties. The penalties are either turned over to the EPA, or, if the court orders, penalties under $100,000 may be used for "beneficial mitigation projects." CAA §304(g), 42 U.S.C. §7604(g). See Garrett and Winner, 1992, p. 10310.

72. The cases are *Lujan v. National Wildlife Federation*, 497 U.S. 871 (1990); *Lujan v. Defenders of Wildlife*, 112 S.Ct. 2130 (1992); and *Air Courier Corp. v. American Postal Workers Union*, 498 U.S. 517 (1991).

73. Mansfield (1993) at 69. Her discussion is at pp. 86–88. Werham (1992) calls this trend the "neoclassical revival" in administrative law. He claims that "the distinguishing trademark, and bite, of the model is its rigid definition of the 'law,' one which limits the concept to the clearly expressed intent of an authoritative lawmaker,

such as Congress, and which thereby denies reviewing courts an active role in the administrative process" (id. at 568). "The dominant theme of the neoclassical decisions is that courts are no longer available to protect those whose *interests* are affected by administrative actors unless the action can be said to violate some *right* held by the affected party" (id. at 620).

74. See chapter 9 for a fuller discussion.

TWO   PUBLIC POLICY ANALYSIS AND THE PATHOLOGIES OF POLITICS

1. Information on environmental conditions in Germany can be found in Germany, Federal Environmental Agency, 1990; Germany, Federal Ministry for the Environment, 1992; and Umweltbundesamt, 1991, 1992a, 1992b. On the special problems raised by German unification, see Palinkas (1992), Rehbinder (1992), Streibel (1992), and Weale (1992) pp. 172–174. East Germany had much higher levels of pollution caused by industrial production than the Federal Republic, but it had lower levels of consumption-related pollution, such as nitrous oxides and household waste (Rehbinder [1992b] pp. 232–234). See table 2.2 for comparative data on sulfur dioxide and nitrous oxides.

2. Dewees (1992a), Freeman (1990), Portney (1990c), and U.S. President's Council on Environmental Quality (1993). Germany and the United States are leaders within the OECD in the proportion of their Gross Domestic Product spent on environmental protection. In 1985 the proportions were 1.52% for Germany and 1.47% for the United States. Pollution control investments as a percent of total national investment were 3.1% in Germany and 2.8% in the United States (OECD 1991a:275).

3. A Social Democrat/Free Democratic coalition controlled the government from 1969 to 1982, when most of the environmental statutes were passed. Müller reports that German civil servants studied the American programs when preparing the Environmental Program of 1971. Between 1971 and 1974, laws were passed concerning airplane noise, lead-free gasoline, waste disposal, DDT, air pollution, and environmental statistics. In addition, many legal regulations and guidelines were issued. The first version of the air pollution guidelines (*Technische Anleitung zur Reinhaltung der Luft*—TA Luft) was issued in 1974. In 1975 a law on laundry detergents was passed, and in 1976 the water law was revised, the nature protection law was passed, and a tax on waste water was instituted. In 1980 the government promulgated statutes on environmental crimes and chemicals. For an overview see Müller (1989).

4. For an introduction to the concept of externalities as it applies to environmental issues see Cropper and Oates (1992) pp. 678–681.

5. Cost-benefit analysis, a test derived from the principles of microeconomic theory, seeks an outcome that maximizes the net benefits of a policy. This is the point where marginal benefits equal marginal costs. For an introduction to cost-benefit techniques see Weimer and Vining (1992). At the level of principle one can argue over both the standard of value chosen and the method of aggregation. In conventional analysis the standard of value is willingness-to-pay or willingness-to-accept measured in dollars, and the method of aggregation is simply to add up the dollars. A

utilitarian would use the same aggregation method but would select "utiles" rather than dollars as the unit. Since no one has a way to measure utiles, the question for the practical-minded utilitarian is whether dollars will do as a rough proxy. A strict majoritarian democrat, in contrast, would reject the idea of weighing people's votes by the intensity of their preferences measured in dollars and would just want to count heads. See Rose-Ackerman (1980).

6. Portney (1990a) and Freeman (1990).

7. For a summary see Portney (1990a).

8. This, of course, is an oversimplification. Policymakers must decide how much and what kind of fish life to encourage, and how much and what kind of diseases to control. Sometimes scientific or engineering thresholds aid decisions. At some point the oxygen level in water falls so low that anaerobic decay occurs, so the goal might be to avoid that threshold. Even here, however, complications are introduced by the water temperature and the flow of the body of water.

9. For more nuanced discussions of rights and charges and reviews of the proposals for using economic incentives to control pollution, see Cropper and Oates (1992), pp. 681–682, 685–692, 699–700, Hahn and Hester (1989), and Tietenberg (1991).

10. American pollution policy is not cost-effective, according to the articles collected in Portney (1990c). Governmental sponsored studies of the benefits and costs of German environmental policies have not addressed this issue. See Germany, Federal Environmental Ministry (1991); Schulz and Schulz; and the discussion in chapter 1. Thus a comparison of the relative efficiency of German and American policies is not possible.

11. The United States discharged 2.2 tons per square kilometer of sulfur dioxide compared with 5.0 for the FRG and 48.5 for the GDR. The U.S. discharged 2.1 tons per square kilometer of nitrogen oxides compared with 11.4 for the FRG and 6.2 for the GDR.

12. United States population density in 1990 was 26.7 people per square kilometer (calculated from data in OECD [1991b] p. 7, and U.S. President's Council on Environmental Quality [1991] p. 263). The German figure in 1990 was 223 per square kilometer (Bauer, Klinke, and Pabst [1992] p. 4).

13. The new American law will cap sulfur dioxide emissions at 8,900 kilotons when the second phase of the program begins in the year 2000 (Clean Air Act [CAA] §403[a], 42 U.S.C. §7651b[a]).

14. Boehmer-Christiansen (1992) pp. 307–308, 311, argues that in Germany it is often taken as the basic goal. An emphasis on discharge reduction rather than environmental quality is also prevalent in American debates.

15. The pollutants are the criteria substances central to implementation of the American Clean Air Act. The figures are averages from the sites in the nationwide monitoring network and thus depend on the location of these monitors.

16. The American numbers are for carbon monoxide, and the German ones are for carbon dioxide. Currie (1982) pp. 362–363, discusses Germany's lack of an ozone standard. The German government seeks to limit smog through controls on stationary sources and emission control devices on new cars. Only recently have traffic controls been considered. Hesse, for example, imposed speed limits during summer

smog alerts for the first time in the summer of 1994.

17. Sulfur dioxide data may be distorted by the unusually mild winters in 1988, 1989, and 1990. In Germany suspended particulates fell from an average of 50 micrograms per cubic meter in the seventies to 30 micrograms per cubic meter by the end of the eighties. In the United States the decline was much less dramatic, and the 1988 average was 50.5 micrograms per cubic meter. Because suspended particulates are often a local phenomenon, however, measurement may be especially sensitive to the location of the meters.

18. About 40% of the imports were from East Germany. Umweltbundesamt (1992b) pp. 212–219. The model was developed by the Cooperative Programme for Monitoring and Evaluation of the Long-Range Transmission of Air Pollutants in Europe. In 1988 the model estimated that the Federal Republic exported 294 kilotons of atmospheric sulfur (sulfur dioxide and sulfates) and imported 357 kilotons. The model estimated that 276 kilotons generated within the FRG stayed there. These numbers imply that 570 kilotons of sulfur were emitted by FRG dischargers. The difference between this figure and the 1250 kilotons of sulfur dioxide listed in table 2.2 is presumably the difference between measuring sulfur alone and weighing the entire compound (Germany, Federal Environmental Agency 1990, p. 109).

19. One exception is a proposed regulation of ambient concentrations of carcinogens. Interview with Eckard Rehbinder, July 1993.

20. Table 2.5 might leave the incorrect impression that old power plants were entirely unregulated in the United States. They are controlled on a state-by-state basis as part of each State Implementation Plan (CAA §110, 42 U.S.C. §7410).

21. In the German air pollution law "state of the art" is defined as: "the state of development of advanced processes, of facilities or of modes of operation which is deemed to indicate the practical suitability of a particular technique for restricting emission levels. When determining the state of the art, special consideration shall be given to comparable processes, facilities or modes of operation that have been successfully proven in practical operation." *Bundes-Immissionsschutzgesetz*-BImSchG §3(6). One of the obligations of a licensed discharger is to install emission control measures that are "appropriate according to the state of the art." BImSchG §5(1)2.

Some flexibility, however, is provided in BImSchG §§7(3) and 17(3a), which permit something that looks like a "bubble" both within one plant and between plants (Bohne 1987). Offsets are also permitted in the eastern Länder for a five-year period (BImSchG §67a[2]). Only a few bubbles have been established. The most important were used for ceramic plants in Rhineland-Palatinate, where major differences in costs between large and small plants promised substantial cost savings. The use of bubbles has been restricted because of an eight-year time limit that is no longer in the statute but remains in the technical guidelines. Furthermore, bubbles are limited to existing sources and can be achieved only through technical measures, not the shutting down of existing sources (Rehbinder 1993, pp. 75–76).

The American Clean Air Act refers to "reasonably available control technology" (RACT) for existing stationary sources. New sources must attain the "lowest achievable emission rate" (LAER). In clean areas sources must use the best available control technology (BACT). Major sources of air toxics must use maximum achievable emission control technology (MACT). CAA §§111(a)(1), 112, 165, 169(3), 171(3), 172(b), 173, 42 U.S.C. §§7411(a)(1), 7412, 7475, 7479(3), 7501(3), 7502(b), 7503, Garrett and Winner (1992) pp. 10173, 10241–10243, 10247–10248.

Although the concept of "feasibility" pervades American administrative law, in one important air quality case the Supreme Court found that the EPA could not invoke feasibility as a criterion. In *Union Electric Co. v. EPA*, 427 U.S. 246 (1976), the Court interpreted the statute to mean that "Congress intended claims of economic and technical infeasibility to be wholly foreign to the Administrator's consideration of a state implementation plan." For cases where feasibility is taken to mean a standard that preserves the viability of a regulated industry, see *Industrial Union Dept. AFL-CIO v. American Petroleum Inst.*, 448 U.S. 607 (1980) and *American Textile Mfrs. Inst. v. Donovan*, 452 U.S. 490 (1981).

22. Burtraw and Portney (1991) pp. 297–299. The Federal Insecticide, Fungicide, and Rodenticide Act, 7 U.S.C. §136(bb) (1988), and the Toxic Substances Control Act, 15 U.S.C. 2605(c)(1), require benefits and costs to be balanced, however (id. at 297).

23. Compare Wolf (1987), who also criticizes the engineering bias in regulatory policy.

24. Burtraw and Portney (1991) pp. 292–293; U.S. Environmental Protection Agency (1992), pp. 1–1 to 1–2. The Clean Water Act (CWA), also called the Federal Water Pollution Control Act (FWPCA) 33 U.S.C. 1251 et seq., requires the EPA to set national, uniform standards based on control technologies that apply to classes of industrial dischargers and public treatment plants. Ambient water quality goals are set in part by the states for each body of water. If these goals are not met, given the technical standards, states must impose additional requirements.

25. CAA §§101–618, 42 U.S.C. §§7401–7671q. For a summary, see Garrett and Winner (1992).

26. For a critique of this practice, see Harrison (1977).

27. CAA §§401–413, 42 U.S.C. §§7651–7651(l); Garrett and Winner (1992) pp. 10253–10256. The program does not account for the differing impact of pollution depending on its source. Power plants in the American Midwest cause more serious pollution problems than those located on the Atlantic Coast. Difficulties in the practical design of the auction system are discussed in Hausker (1992).

28. CAA §§181–184, 42 U.S.C. §7511; Garrett and Winner (1992) pp. 10176–10181.

29. CAA §249, 42 U.S.C. 7589; *Environmental Reporter* 24:814, 819 (1993).

30. See "Northeast States Weigh NO_x Reductions, Trading Schemes to Meet Air Act Reduction Goal," *Environmental Reporter* 23:3192–3193 (April 23, 1993); "California: Emissions Baselines, Monitoring Critical to Success of Trading Program, Official Says," *Environmental Reporter* 24:18 (May 7, 1993); "State Officials Agree to Framework for Establishing NO_x Trading Program," *Environmental Reporter* 24: 135–136 (May 21, 1993).

31. Some policy-makers argue that once technically based standards have been met, tradable permits could be used to achieve water quality goals in bodies of water not yet in compliance with the law. They interpret the act's failure to address the issue as permitting the establishment of such systems. (U.S. Environmental Protection Agency, 1992). Only one such system has been established, and it has not resulted in

any economically motivated trades. Studies of the program suggest that its design gave dischargers insufficient incentives to trade. A study commissioned by the EPA calculated that of the 1,083 bodies of water with non-attainment status for which data are available, 39% could benefit from a trading system even with no change in the technical standards under law.

32. Boehmer-Christiansen (1992) pp. 307–308 points out that German terminology ratifies the emphasis on technical or engineering solutions. She points out that in German, " 'pollution' is described as an attribute of the pollutant, as harmful material, 'Schadstoff.' A physical burden placed upon nature, 'Umweltbelastung,' literally means a burden upon the world. English takes a more scientific approach and defines pollution not as the introduction of pollutants as such, but as an effect on the environment that is judged harmful by society. The step between pollution and abatement action of one sort or another is therefore shorter in German perception."

33. The air and water statutes are modelled after the Prussian law for licensing business enterprises. The statute governing air pollution and noise includes a presumption in favor of granting a license with the burden on government to demonstrate why denial is justified. The license, once granted, acquires the status of a property right and can give rise to claims for compensation if the government attempts to modify or rescind the license (BImSchG §§6, 21(4). See Bohne (1987); Currie (1982); Jacob (1963) p. 55; Schmidt-Aßmann (1992) p. 11; and Wolf (1987).

34. BImSchG §§47, 47a; Currie (1982) pp. 374–380; Weidner (1986) p. 83. Plans are required only for "heavily polluted" areas, and even for such areas, the Länder have been slow to promulgate plans (Weidner [1986] pp. 83–85).

35. BImSchG §17(1), (2). In addition, if ambient standards are close to being violated, higher treatment requirements may be imposed on applicants for new licenses (letter from Gertrude Lübbe-Wolff, August 1994).

36. TA-Luft nos. 2.6.2.2, 2.6.2.3. See Hansmann (1987) pp. 146–152; Bohne (1987) p. 142, n. 41.

37. Ordinance Concerning Large Combustion Plants (*Verordnung über Großfeuerungs-anlagen*—13.BImSchV), June 22, 1983.

38. Rat von Sachverständigen für Umweltfragen, Waldschäden und Luftverunreinigungen, 1983.

39. Scientists believe that air pollution is only one factor affecting the health of forests (Boehmer-Christiansen and Skea [1991] pp. 38–41). Boehmer-Christiansen (1992) p. 311 argues that political actors converged on the use of simple criteria for success. "These were not the health of the forests or a reduction in cancers (that is, scientific criteria), but the reduction of SO_2 emissions or the increase in the number of cars with autocatalysts."

40. See 13.BImSchV §§8, 12, 17.

41. 13.BImSchV §§6(5), 11(5).

42. "Trotz Erfolge bei der Luftreinhaltung: Der Wald gesundet nicht," *Umwelt und Entwicklung*, December 1991, p. 14. In 1988, 52% of total forest area was damaged, with 15% moderately or severely damaged. Pratt (1992) p. 82. In 1993 the percentages were 61 and 21, respectively, lower than in 1992. Experts, however, argued that the improvement was not tied to reductions in air pollution and in addition was not

even a relevant measure of the health of the German forests. Hans Schuh, "Wald-forschung in der Sackgasse," *Die Zeit*, December 10, 1993, p. 17.

43. One observer, who may be excessively cynical, argues that the policy became a way to raise the acceptability of nuclear power, benefit the southern Länder, and justify subsidies to coal-burning plants in the Ruhr (Boehmer-Christiansen [1992]). The subsidies took the form of tax relief and government underwriting of the capital risk rather than direct grants. Low-interest loans were provided by the *Kreditanstalt für Wiederaufbau* or Reconstruction Loan Corporation (Boehmer-Christiansen and Skea [1991] pp. 202–203; Weale, O'Riordan, and Kramme [1992] p. 186).

44. See Brown and Johnson (1984), who do, however, recognize that the program differs from an economically efficient scheme. The Effluent Charge Law (*Abwasserabgaben-gesetz*-AbwAG) was originally passed in 1976 and amended most recently in 1991.

45. The *Wasserhaushaltsgesetz*—WHG requires those obtaining discharge permits to comply with generally acknowledged rules of technology (*allgemein anerkannten Regeln der Technik*). If the wastewater contains "hazardous substances," then the possibly more stringent "Stand der Technik" applies [WHG §7a]. Article 6 makes it possible for the authorities to consider ambient water quality. If water quality is below Länder quality guidelines, dischargers may be denied a license. The guide-lines, however, permit exceptions if the public interest would be served. However, if a license is granted under such conditions, the discharger may be held to a higher level of treatment than mandated by WHG §7a. This feature of the implementation process is quite important since many watercourses do not comply with ambient standards (letter from Gertrude Lübbe-Wolff, August 1994).

46. AbwAG §§3, 4, 9, Annex A; Jarass and DiMento (1993) p. 62.

47. For river sewage plants, however, the fee is determined on the basis of water quality downstream from the plant (AbwAG §3[2]).

48. The 50% reduction applies to those required to use "generally acknowledged rules of technology." Those required to meet the "Stand der Technik" obtain an 80% reduction if they comply. AbwAG §9(5),(6).

49. Hansmeyer and Gawel (1993); Rehbinder (1993) pp. 72–74. Firms may request more restrictive permits as a means of limiting charges (Jarass and DiMento [1993] p. 62). According to Hansmeyer and Gawel (1993), even this incentive aspect of the law would be reduced if a proposed fourth amendment to the law is passed. The proposed amendment would reduce tax rates and increase inefficient investment subsidies to industry. The authors fear that the law's incentive function will be eliminated.

50. See, for example, Ackerman and Hassler (1981).

51. Rehbinder and Stewart (1985) p. 94; Salzwedel and Preusker (1982), pp. 26, 48, 287–289. See *Chemikaliengesetz*—ChemG §§4–12, 16–16. Under the Immission Control Act, the regulation covering air pollution from large combustion plants distinguishes between new and old plants but does require retrofitting of old plants. Old plants are given until 1993 to meet the same sulfur dioxide standards as new plants. (13.BImSchV §§3–12, 17–20, Rissberger [1985] p. 338; Weidner [1986] pp. 79–80).

52. Pashigian (1985) presents data suggesting that the Prevention of Significant Deteri-

oration provisions in the Clean Air Act Amendments of 1977 allow northern cities to obtain improved air quality while limiting the transfer of resources to rural and less-developed regions.

53. The European Union has approved transition measures to be applied only to existing enterprises. The transition period lasts until 1995 or 1996. The measures are mostly concerned with waste, water, and air. They do not apply to nuclear power, and as a consequence all the nuclear reactors in the eastern part of Germany have been shut down (Palinkas [1992]; Streibel [1992]).

54. Boehmer-Christiansen (1992).

55. Pehle (1988a, 1988b, 1988c) argues that farm interests and the chemical industry have veto power (*Vetomacht*) over environmental policy.

56. Brickman, Jasanoff, and Ilgen (1985) pp. 230–233, 252–256; Paterson (1989b); ChemG §§4–12, 16–16c.

57. *Bundesnaturschutzgesetz*—BNatSchG §§1(3), 8(7); WHG §19(4).

58. Rehbinder (1992b) p. 228.

59. Bosso (1987) pp. 161–166.

60. "Two Senators Propose Rewrite of Clean Water Law," *Congressional Quarterly*, June 26, 1993, p. 1652. The Clean Water Act has only a voluntary program for non-point sources of pollution (CWA §319, 33 U.S.C. 1329).

61. The bill, S. 2093, was approved by the Environment and Public Works Committee on February 24, 1994. By mid-1994 the House Public Works and Transportation Committee had not reported a bill. "Senate Will Wait for House Panel Markup Before Beginning CWA Consideration on Floor," *Environmental Reporter*, June 17, 1994, pp. 308–309; "Need for Non-point Controls Stressed in Reauthorization of Clean Water Act," *Environmental Reporter*, July 23, 1993, pp. 513–514; "Congress Bracing to Renew 1972 Clean Water Law," *Congressional Quarterly*, January 29, 1994, pp. 164–166.

62. Ackerman and Hassler (1981) describe the alliance between American producers of "locally-produced," or high-sulfur, coal and environmentalists in seeking to enshrine the scrubber.

63. CAA §§401–413, 42 U.S.C. §§7651–7651*l*; Garrett and Winner (1992) pp. 10253–10256.

64. Boehmer-Christiansen (1992) p. 316. The regulation governing air pollution from large combustion plants imposes different standards on plants using solid fuels and plants using liquid fuels or natural gas. The standards for solid fuel (that is, coal) are generally more lax (13.BImSchV §§3–16). The standards are, nevertheless, quite tough and have been interpreted to require flue-gas desulfurization equipment ("scrubbers") on coal-fired power plants, a regulation that favors high sulfur coal [Rissberger [1985] p. 335). In North Rhine-Westphalia, before the federal government promulgated its regulation, a study written in 1983 reported that "sixteen of the state's largest lignite-burning plants with a total capacity of 6,600 megawatts (MW) will be equipped with flue gas desulfurization equipment, while six older plants will be closed and replaced with four newer, less polluting power stations" (Wetstone and Rosencranz [1983] p. 85).

65. Council Directive of November 24, 1988, on the Limitation of Emissions of Certain

Pollutants into the Air from Large Combustion Plants, 88/609/EEC. The exception for Spain is in article 5.

66. For a critical overview of the EPA through the Reagan administration, see Landy, Roberts, and Thomas (1990).

67. Eads and Fix (1984) pp. 140–148; Harris and Milkis (1989) pp. 6, 113–124; Kraft and Vig (1984) pp. 426–428; Crandall and Portney (1984) p. 62. Crandall and Portney, p. 62, claim that at the EPA "[g]roups outside the agency prepared 'hit lists' of supposedly pro-environmental EPA employees and the new leadership appeared to respond to them by, for example, replacing several members of the EPA Science Advisory Board. Many senior employees left, while others became resentful and distrustful of the new team."

68. The positions of EPA administrator and deputy administrator were not filled in the first six months of Reagan's term. Crandall and Portney (1984) p. 62.

69. Crandall and Portney (1984) p. 72.

70. Kraft and Vig (1984) pp. 428–429, Crandall and Portney (1984) p. 69.

71. Crandall and Portney (1984) p. 69.

72. Harris and Milkis (1989) pp. 255–256, Kraft and Vig (1984) pp. 430, 431.

73. Russell (1990) p. 263.

74. EPA civil referrals to the Department of Justice rose from a low of 112 in 1982 to 251 in 1984, peaking at 372 in 1988. EPA administrative actions were 864 in 1982, 1,848 in 1983, and 3,124 in 1984. After falling off a bit in 1985 and 1986, actions rose to 3,194 in 1987 and 3,085 in 1988. Although the number of criminal prosecutions remained small, the increase was large—from seven in 1982 to twenty-seven in 1987 (Russell 1990, pp. 263–267). Wood and Waterman (1991) document the increase in hazardous waste site inspections. After Congress increased the EPA budget in 1984, inspections soared to a new high of 163 inspections per month compared with 27 at the time of the Burford contempt citation (id. pp. 818–821).

75. Warren and Chilton (1990).

76. Administrative actions increased from 3,085 in 1988 to 4,136 in the first year of the Bush administration. By 1992 the total had fallen back to 3,607. Civil referrals to the Department of Justice ranged from 361 to 393 during the Bush presidency. Criminal referrals jumped from 59 in 1988 to 81 in 1991 to 107 in 1992. U.S. EPA Enforcement Accomplishment Reports, 1988–1992.

77. For example, the Bush administration played an important role in designing the sulfur dioxide trading system in the Clean Air Act Amendments of 1990.

78. For a history see Müller (1986, 1989). See also Boehmer-Christiansen and Skea (1991) pp. 106–109; Weale, O'Riordan, and Kramme (1991) pp. 122–132.

79. Katzenstein (1987); Leonardy (1991); Mayntz and Scharpf (1975).

80. "Senate Passes $6.7 Billion EPA Budget, Extends Funding for White House Council," *Environmental Reporter* 24:899 (September 24, 1993).

81. Wood and Waterman (1991) p. 818.

82. Bundesministerium für Umwelt, Naturschutz und Reaktorsicherheit, *Das Bundesumweltministerium*, pamphlet, Bonn, 1991, p. 4, and Umweltbundesamt (1991) p. 6.

83. Bundesministerium für Umwelt, Naturschutz und Reaktorsicherheit, *Das Bundesumweltministerium*, pamphlet, Bonn, 1991, p. 6. At least a third of the budget went to

special-purpose grants for the new eastern Länder. The same publication points out, however, that spending on environmental affairs by the government as a whole totals DM 9,616 million, of which DM 2,645 million is for "credits for environmental measures."

84. The 1994 budget includes $2.5 billion for water programs and $1.5 billion for the hazardous substances Superfund. "Senate Passes $6.7 Billion EPA Budget, Extends Funding for White House Council," *Environmental Reporter*, September 24, 1993, p. 899. The large-scale program of matching grants for constructing sewage treatment plants was phased out in 1991, replaced by contributions to a state-managed revolving loan fund (Freeman, 1990, p. 138). Federal fund authorizations for this program expire in 1994. "Two Senators Propose Rewrite of Clean Water Law," *Congressional Quarterly* June 26, 1993, p. 1652.

85. Weidner (1989).

86. In the early nineties most of these funds are being spent in the new Länder of the east. Bundesminister für Umwelt, Naturschutz und Reaktorsicherheit, "Umwelt Union: Deutsche Einheit, Neue Aufgaben," pamphlet, Bonn, 1990.

87. In addition to revenue-sharing funds provided by formula to the Länder, the federal government also makes below-market-interest-rate loans to lower-level governments that can be used for sewage treatment plants. The loans are made through a public corporation [the Kreditanstalt für Wiederaufbau, or Reconstruction Loan Corporation] originally established to administer European Recovery Program funds after World War II (interview with Michael Bothe, July 1993, and Boehmer-Christiansen and Skea (1991) p. 125). Other subsidies involve tax benefits and subsidies for measures that reduce pollution and save energy (Weidner 1986:93–98, Kloepfer 1989:167–175).

88. Pehle (1988a), (1988b), (1988c); Weidner 1989.

89. Müller (1990), Weidner (1989) p. 18.

90. Hartkopf and Bohne (1983), pp. 150–151, writing before the establishment of the Environmental Ministry, raise this possibility.

91. 13. BImSchV. See Weidner (1989) p. 16.

92. Boehmer-Christiansen (1992) and Boehmer-Christiansen and Skea (1991) provide a political analysis of this case. See also Weale (1992) pp. 169–171.

93. Sellers (1994), in his study of land-use regulation in Freiburg, discusses the impact of Green party members on policy debates. "By framing issues of environmental policy as matters of partisan ideological disagreement . . . the Greens removed decisions from the preserve of rationalistic administration" (chapter 3, p. 68).

94. In the United States, Bosso (1987) describes how pesticide regulation evolved from a simple "food-versus-famine" issue to a complex, multidimensional problem. One environmentalist interviewed in the eighties said, "These are the 'nuts and bolts' days, unlike the earlier days when all you had to do was say, 'trees,' and a lot of people would lend their support. You just can't say 'trees' like in the old days. Everyone now realizes the complexity of the issues involved, though everyone publicly may argue that it is a 'black-versus-white' issue" (id. p. 217).

95. Dower (1990), p. 189. concludes that "our state of knowledge concerning the benefits and costs of hazardous waste control is shockingly poor." Shapiro (1990), p. 236,

finds that "despite considerable public concern about the dangers of exposure to toxic chemicals, for the majority of chemicals in commerce the available data are grossly inadequate to characterize potential chronic hazards, let alone determine whether the risks are unreasonable and permit selection of appropriate regulatory strategies."

96. Freeman (1990) p. 127.

97. Portney (1990b) estimates that by 2005 the Clean Air Amendments of 1990 will add $20–36 billion to annual compliance expenditures. He expects the benefits to fall between $6 billion and $25 billion, with the most likely estimate $14 billion.

THREE POLLUTION AND FEDERALISM

1. For an introduction to the problems of depletion of the ozone layer, see Gallagher (1992) pp. 270–277; on global warming see Morgenstern (1991) and Nordhaus (1991).

2. Pearce (1991) p. 259 estimates that if each "adult person in the wealthy part of the world [Western Europe, North America, Australia] would be willing to contribute $8 per annum to an 'Amazon Conservation Fund,' the resulting $3.2 billion would enable the people responsible for more than 25% of the economic output of Amazonia to be compensated for ceasing their activities." Pearce considers $8 to be a conservative estimate of the value placed on rain forest species ([1991] p. 258).

3. Some policies involve limiting uses—for example, banning the use of chlorofluoro-carbons in spray cans to protect the ozone layer [McInnis, 1992]. Such regulations prejudge the relative importance of various uses rather than leave it to the market to allocate the reduced supply through higher prices.

4. Tietenberg (1991) pp. 106–107. For an analysis of a system of carbon emission rights to control greenhouse warming, see Manne and Richels (1991). A carbon tax is analyzed in Christian (1992).

5. For an attempt to develop such a scheme, see Aronson (1993). Such proposals, of course, have a somewhat utopian air, because no global authority exists that is capable of administering such a program. See Barrett (1991) for a discussion of how global cooperation can arise under certain conditions.

6. Burtraw and Portney (1991) p. 311, for example, report that in Baltimore the economically efficient standard for total suspended particulates, that is, the point where marginal benefits equal marginal costs, is nearly 50% greater than the optimal standard for St. Louis.

7. See, for example, Oates (1972) and Olson (1979).

8. See, for example, Breton (1965) and Oates (1972).

9. For example, in the American chemical industry, national firms appear to have a relatively weak bargaining position at the state level: moving costs are high once capital is in place, and the industry is very capital intensive. Large chemical companies have thus actively supported uniformity in a number of regulatory areas. The chemical industry joined with OSHA in support of uniform national labeling standards (Eads and Fix, 1984, p. 152). Under the Resource Conservation and

Recovery Act, the Chemical Manufacturers Association (CMA) favored uniform federal standards. The CMA worried that "variations in state priorities could result in cost disadvantages for existing facilities due to geographic location" (Comments of the Chemical Manufacturers Association on EPA's Proposed Consolidated Permit Regulations #189 [September 12, 1979] p. 181, cited in Schnapf [1982] p. 712, n. 136).

10. In other words, the tax in the first town has been set to give the noise producer an incentive to reach the noise level mandated in the second town.
11. For example, see Oates and Schwab (1988) p. 336, n. 2. They assume that each community sets the ratio of emissions to labor force. They also note that the results would not be changed "if communities use certain other policy tools such as Pigouvian taxes on emissions rather than the command and control strategy." They do not, however, consider the case in which some communities use fees and others use standards.
12. See Oates and Schwab (1988). These authors go on to consider cases where efficiency does not prevail. The recent theoretical articles are summarized for a legal audience in Revesz (1992).
13. "It is one of the happy incidents of the federal system that a single courageous state may, if its citizens choose, serve as a laboratory, and try novel social and economic experiments without risk to the rest of the country" *(New State Ice Co. v. Liebman*, 285 U.S. 262, 311 [1932] [Brandeis, J., dissenting]).
14. Rose-Ackerman (1980b). See also Gey (1989–1990) p. 72.
15. For a discussion of the way a "prisoner's dilemma" operates when local governments compete, see Mashaw and Rose-Ackerman (1984), Revesz (1992) pp. 1213–1227, and Rose-Ackerman (1992b) pp. 166–170. The prisoner's dilemma may not, however, be very important for environmental policy. The U.S. evidence suggests that even when interjurisdictional policy differences were large, they were not a major determinant of firm location. Interstate differences in pollution control costs are a relatively small fraction of siting costs. For empirical work see Bartik (1988); Duerksen (1983) pp. 56–71; and McConnell and Schwab (1990).
16. See Gey (1989–90) p. 75: "The attraction of decentralization is that it disperses political power. But concerted private interests have typically found it easy to counter dispersed political power. . . . [A] decentralized political structure [is] . . . vulnerable to challenge by . . . concentrations of wealth . . . as well as to challenges by multinationals." See also Gey (1989–1990) pp. 56–60 which characterizes the situation as a "battle" between states and large corporations.
17. Revesz (1992). Farber (1986) p. 413 argues that in general "the market exacts its own inexorable penalties for needlessly burdensome regulations."
18. The most sophisticated is Oates and Schwab (1988).
19. See Markusen, Morey, and Olewiler, forthcoming. Their model can produce pollution levels that are either too high or too low, depending upon whether the disutility of pollution is relatively low or high. See also Markusen, Morey, and Olewiler (1993).
20. Waste disposal becomes a regional problem when it contaminates regional air or water basins. The most principled response here would be to regulate the produc-

tion of air and water pollution nationally and let local communities decide for themselves how to administer their waste collection systems subject to the caveats discussed in the text.

21. Davis and Lester (1989) p. 59.

22. This issue does not arise for old sites that those purchasing land in the region knew to be hazardous. In such situations the danger would be incorporated in the sale price. As long as new owners are informed of their responsibility prior to purchase, there is no unfairness in requiring them to follow through. The problem is then pushed back a step to the seller who bore the cost in the form of a reduced price.

23. U.S. Constitution, Article I, §8. Tribe (1988) §§5–4 to 5–6. *Hodel v. Indiana,* 452 U.S. 314, 323 (1981) states that the Supreme Court will invalidate legislation enacted under the Commerce Clause "only if it is clear that there is no rational basis for a Congressional finding that the regulated activity affects interstate commerce, or that there is no reasonable connection between the regulatory means selected and the asserted ends."

A federal appeals court recently suggested limits to the Court's permissive jurisprudence at least in the criminal justice area. The Fifth Circuit held unconstitutional a federal law outlawing guns in the vicinity of schools, *U.S. v. Lopez,* 2 F. 3d 1342 (5th Cir. 1993), cert. granted, 114 S. Ct. 1536 (1994). The court based its decision on Congress's failure to mention any link to interstate commerce (id. at 1354–1355. But see the contrary holding in *U.S. v. Ornelas,* 841 F. Supp. 1087 [D.C. Col. 1994]). The judge in the latter case believed that precedent required him to uphold the law, but he states that if he could, he would hold the law unconstitutional as a violation of the Tenth Amendment (id. at 1094, n. 11).

24. A recent attempt to challenge the constitutionality of the regulation of intrastate wetlands under the Clean Water Act (CWA) failed. A panel of the Seventh Circuit held that the federal regulation of isolated, intrastate wetlands was both contrary to the CWA and unconstitutional under the Commerce Clause (*Hoffman Homes v. EPA,* 951 F.2d 1310 [7th Cir. 1992]). Even this panel was careful to point out that it agreed with courts that have upheld the constitutionality of federal regulation of environmental hazards with interstate impacts (id. at 1317). Subsequent to this decision, the EPA requested a rehearing, the original order was vacated, and a majority of the same panel wrote a narrow opinion holding that the jurisdiction of the CWA did not extend to the particular property at issue (*Hoffman Homes v. EPA,* 999 F. 2d 256 [7th Cir. 1993]). The author of the original opinion wrote a concurrence in which he continued to maintain that federal regulation of intrastate wetlands was unconstitutional (id. at 262 [Manion, J.,concurring]).

25. For a summary see Burtraw and Portney (1991) and the articles collected in Portney (1990c).

26. *Oregon Waste Systems v. Envl. Dep't.,* 114 S.Ct. 1435 (1994) and *Chemical Waste Management, Inc. v. Hunt,* 112 S.Ct. 2009 (1992). The decisions build on *Philadelphia v. New Jersey,* 437 U.S. 617 (1977), which voided a New Jersey law prohibiting the import of out-of-state solid waste. See also *New Energy Co. of Indiana v. Limbach, Tax Comm'n of Ohio,* 486 U.S. 269 (1988) holding a lower tax on Ohio-produced ethanol unconstitutional.

27. *Fort Gratiot Sanitary Landfill, Inc. v. Michigan Dep't. of Natural Resources*, 112 S.Ct. 2019 (1992), and *C. & A. Carbone Inc. v. Clarkstown*, 114 S.Ct. 1677 (1994).

28. *Alliance for Clean Coal v. Craig* 840 F. Supp. 554 (N.D. Ill., 1993). The Illinois Coal Act required public utilities to take into account "the need to use coal mined in Illinois" and "the need to preserve as a valuable state resource the mining of coal in Illinois," when they formulated their Clear Air Act compliance plans. The act also required the four largest utilities to install devices to control sulfur dioxide emissions ("scrubbers"), a requirement that would decrease the benefits of using low-sulfur, out-of-state coal [id. at 557]. The District Court found that the statutory language represented "pure protectionism" (id. at 559).

29. See Ackerman and Hassler (1981).

30. See *Chemical Waste Management*, 112 S.Ct. 2009 at 2019 (Rehnquist, J., dissenting). The market participant doctrine is stated in *Hughes v. Alexandria*, 426 U.S. 794 (1976).

31. *Illinois v. Milwaukee*, I, 406 U.S. 91 (1972); II, 451 U.S.304 (1981); III, 731 F. 2d 403 (1984), *cert. denied*, 469 U.S. 1196 (1985).

32. *International Paper Co. v. Ouellette et al.*, 479 U.S. 481 (1987).

33. Low Level Radioactive Wastes Policy Act of 1985, 42 U.S.C. §§2021b et seq. (Supp IV 1980). The act was originally passed in 1980. In drafting both the original act and the 1985 revision, Congress relied heavily on reports submitted by the National Governors' Association (*New York v. United States*, 112 S.Ct. 2408, 2415 and 2435–2438 [White, J., dissenting] [1992]).

34. *New York v. United States*, 112 S.Ct. 2408, 2428.

35. *New York v. United States*, 112 S.Ct. 2408, 2438. He argued that the State of New York "should be estopped from asserting the unconstitutionality of a provision that seeks merely to ensure that, after deriving substantial advantages from the 1985 Act, New York must in fact live up to its bargain . . . " (id. p. 2440).

36. Ashe (1993) pp. 284–285.

37. *New York v. United States*, 112 S.Ct. 2408, 2431–2432. The Court's argument for this position is that the constitutional division of authority between federal and state governments is for the protection of individuals, not for the benefit of the states.

38. GG art. 74(11a), (18), (24).

39. GG art. 75(3), (4).

40. GG art. 72(2).

41. For more on the constitutional provisions, see Currie (1994) pp. 33–101.

42. GG art. 72.

43. GG art. 89.

44. *Entscheidungen des Bundesverfassungsgerichts*—BVerfGE (Decisions of the German Federal Constitutional Court) 15, 1 (1962); BVerfGE 21, 312 (1967).

45. Currie (1994) pp. 44–45 discusses this case and argues that it was correctly decided. Constitutional amendments to give the federal government preemptive power over the Länder in the area of water pollution failed to pass in 1973, 1974, and 1975. Brown and Johnson (1984) p. 930.

46. The existing federal framework laws governing water pollution are the *Wasserhaus-*

haltsgesetz-WHG, as amended in 1986, and the *Abwasserabgabengesetz*-AbwAG, as amended in 1990. The WHG §§36, 36b requires that each Land draw up both an overall plan and specific plans for each body of water. Interstate agreements on the use and condition of water are a reason for requiring a plan [WHG §36b(2)(2)], and the federal government can use administrative guidelines to influence the content of plans [WHG §§36(3), 36b(7)]. Neumann, Schultz-Wildelau, and Schilling (1990) p. 259, list the thirty general planning areas in the western part of Germany.

47. The first such body, the *Emscher Genossenschaft*, was established in 1902 in response to a discharge of dye into the Rhine. It was followed by the establishment of similar bodies on the Wupper, Lippe, and Ruhr. The associations include riparian businesses and communities and the water industry. Weale (1992) p. 162.

48. Umweltbundesamt (1991) p.254. The Commission was established in 1990 between Germany and Czechoslovakia. There are also specific conventions for the Rhine that include the European Union as a signatory (Convention on the Protection of the Rhine Against Chemical Pollution, December 3, 1976, 16 I.L.M. 242; Convention on the Protection of the Rhine Against Pollution by Chlorides, December 3, 1976, I.L.M. 265). The Elbe is much more polluted than the Rhine. *Umwelt*, October, 1993, p. 407 compares the two rivers in 1990.

49. GG arts. 83–85.

50. GG arts. 104a, 106, 107.

51. BVerfGE 39, 96 (1975); BVerfGE 41, 291 (1976). These cases are discussed by Blair (1991) pp. 78–79 and Currie (1994) pp. 57–58, pp. 83–84 at notes 126–132.

52. BVerfGE 72, 330 (1986). For discussions see Blair (1991) pp. 79–81, Currie (1994) pp. 58–60, 84–86, at notes 133–142; Kommers (1989) p. 100. The political wrangling that produced the unconstitutional allocation is described in Renzsch (1989).

53. BVerfGE 72, 330, 402ff (1986). By the end of 1992 the federal government had spent DM 1.6 billion for 1800 special environmental protection projects in the east. "Umweltsituation in den neuen Ländern spürbar verbessert," *Umwelt*, December 1993, pp. 474–475. In addition to direct subsidies, the federal government provides tax benefits and borrowing subsidies throughout the country to encourage energy efficiency and environmental protection. See Kloepfer (1989) pp. 167–175 and Weidner (1986).

54. Friedrich Adolf Jahn MdB, CDU/CSU, "Keine Totalrevision des Grundgesetzes"; Detlef Kleinert MdB, FDP, "Als verläßliche Grundlage anerkennen"; Hans-Jochen Vogel MdB, SPD, "Vom Grundgesetz der alten Bundesrepublik zur Verfassung der neuen Bundesrepublik," *Das Parlament*, April 10, 1991, p.13.

55. Currie (1993) pp. 238–239; Davis and Linnerooth (1987) pp. 97–99; Leonardy (1991) p. 54.

56. Mayntz (1978) pp. 204–205.

57. Mayntz (1978) p. 205. For example, Baden-Württemberg's efforts to clean up Lake Constance involved subsidies for sewage treatment that favored the construction of small, inefficient plants (Scharpf, Reissert, and Schnabel [1978] pp. 78–83).

58. See Rehbinder (1976b). Not surprisingly, the Länder officially rejected the notion of a deficit in enforcement. According to Rehbinder [id. p. 374], however, "many

Land officials, in particular those on the lower administrative levels, privately admit the existence of the enforcement deficit." Boehmer-Christiansen and Skea (1991, p. 178) claim that the Länder vary widely in the quality of plant licensing processes under the federal pollution control laws. Brickman, Jasanoff, and Ilgen (1985, pp. 49–50) make the same claim with respect to the enforcement of the chemical control law. Lübbe-Wolff (1992) argues that although building projects seldom begin without the requisite permits under the *Bundes-Immissionsschutzgesetz,* water permits are not always issued when required by law and, if issued, are not well enforced.

59. The existence of this public perception is reported in letters from Philip Kunig, June 4, 1993, and Fritz Scharpf, June 1, 1993. Lübbe-Wolff (1993), however, contests this claim.

60. Bohne (1987) compares air pollution policy in Germany and the United States. For a general discussion of the impact of American federalism on air and water pollution policy, see Lowry (1992).

61. CAA §110, 42 U.S.C. §7410.

62. Melnick (1983) pp. 193–238.

63. The Clean Water Act (CWA), also called the Federal Water Pollution Control Act (FWPCA), 33 U.S.C. §1281 et seq.

64. The matching grant program is being replaced with a revolving loan program (CWA, 33 U.S.C. 1383; Freeman [1990] pp. 97–150). See "Grant-to-Loan Transition in Water Act Heralds New State, EPA Roles, Quigley Says," 17 *Environmental Reporter* 1789 (February 20, 1987).

65. Bennett and von Moltke (1990) p. 128 describe the importance of subsidies and tax benefits in administering pollution policy in Hamburg.

66. The air pollution statute permits interstate differences in air quality plans, subject to federal guidelines; but these are tied to state boundaries, not air basins. CAA §110(a)(2), 42 U.S.C. §7410(a)(2) requires each state to develop and submit a plan to the EPA.

67. Davis and Lester (1989) 71–83 document differences in state's commitments to environmental protection as a policy goal and in their dependence on federal funds.

68. Davis and Lester (1989) p. 62.

69. National Governors' Association, Environmental Subcommittee, "Report of Work Group on Delegation and Oversight," mimeograph, December 1982.

70. Burtraw and Portney (1991) pp. 307–308; Dower (1990) pp. 168–177. The formal name of the act is the Comprehensive Environmental Response, Compensation, and Liability Act (CERCLA) 42 U.S.C. §§9601 et seq. (1988).

71. Dower (1990) pp. 168–190. The program is very expensive. The cumulative authorized commitment of federal tax dollars in $15.2 billion, and estimates of total costs range from $100 billion to $1.7 trillion (Church and Nakamura [1993] p. 3). The search for responsible parties and the conflicts between them over liability have slowed down the process of cleanup and produced a heavy judicial caseload as "potentially responsible parties" sue each other (id. pp. 7, 24–28). Government seeks to collect cleanup costs and the value of damages to natural resources from those waste producers who used a particular site. CERCLA §107(a), 42 U.S.C.

§9607(a). The executive branch, not the courts, sets standards for damage assessment (see *State of Ohio v. United States Department of the Interior,* 880 F. 2d 432 [D.C. Cir. 1989], reviewing the regulations for damage assessment and finding fault with some aspects).

72. Under such a system, one would need to determine the proper amount of compensation based on the health risks and other costs of the waste site. The major argument against such a locally based system is the political reality of local government decision-making. Those harmed by the site may not be involved in making the choice, and if the damages are paid to local governments, those harmed may not receive compensation for their injuries.

73. A soil pollution act is, however, in the draft stage. The 1991 Environmental Liability Law (*Umwelthaftungsgesetz*—UmweltHG) does not extend liability to waste generators and transporters, and it has only prospective application. Landowners, rather than generators, have primary responsibility for cleanup under German police law [Church and Nakamura, 1994, pp. 25–29]. Generators, however, could be liable if they are negligent in the selection of a waste transporter or operator of a waste disposal facility. Letter from Eckard Rehbinder, 1993. See also chapter 7.

74. Church and Nakamura (1994) pp. 25–29. The states with the most active programs are, according to Church and Nakamura (p. 24), Hesse, North Rhine Westphalia, Rhineland Palatinate, Baden-Württemberg, and Bavaria.

75. In Hesse, for example, cleanup is managed by a specially created private law corporation, the Hessische Industriemüll GmbH, which is owned 27% by Hesse and 73% by the generators. This corporation also disposes of current wastes, with the costs covered by fees levied on dischargers (interview with Michael Bothe, July 1993). Davis and Linnerooth (1987) pp. 103–106 report that at the time of their study, the state of Hesse heavily subsidized this corporation. See also Church and Nakamura (1994) pp. 24–25.

76. Blankenburg (1985). He relies on detailed case studies performed in the seventies by Hucke, Müller, and Wassen (1980). Blankenburg (1985) pp. 484–485 reports that for waste disposal in general, local authorities tend to be stricter where industrial waste problems are small and more lenient where they are large.

77. Davis and Linnerooth (1987) pp. 101–106 describe how the wealthy states of Hesse and Bavaria subsidize hazardous waste management activities from general public funds and also charge the companies that generate waste.

78. According to a Greenpeace report, 400,000 tons of hazardous waste per year—as well as large quantities of other kinds of waste—were shipped to depositories in East Germany (Andreas Bernstorff, "Müllkolonie DDR," *Natur* [January, 1990] p. 10).

79. GG arts. 104a, 106, 107. BVerfGE 39, 96 (1975); BVerfGE 41, 291 (1976). But see BVerfGE 72, 330, 402ff (1986).

80. By the end of 1992, DM 248 million had been provided by the federal government for waste disposal projects in the east. See also "Ziele der Bundesregierung zur Erfassung, Sicherung und Sanierung von Altlasten in den neuen Bundesländern," address by Dr. Bertram Wieczorek, Parlamentarischer Staatssekretär beim Bundesumweltminister, *Umwelt,* April 1993, pp. 139–143. The federal government

acting through the Treuhandanstalt provides between 60% and 75% of the funding. The remainder is provided by the eastern Länder.

81. Ordinance on the Avoidance of Packaging Waste (*Verpackungsverordnung*—VerpackVO) of June 12, 1991, art. 4. Fishbein (1994).

82. VerpackVO art. 6. Participation in the private system also exempts distributors from having to take back drinks packages or containers for paints or washing and cleaning agents. VerpackVO articles 7–9.

83. VerpackVO, Annex to Art. 6 para. 3. "Recycling Germany: A Wall of Waste," *Economist*, November 30, 1991, pp. 9–12; "Abolishing Litter," *Economist*, August 22, 1992; Rüdiger Jungbluth, "Ein Schritt zur Müllvermeidung," *Tagesspiegel*, December 1, 1991. By July 1, 1995, 80% by weight of packaging waste must be collected. The law requires not only collection but also recycling. Of the waste collected, 90% of glass and metal must be recycled and 80% of plastics and paper by July 1, 1995. Germany is also considering a statute to require manufacturers to take back discarded products as well as packaging. Fishbein (1994) pp. 131–156.

84. "Falling Victim to Its Own Success—Germany's Recycling Scheme Is under Attack from Both Industry and Environmentalists," *Financial Times*, January 27, 1993.

85. In 1992 packaging materials fell by half a million tons, or 3.1% from the previous year. "Trendwende beim Packmitteleinsatz," *Umwelt*, September 1993, pp. 364–365. German waste levels were much lower than in the United States even before the ordinance went into effect. In 1989 per capita municipal waste was 864 kilograms in the U.S. and 318 kilograms in the FRG. Per capita waste increased by 16.2% in the U.S. between 1985 and 1989 and by only 0.2% in Germany. In 1985 the U.S. recycled 20% of paper and cardboard and 8% of glass, and Germany recycled 44% and 36% respectively (OECD 1991a, Tables 7.2A and 7.5, pp. 133, 147).

86. "Punkte gegen die Umwelt," *Die Zeit*, January 14, 1994; "Falling Victim to Its Own Success—Germany's Recycling Scheme Is under Attack from Both Industry and Environmentalists," *Financial Times*, January 27, 1993; Fishbein (1994) pp. 113–130.

87. Fishbein (1994) pp. 59–60, 197–200.

88. "Falling Victim to Its Own Success—Germany's Recycling Scheme Is under Attack from Both Industry and Environmentalists," *Financial Times*, January 27, 1993; "Töpfers Entwurf für neue Verpackungsverordnung," *Handelsblatt* December 4, 1993.

89. "Falling Victim to Its Own Success—Germany's Recycling Scheme Is under Attack from Both Industry and Environmentalists," *Financial Times*, January 27, 1993. The Environmental Ministry admits that a problem exists for recycling plastic, "Trendwende beim Packmitteleinsatz," *Umwelt*, September 1993, p. 364.

90. "Töpfers Entwurf für neue Verpackungsverordnung," *Handelsblatt*, December 29, 1993; Fishbein (1994) pp. 200–201.

91. One of the main problems of plastics recycling is that some kinds of plastic cannot be combined. Federal standards for plastics could solve this incompatibility. As yet Germany, like the United States, has no such regulations. Letter from Gerd Winter, July 1993.

92. The agreement, called the Montreal Protocol, was signed in September 1987 by 25 participants, including the U.S. and Germany. Fifty-six countries signed the London Amendments to the Protocol in June 1990. The original document required a 50% reduction in the consumption and production of chlorofluorocarbons (CFCs) by 1999 (Jachtenfuchs 1990). The Amendments of 1990 speed up that timetable and contain provisions designed to aid poorer countries in reducing CFCs and other ozone-depleting chemicals (Gallagher [1992]; Raiczyk [1991]).

    Of course, in this field, as in others, there is considerable disagreement among experts about the seriousness of the problem. Despite several large-scale research projects, doubt remains about the contribution of chlorofluorocarbons to the thinning of the ozone layer and about the link between a damaged ozone layer and skin cancer or other harms (McInnis 1992).

93. Evidence on ozone depletion was reported by the U.S. National Aeronautics and Space Administration in both 1991 and 1992 (Gallagher [1992] p. 277; Raiczyk [1991] p. 367) and by the United Nations in October 1991. "Stratospheric Ozone Hole Found to Occur in Mid-Hemisphere, New Information Shows" (*Current Reports, International Environmental Reporter* 14:590 [Nov. 6, 1991]). Shorter timetables were announced by the United States in February 1992 and proposed by the European Commission in March. The Commission proposal of 1992 is compared with earlier standards and the amended Montreal Protocol in Kraemer (1992) p. 13. See also Raiczyk (1991) pp. 373–374; Keith Schneider, "Bush Orders End to Ozone Destroyers by 1996," *New York Times*, February 12, 1992, and "Holestoppers: CFCs Will Be Phased Out Faster Than Once Expected, but This May Be Costly," *Economist*, March 7, 1992, p. 72.

    In May 1991 Germany promulgated a regulation prohibiting certain ozone-depleting halogenated hydrocarbons (*FCKW-Halon-Verbots-Verordnung*). The ordinance goes beyond the Montreal Protocol and European Union regulations. If the ordinance is enforced, Germany will stop using fully halogenated CFCs and halons by 1995. Germany, Federal Ministry for the Environment (1992) p. 136; Raiczyk (1991) p. 375.

94. Kraemer (1992); "Ozone Hole Rescue Moves Lead to a Tussle," *Financial Times*, November 23, 1992; "A Quick Fix on Ozone," *The Economist*, November 28, 1992. The ninety-three nations meeting in Copenhagen in November 1992 agreed to set up a fund to help poor countries, to tighten the timetable to phase out chlorofluorocarbons, and to add two new substances to the restricted list.

95. McInnis (1992) demonstrates that under the original protocol the American chemical industry would have earned substantial oligopoly profits from the restrictions on production because it had a head start on developing substitutes. Subsequent amendments, however, that sped up the timetables, cut these gains.

96. McInnis (1992).

97. See Rose-Ackerman (1981) for a general discussion of this phenomenon. In the American federal system, where states have substantial independent regulatory authority, the regulation of automobile exhaust followed this pattern. California, a large state (and therefore a large market for car sales) passed a law stringently regulating automobile exhaust. As a consequence, the automobile industry began

to support preemptive federal legislation. Similar to the case of CFCs, however, the subsequent federal law was so strict that it cast doubt on the wisdom of the industry's strategy. See Elliott, Ackerman, and Millian (1985).

98. United Nations, Convention on Climate Change, 1992. "UNCED" (1992) p. 207. The Convention had been ratified by 55 of the 160 signatory states by February 1994. It went into effect March 21, 1994 ("U.N. Conference Finds Greenhouse Gases Must Be Cut," Reuters, February 18, 1994, NEXIS). The United States was the first industrial nation to ratify the convention in October 1992.

99. "UNCED" (1992) p. 207; "U.S. Signs Accord on Biodiversity," *Chicago Tribune,* June 5, 1993.

100. Margaret Katz, "Lukewarm," *National Journal,* August 14, 1993, pp. 2028–2031; "Clinton Urging Voluntary Goals on Air Pollution," *New York Times,* October 19, 1993.

101. Cavender and Jäger (1993) provide a history of the climate change policy debate in Germany. They stress the role of the nuclear industry, particularly in the aftermath of Chernobyl, in using fears of the greenhouse effect as an argument for nuclear power.

102. "German Industry Snubs Carbon Tax," *Financial Times,* September 30, 1992, p. 12.

103. At Rio, Chancellor Kohl stated that Germany planned a 25–30% cut in carbon dioxide emissions by 2005 relative to 1987 levels. Töpfer claims that a carbon tax is necessary to meet this goal—a method opposed by German industry ("German Industry Snubs Carbon Tax," *Financial Times,* September 30, 1992, p. 12).

104. "U.S. Signs Accord on Biodiversity," *Chicago Tribune,* June 5, 1993. The pact had not been ratified by the U.S. by mid-1994. The Convention entered into force on December 29, 1993, once thirty countries had ratified it (*International Environmental Reporter* [BNA] 17:3 [January 12, 1994]).

105. The Biodiversity Convention would encourage the transfer of biotechnology to developing countries (United Nations, Convention on Biological Diversity, 1992, art. 16[1],[2]). "The U.S. was afraid that the Convention . . . might slow down the application and industrialisation of bio-technologies and would not afford protection for intellectual property and could reduce royalties, especially for pharmaceutical companies, needing vital raw material, for life-saving drugs. . . . The U.S. was, however, the only industrialised country not to have signed the Convention" ("UNCED" [1992] pp. 206–207). See also Graeme Browning, "Biodiversity Battle," *National Journal,* August 8, 1992, pp. 1827–1830. Browning suggests that the Industrial Biotechnology Association, representing 80% of the industry, could have accepted the treaty. In fact, the language of the Convention is protective of intellectual property. Article 2, in discussing technology transfers to developing countries, states that "in the case of technology subject to patents and other intellectual property rights, such access and transfer shall be provided on terms which recognise and are consistent with the adequate and effective protection of intellectual property rights." The text of the Convention is reproduced in *Environmental Law and Policy* 22 (1992):251–258.

106. In spring 1993 the industry was urging the administration to sign so that the United States could participate in the international negotiations over the interpretation of the intellectual property portions of the treaty. Bureau of National Affairs, *International Trade Reporter,* LEXIS-NEXIS, June 9, 1993.

107. Germany's politicians are on record as being concerned about endangered species and the loss of the rain forest. *Das Parlament,* June 5, 1992. According to Töpfer, "international species protection must have priority over the economic interests of individual states and traders." Gabrielle Wille, " 'The Future's Ark' Mustn't Become Empty," press release, Inter Nationes, 1992. According to Chancellor Kohl: "Die Vernichtung der tropischen Regenwälder und das Ozonloch . . . betreffen die Menschen in Lateinamerika ebenso wie in Europa, in allen Kontinenten gleichermaßen." Presse- und Informationsamt der Bundesregierung, *Umwelt und Entwicklung,* November 1991, p. 1.

108. Similar points were made by opposition party members in the Bundestag debate over the Rio Conference. "Regierungserklärung zum Rio-Umweltgipfel: Zwischen Chancen und Skepsis," *Das Parlament,* June 5, 1992.

109. Monetary contributions to international projects can also be good for one's image without imposing much pain. Thus Germany has contributed DM 250 million to help fund a three-year pilot project on rain forest preservation sponsored by the World Bank. This contribution is 15% of the project's budget. See "Tropenwalderhaltung," *Umwelt,* January 1992, pp. 13–14; Presse- und Informationsamt der Bundesregierung, " 'Ein Alarmsignal zum Handeln': Bericht der Bundesregierung über den Stand der Maßnahmen zum Schutz der tropischen Wälder," *Umwelt und Entwicklung,* December 1991, pp. 6–8.

FOUR   GERMAN ENVIRONMENTAL POLICY-MAKING PROCESSES

1. Böhret (1983). German political scientists who study the administrative system, however, have no trouble acknowledging the close connection between policy and politics. See, for example, Seibel (1992b).

2. Ossenbühl (1988b) p. 389.

3. In that same year, 300 laws were passed by federal and state legislatures and 880 legal regulations were promulgated [Katzenstein (1987) p. 382].

4. GG art. 20(2) states: "All state authority emanates from the people. It shall be exercised by the people by means of elections and voting and by specific legislative, executive, and judicial organs." Separation of powers also refers to the division of powers between the state and federal governments.

5. "Bei der Gewaltenteilung geht es nicht lediglich um eine Teilung und Trennung staatlicher Funktionen und um eine Zuweisung an verschiedene staatliche Organe, sondern vor allem um eine gegenseitige Hemmung und Kontrolle dieser Gewalten." Maunz (1991) p. 5. Maunz's language is practically identical to BVerfGE 34, 52, 59 (1972). Currie (1993) focuses on this principle.

6. GG art. 80(1) states, "The Federal Government, a Federal Minister or the Land governments may be authorized by a law to issue ordinances having the force of law [*Rechtsverordnungen*]. The content, purpose, and scope of the authorization so

conferred must be set forth in such law. This legal basis must be stated in the ordinance. If a law provides that such authorization may be delegated, such delegation shall require another ordinance having the force of law."

7. Maunz (1991) pp. 12–16, Ossenbühl (1988b) pp. 395–397; Ramsauer (1989) pp. 583–589; Richter and Schuppert (1991a) pp. 511–518. For a more extended discussion see Currie (1989), who stresses the strength of the German doctrine relative to the American nondelegation doctrine.

8. BVerfGE 56, 1, 12–14 (1981). The case concerns a statute providing benefits to victims of World War II. The law did not explicitly authorize legal regulations but was written to give considerable discretion to those administering the law.

9. BVerfGE 58, 257, 278 (1981) (challenge to an ordinance regulating the promotion of students). In general, the Court will scrutinize delegations in the area of criminal law and tax law with particular care (Maunz, 1991, p. 15).

10. BVerwG, May 11, 1993, *Umwelt- und Planungsrecht* 1993, pp. 383–384.

11. GG art 80. The Bundesrat also must approve ordinances that concern the railroads and the post office, the two largest operating federal agencies. GG art. 80(2) states, "The consent of the Bundesrat shall be required, unless otherwise provided by federal legislation, for ordinances having the force of law [*Rechtsverordnungen*] issued by the Federal government or a Federal Minister concerning basic rules for the use of facilities of the federal railroads and of postal and telecommunication services, or charges therefore, or concerning the construction and operation of railroads, as well as for ordinances having the force of law issued pursuant to federal laws that require the consent of the Bundesrat or that are executed by the Länder as agents of the Federation [*im Auftrage des Bundes*] or as matters of their own concern [*als eigene Angelegenheit*]."

12. GG arts. 76, 77 describe the role of the Bundesrat in the legislative process. Bundesrat approval is required for some laws; for others, the Bundestag can overrule a negative decision of the Bundesrat.

13. Kommers (1989) pp. 106–113; Leonardy (1991); Maunz (1991) p. 23. See BVerfGE 8, 274, 321 (1958).

14. GG arts. 84(2), 85(2). The terminology is not standardized. Verwaltungsvorschriften are also called *Verfügungen, Dienstanweisungen, Richtlinien, Anordnungen,* and *Grundsätze*. Guidelines do not require Bundesrat approval if they are not to be administered by the Länder. A third category, called *Satzungen,* are used primarily to structure self-governing quasi-governmental organizations. Ossenbühl (1988a) pp. 427–429.

15. The Constitutional Court ruled that article 80 applies only to federal Rechtsverordnungen, not to other forms of administrative action, such as administrative guidelines (*Verwaltungsvorschriften*), or to state laws and regulations (Maunz [1991] pp. 6–8; Ossenbühl [1988a] p. 458; Ramsauer [1989] pp. 573–575). Nevertheless, guidelines can be issued only on the basis of an underlying legislative authorization (Currie [1993] pp. 222–223).

16. For example, the ordinance of June 12, 1991, on avoiding packaging waste (*Verpackungsverordnung*-VerpackVO) provoked controversy in the Bundesrat and was passed only after the Bundesregierung modified its proposal to obtain the support

of several Länder controlled by the Social Democrats. The Bavarian Christian Social Union, which is generally in partnership with the Christian Democrats, refused
to go along with the government proposal even as amended. "Töpfers Verpackungsverordnung kam im zweiten Anlauf durch," *Frankfurter Rundschau,* April 4,
1991; "Mit SPD-Hilfestellung über die Hürde," *Tageszeitung,* April 4, 1991.

17. Mayntz and Schrapf (1975) pp. 36–37 discuss the reverse situation when the
    CDU/CSU controlled the Bundesrat and an SPD/FDP coalition controlled the
    central government.

18. Such vetoes could involve the entire Bundestag or a specified committee. Lorenz
    (1980) pp. 563–564; Maunz (1991) pp. 15–16; Ossenbühl (1988b) pp. 409–414;
    Ramsauer (1989) p. 508; Currie (1993) p. 233. In a tax case, the Constitutional
    Court held that statutes can include a requirement of Bundestag approval for
    regulations in which parliament has a legitimate interest. BVerfGE 8,274 (1958).
    The Court stated that it was up to the Bundestag, not the courts, to determine
    which issues were important. According to Ossenbühl (1988b) p. 412, Bundestag
    approval of rules is legitimate but only if the idea of the "legitimate interest of the
    legislature" is taken as a serious constraint. Committee vetoes are much more
    controversial, and many legal issues are undecided (id., p. 413).

19. *Gesetz über die Umweltverträglichkeitsprüfung*—UVPG, February 2, 1990, §3; im-
    plementing European Community directive 85/337/EEC.

20. *Bundes-Immissionsschutzgesetz*—BImSchG §48a.

21. Environmental Liability Law (*Umwelthaftungsgesetz*—UmweltHG) §20(2). The
    Bundestag can amend or reject the regulations. If the Bundestag has taken no
    action within three weeks, the government can proceed to seek Bundesrat approval.

22. Mayntz and Scharpf (1975) pp. 36–37.

23. APA, 5 U.S.C. §553.

24. Verwaltungsverfahrensgesetz—VwVfG, May 25, 1976, as amended on September
    12, 1990. A major portion of the act is directed toward administrative acts [*Ver-
    waltungsakte*], VwVfG §35(1). The act does recognize the possibility of a general
    order (*Allgemeinverfügung*), but it is defined as an administrative act "which ad-
    dresses a category of persons who are determined or are determinable by common
    characteristics or which concerns the public law quality of a thing or its use by the
    general public" [VwVfG §35(2)]. Although such decisions may be "general" in the
    sense that many people are affected, the act is nevertheless designed to control only
    particular cases.

25. See chapter 6 for a discussion of proceedings governed by legal procedural require-
    ments of the VwVfG.

26. *Gemeinsame Geschäftsordnung der Bundesministerien*—GGO II §§24, 63ff, 78. The
    provision also applies to statutory proposals.

27. Ossenbühl (1988b) pp. 416–417. Maunz (1991) p. 22, explains that GG art. 80 does
    not apply to these ordinances. Thus they have no external legal force.

28. My view of the German administrative process differs from that of Weale (1992).
    He finds the process "juridified" and heavily focused on due process. Although I
    agree with this characterization of low-level administrative procedures that imple-
    ment policies, my research suggests that high-level policy-making is constrained

very little by legal procedures. Weale, however, does agree that a "cult of expertise" exists in which lawyers and engineers are dominant and that environmental groups play little role in the advisory process (id. pp. 177–180).

29. Maunz (1991) pp. 9–10; Ossenbühl (1988a) p. 460. The Federal Administrative Court ruled that it was constitutionally permissible for the Berlin government to refuse to reveal administrative guidelines implementing the law concerning aliens to a lawyer representing people claiming to have been unfairly treated (BVerwGE 61, 15 [1980]). The lawyer claimed a right to examine these documents under the constitutional right to free choice and exercise of one's profession (GG art. 12[1]). The court did rule, however, that one may have a right to examine such guidelines outside of a specific administrative process if the applicant can show a "legitimate interest" ("In der Rechtsprechung ist allerdings anerkannt, daß auch außerhalb eines Verwaltungsverfahrens ein berechtigtes Interesse bestehen kann, Einsicht in verwaltungsbehördliche Akten und Unterlagen zu nehmen" [BVerwGE 61, 15, 22]). Some German scholars have argued for a broader public right to information to improve the transparency of the administrative process. Gurlit (1989) pp. 113–115.

30. BImSchG §48. For discussions, see Maunz (1991) p. 9; Ramsauer (1989) p. 573; Rehbinder (1976).

31. Maunz (1991) pp. 15, 28; Ramsauer (1989) pp. 593–594.

32. Ossenbühl (1988b) p. 414 provides examples of statutes that require the participation of incorporated groups, organizations, or individual experts. According to him, these requirements bring expertise and experience to the norm-setting process, thus improving it. A hearing of interest groups (*Interessenverbänden*) lets the executive branch learn the views of such groups at an early stage.

33. BImSchG §51 lists the types of participants that should be included in a hearing.

34. Maunz (1991) p. 15. The case is BVerfGE 10, 221ff (1959). It concerned the postwar implementation of a National Socialist law regulating the rents that could be charged for houses built on small garden plots. For obvious reasons, "legislative intent" was not a factor in interpreting the statute.

35. BVerfGE 10, 221, 226.

36. BVerwGE 59, 48 (1979).

37. Id.

38. Id. at pp. 55–56.

39. Id. at p. 51.

40. Id. at p. 50. According to the 1979 Court, the earlier opinion should not be read to mean that every violation of procedures invalidates an ordinance.

41. Greve (1987) p. 284; Nelkin and Pollak (1981) p. 177; Paterson (1989b) p. 75. Nelkin and Pollak argue that the group is too inclusive to be an effective environmental lobby. In a pamphlet, the Umweltbundesamt lists the organization as one with which it consults (Federal Environmental Agency, "Partners in Environmental Protection" [1988]). It is the only environmental organization mentioned.

42. The Council had seven members in 1992, down from twelve in earlier years.

43. For a comparison of the two economic advisory groups, see Wallich (1968).

44. For an overview of the Council's responsibilities, membership, and work product, see Rat von Sachverständigen für Umweltfragen (1992).

45. As examples of each category, see in the waste disposal field Rat von Sachverständigen für Umweltfragen (1991) (a 700-page study of waste disposal) and (1993) (a fifteen-page response to a particular draft law).

46. Schmölling (1986) pp. 77–85. The group's background study is Rat von Sachverständigen für Umweltfragen (1983).

47. Umweltbundesamt (1991), (1992a).

48. Umweltbundesamt (1991) table 2, p. 7. The table lists 416 professionals, of which 3 are economists and 15 are trained in political science. Umweltbundesamt (1992a) table 1, p. 6.

49. Umweltbundesamt (1991) pp. 44–47; Umweltbundesamt (1992a) pp. 13–15; Germany, Federal Ministry for the Environment (1991); and Schulz and Schulz (1991).

50. Umweltbundesamt (1992a) p. 33.

51. In all fields the number of advisory committees grew from 91 in 1962 to 358 in the mid-seventies. These committees included 5,600 scientists and other experts. The field of nuclear power has a particularly complex array of advisory groups; most important are the Nuclear Reactor Safety Commission, the Radiation Protection Commission, and the Nuclear Technology Committee. Brohm (1988) pp. 223–224; Steinberg (1994).

52. Grefen (1991) sect. 3.14. The legal status of norms set by these groups is a controversial issue in German law. A law that permits the technical norms to be read into the language of an existing statute has the advantage of flexibility. Such a "fill-in-the-blanks" law, however, can be criticized for delegating lawmaking authority to a private group. On the one hand, safety standards can be easily adapted to technical changes, and standard setting by those affected will produce outcomes that the regulated firms can live with. On the other hand, there is a risk that the process will become a political negotiation but with important interests, such as consumers, omitted from the process. The general problem is discussed in Denninger (1990) and in a symposium sponsored by the Deutsches Institut für Normung (1982). See especially the contribution by Marburger (for a brief discussion in English, see Brüggemeier and Falke [1991] pp. 6–12).

53. Denninger (1990), Führ (1993), Lamb (1993), Lübbe-Wolff (1991b). Such groups also influence standard-setting in the regulation of atomic power, chemicals, workplace health and safety, food, and consumer products. Brickman, Jasanoff, Ilgen (1985) p. 168; Kilimnik (1988) pp. 201–203.

54. Brüggemeier and Falke (1991) pp. 50–74, Führ (1993), and Lamb (1993) discuss the work of the DIN. As of 1990 the DIN had 20,988 standards on its books. Almost 4,000 committees of the DIN exist to set standards in a variety of fields [Grefen (1991) p. 15]. The DIN contract with the federal government, which dates from 1975, requires the DIN to take the public interest into account when setting standards. The document does not explain how to accomplish this (Gusy [1986] p. 245).

55. The VDI, founded in 1856, has 110,000 individual members. It established a Clean Air Committee in 1955. Grefen (1991) p. 2; Weale, O'Riordan and Kramme (1991) p. 44. Also important are the Verband Deutscher Elektrotechniker (VDE) and the Deutscher Verein des Gas- und Wasserfaches (DVGW), the Abwassertechnische

Vereinigung (ATV) and the Deutsche Verdingungsausschuß für Bauleistungen (DVA) (Lamb [1993] p. 97).

56. Grefen (1991); Kommission Reinhaltung der Luft im VDI und DIN (1991). Before this commission was established, the VDI had an official mandate from the federal Environmental Ministry "to establish guidelines and standards and to review proposals submitted by interested groups or the Environmental Ministry." Grefen (1991) p. 2.

57. See BVerwGE 77, 285 (1987) on the use of DIN and VDI norms in setting noise standards in *Technische Anleitung zum Schutz gegen Lärm*—TA Lärm.

58. Kilimnik (1988) pp. 212–213, n. 486 mentions one civil case in which the court refused to apply an eighteen-year-old and out-of-date soundproofing standard. The legal adviser of the DIN told Kilimnik in an interview that he was aware of only one other example of this sort.

59. Langbein (1985) pp. 835–841 defends the use of court-appointed experts in private law, but this defense has less force here. The official government lists of experts used by the courts are likely to include the same people called on by the DIN or the VDI to write the standards.

60. According to Grefen (1991) sect. 3, "In Germany many engineering rules, including especially VDI guidelines and DIN standards on air quality, are closely related to established national laws or administrative instructions. By being quoted in legally binding standards they have quasi-legal status. Since its foundation in 1957, the VDI Commission and since 1971 the DIN Standardization Committee have contributed decisively to the various versions of the Technical Instructions for Clean Air (TA Luft) of 1964, 1974 and 1983/86, the most important administrative instruction for air pollution abatement in the Federal Republic of Germany. They frequently refer to VDI guidelines and DIN standards directly or indirectly."

61. TA Luft, Nos. 2.6.2.7, 3.1.1, 3.1.10, 3.2.1, apps. F and G. Ossenbühl (1987) p. 41 counted 48 norms that incorporated VDI guidelines. This is, however, only a small proportion of the norms included in the TA Luft. Overall the VDI has issued over 200 technical guidelines on pollution control [Boehmer-Christiansen and Skea (1991) pp. 169–170].

   In the field of workplace safety and health, standards for carcinogens are set by the Committee for Dangerous Substances [Ausschuß für Gefahrstoffe], an advisory committee to the Ministry of Labor and Social Order. The Ministry publishes these standards without change. Tilmann (1987) p. 251. Tilmann criticizes the process for not permitting a hearing of those affected and for failing to weigh the interests sufficiently. According to him, the committee's work overemphasizes technical expertise (id. at pp. 266–267).

62. Ossenbühl (1988a) pp. 454–455.

63. Grefen (1991); Kommission Reinhaltung der Luft im VDI und DIN (1991).

64. Grefen (1991), Kommission Reinhaltung der Luft im VDI und DIN (1991). The committee on measurement technology has a task that is easiest to justify in terms familiar to the other work of the DIN. A standardized set of measurement techniques would greatly facilitate international comparisons of environmental quality and treatment efficacy.

65. The breakdown in 1991 for those who participated as voluntary members of the commission's committees was as follows: 50% from industry, 20% in teaching and research, 20% government officials, and 10% from technical scientific organizations or self-employed. Their fields of specialization were: 80% engineers, chemists, physicists, meteorologists, and mathematicians; 15% medical doctors, biologists, botanists, foresters, and agricultural experts; and 5% lawyers, economists, art historians, and other disciplines ("Juristen, Volkswirtschaftler, Kunsthistoriker und andere Disziplinen") (Kommission Reinhaltung der Luft im VDI und DIN, 1991, p. 2). The paid professional staff appears to consist entirely of engineers and scientists (id. p. 70).

66. In contrast, DIN consumer product standard committees include representatives of consumer groups. In 1974 a publicly financed body was set up under DIN to improve consumer representation. The five members of this Consumer Council are appointed by the head of the DIN in consultation with the Federal Minister for Economic Affairs and the Consumers' Working Group (*Arbeitsgemeinschaft der Verbraucher*). Most of the seven-member professional staff of the Council are engineers. Brüggemeier and Falke (1991) pp. 68–72.

67. Führ (1993); Gusy (1986); Lübbe-Wolff (1991b), pp. 227–231; Lamb (1993).

68. Führ (1993).

69. The new office is discussed in Führ (1993) pp. 101–102.

70. Führ (1993); Lamb (1993). Wagener (1988) p. 74 argues that in setting air pollution standards, the VDI is biased in favor of industry. Gusy (1986) discusses DIN standard-setting outside of the environmental area. He views standard-setting as a "political" process in which quality is traded off against cost. Steinberg (1994) notes that DIN Normenausschuß Kerntechnik, dealing with nuclear engineering, is composed only of representatives of manufacturers, power companies, and research bodies.

71. For a defense of the work of the VDI-DIN Commission, see Grefen (1991) and Kommission Reinhaltung der Luft im VDI und DIN (1991).

72. Ossenbühl (1987) p. 47 argues that when an outside commission is used to set standards, its members should be interdisciplinary, independent, and neutral. The process it uses should be transparent—e.g., it should use well-accepted methods of analysis—and the decision should be backed with reasons and should take all interests into account. Denninger (1990) pp. 130–147 argues that the constitutional "Democracy Principle" forbids the use of private organizations to set legally binding standards. Even if such groups are consulted, the basic responsibility for rules and guidelines lies with the government. Lübbe-Wolff (1991b) p. 234 argues that the processes used by the private groups should conform to democratic norms of openness and broad participation as a condition for giving their decisions legal legitimacy. See also Führ (1993) and Lamb (1993). The Administrative Conference of the United States has promulgated similar recommendations: 1 CFR (January 1, 1993 Edition) 93, §305.78–4, Federal Agency Interaction with Private Standard-Setting Organizations in Health and Safety Regulation (Recommendation No. 78–4).

73. Denninger (1990); Wagener (1988); Winter (1986) pp. 140–141; Wolf (1987).

74. See chapter 2 and Wolf (1987). The DIN views standard-setting and policy-making as equivalent. According to a representative of DIN, "to solve the pending problems in the field of environmental protection [created by the Internal Market in Europe] a still closer cooperation of all standardization organizations in Europe and around the world is necessary" (Grefen [1991]).

75. Brown and Johnson (1984) pp. 938–940.

76. The three groups are the Committee on Hazardous Substances in the Workplace, the Committee of the Deutsche Forschungsgemeinschaft (German Research Society), and the Beratergremium für unweltrelevante Altstoffe of the Society of German Chemists. Brickman, Jasanoff, and Ilgen (1985) pp. 162–167; Kilimnik (1988) pp. 203–204.

77. *Gefahrstoffverordnung*—GefstoffV §44. For workplace chemicals, however, the problem of representation is not as serious as in other environmental fields, because labor unions can represent the interests of those exposed.

78. Umweltbundesamt (1992a) p. 22. Draft substance reports are prepared by industry for submission to the committee. The Umweltbundesamt reviews reports for validity, plausibility, and completeness. In 1991 the committee prepared thirty reports; twenty were in progress. The committee is industry-financed and evaluates the existing state of the art (interview with Eckard Rehbinder, July 1993).

79. Steinberg (1994); Czada (1993) pp. 78–79. Nelkin and Pollak (1981) pp. 19–20, claim that 80% of the experts consulted in the mid-seventies were from science or industry. See Ossenbühl (1987) pp. 41–42.

80. Steinberg (1994).

81. Führ (1993). Steinberg (1994) makes this criticism of the committees in the nuclear power field.

82. Steinberg (1994) argues that the usual pattern of delegation does not apply in nuclear power. The conventional pattern is to have laws authorizing regulations that authorize administrative guidelines that authorize technical rules that are applied in individual cases. In contrast, the technical standards set by these committees essentially determine the content of the laws and regulations covering nuclear power.

83. Czada (1993) pp. 79–81 describes the industrial self-regulation organizations that implement nuclear safety policy. Czada argues that the German system is desirable because it provides insulation from party competition and extra-parliamentary protest. Further, state-level political pressures for a nuclear freeze have encouraged producers of nuclear power to emphasize safety (id. pp. 86–87).

84. Kitschelt (1986) pp. 62–64 describes the differences between the anti-nuclear movements in the United States, Germany, France, and Sweden. He argues that Germany has closed, and the United States has open, political input structures. German opponents of nuclear power have relied much more on mass protests than their American counterparts have, because Americans have greater access to the political, bureaucratic, and judicial processes. In both countries, however, construction delays for nuclear power plants increased dramatically as a result of public protests (id. p. 80).

85. Interviews with Rolf Giebler and Eberhard Bohne, February 1992; Jarass and

DiMento (1993) p. 55; Schmölling (1986) p. 84. Such committees are important in other areas of German law as well (Brickman, Jasanoff, and Ilgen [1985] p. 66; Leonardy [1991]).

86. Umweltbundesamt (1992a) pp. 46–47.

87. No rules guide the setting of wastewater guidelines under the Water Management Law (*Wasserhaushaltsgesetz*—WHG) §7a. Lübbe-Wolff (1991b) pp. 229–231. Environmental Ministry officials refused to respond to her requests for basic data about working groups and advisory bodies. Their response does not indicate an unwillingness to cooperate; rather, it suggests that this information was not routinely available to members of the public and opposition politicians.

88. BImSchG §51 defines the "parties concerned." Identical language is in the Waste Avoidance and Waste Management Act of 1986 (*Abfallgesetz*—AbfG) §16. The sections of the BImSchG requiring such a hearing are: §§4(1), 5(2), 7(1), 23(1), 26(2), 27(4), 29a(2), 32(1), 33(1), 34(1),(2), 35(1), 37, 38(2), 40(2), 43(1), 48, 53(1), 55(2), 58a(1).

89. *Chemikaliengesetz*—ChemG §17(1), AbfG §16. Under the Chemicals Act, the ministry is instructed to consult selected representatives of science, consumer protection groups, labor unions and industrial peak associations, affected industry, and public health groups, as well as representatives of environmental, animal protection, and nature protection organizations. ChemG §17(7).

90. GGO I §61. Brohm (1988) p. 222 writes, "In der Regel werden die Sachverständigen zur Dienstverschwiegenheit verpflichtet." Thus experts have the same duty of nondisclosure as public officials.

91. Brickman, Jasanoff, Ilgen (1985) p. 92; Greve (1987) p. 283. According to Greve, environmental groups have come to expect that they will be consulted on legislative and regulatory matters, and they complain vocally if excluded.

92. The BBU, established in 1972, is a peak association of citizens' initiatives in the environmental area. These groups formed around local issues, such as the location of nuclear power plants. The BUND, founded in 1970, is a more conventional interest group with individual members. Among its backers are owners of large forests (Boehmer-Christiansen and Skea [1991] pp. 85–86; Paterson [1989a] pp. 268–269).

93. Interviews with Eberhard Bohne and Eckart Meyer-Rutz, officials of the Environmental Ministry, February 1992. The Kohl government has followed the practice of refusing to place on the cabinet agenda issues that have not been resolved at the ministerial level. Thus the ministries with the most interest in a policy must negotiate over a draft regulation or law before it can be approved by the government. This practice can bottleneck controversial initiatives. According to Eckard Rehbinder (interview, July 1993) the law to implement the European Union directive on freedom of information about the environment had not come before the cabinet as of July 1993 because of the Transportation Ministry's failure to accept the Environmental Ministry's definition of "environmental information."

94. Ossenbühl (1988b) p. 419. A statement of reasons [Begründung] is necessary when Bundesrat approval is required, when the rule has financial effects on government budgets, or when the rule affects prices. These requirements, however, affect only

internal procedures. They are not directed toward informing those affected by the norm.

95. Maunz (1991) p. 9. Because many environmental guidelines are technical standards that affect the pollution control activities of private organizations, they must be publicly available to dischargers. According to Ossenbühl (1988a), all guidelines that set norms must be made public.

96. Breuer (1990) pp. 250–251; Winter (1985). According to Bohne (1990) p. 219, "since there are no public hearings and no public record on the bargaining results, agencies and industries considerably diminish the risks of coming under public scrutiny and suffering from negative publicity."

97. *Wasch- und Reinigungsmittelgesetz*—WRMG §9.

98. Bohne (1990) pp. 222–223.

99. Bundesanzeiger, Vol. 41, Nr. 40a, 3–10 (February 25, 1989).

100. Breuer (1990) pp. 250–251. This agreement is only one step away from the German tradition of industrial self-regulation, which was the chemical industry's preferred method of dealing with environmental harms (Paterson [1989b] p. 78). Paterson wonders whether the partial collapse of industrial self-regulation "will lead to a wider redefinition of the relationship between sectoral business interest associations and government in the Federal Republic." He doubts that such a change will occur (id. p. 89).

101. Interview with Eberhard Bohne, February 19, 1992.

102. Compare Breuer (1990) p. 251.

103. The Umweltbundesamt (1992) provided technical support to the Länder Committee on Immission Control and the Länder Working Party for Waste. The Umweltbundesamt participated in international efforts to set standards for noise by contracting with the DIN. A DIN noise standard is described as being worked out with the help of Umweltbundesamt staff (Umweltbundesamt [1992] pp. 33–40).

104. Denninger (1990), Mayntz and Scharpf (1975) pp. 135–142, Winter (1986) pp. 140–141.

105. BImSchG §3(1).

106. The description is taken from Schmölling (1986) pp. 73–77. As an example, he describes the process for cadmium. In 1975 the Umweltbundesamt was charged with the task of producing a criteria document. After consulting with scientists from seventeen different institutes, the agency in 1977 produced a document that recommended a minimum standard of 20 nanograms per cubic meter (ng/m^3) to protect the public health. An expert opinion from a medical institute in Düsseldorf supported this conclusion. In early 1978 the plan was made public and a hearing of experts held. The proposals ranged from 20 to 40 ng/m^3. In the context of the hearings it became clear that the benefits of the tougher standards could be better achieved by regulating cadmium in dustfall. Thus the final proposal was 40 ng/m^3 for suspended dust, 5 micrograms per square meter (μg/m^2) per day for dustfall, and half that amount of dustfall in farming areas where cadmium could endanger farm animals. The Bundesregierung adopted the basic standards for suspended particles and dustfall but reconsidered the tougher standard for farm areas. Because the evidence of "considerable" (*erheblich*) damage was not clear, the

government was able to exercise discretion. It selected the standard in the original recommendation, arguing that it could be waived in cases of hardship. Id. at pp. 76–77.

107. *Stand der Technik*, BImSchG §5(2).

108. Schmölling (1986) pp. 77–85. He reviews the process by which a sulfur dioxide standard was issued as part of the implementation of the regulation covering emissions from large plants (13.BImSchV). A wide range of technical possibilities existed for reducing emissions. In November 1983 the Council of Environmental Experts issued a tough proposal. The state of Baden-Württemberg also proposed standards for plants under its jurisdiction that set a basic standard effective immediately and secondary standards to be met by 1988. Old plants were given until 1990 to comply with the secondary standards. Six national firms pledged to meet this secondary standard for new investment. The Länder Committee for Immission Protection met in February 1984 and recommended relatively lax standards for old coal-fired plants, but with a short time limit. The committee report was not supported by all members. Because of the uncertainty introduced by these various proposals, a clear decision by the government was needed. The Conference of Environmental Ministers of the States and Federal Government came to a decision in April 1984. The basic regulation was not changed, but members of the conference set secondary standards, which were more stringent for larger plants independent of the fuel used. Old plants would have to meet the same standards as new plants but would be allowed more time to comply. Plants were given some discretion in deciding how to combine primary and secondary standards, but the degree of tradeoff depended on the type of plant.

109. Lübbe-Wolff (1991b) pp. 229–231.

FIVE   JUDICIAL REVIEW IN GERMANY

1. GG art. 19(4).

2. Review may be based on constitutional failings or on statutory violations. Neither here nor in the next chapter do I attempt a general treatment of judicial review of administrative actions. English-language overviews are provided by Schwarze (1992) pp. 114–127, 270–279, and Singh (1985) pp. 64–136. Instead, I focus on types of judicial review with implications for the federal policy-making process.

3. Rehbinder (1976b), Böhret (1983), Schäfer (1963) p. 170, Steinberg (1984) p. 358. Currie (1993) pp. 251–259 stresses the importance of judicial review in Germany, but his focus is on the protection of individual rights. Lorenz, a German professor of public law, draws a sharp distinction between law and administration. "The supervision of the judiciary over administrative agencies is restricted to . . . a review of decisions already made. This follows from the different goals of the judiciary and the agencies; the latter have as their task the creative and political shaping of various spheres of life. In this regard, the law provides the basis and defines the limits of the activity, but administrative actions do not serve to implement the *law as such*. Judicial control of the administrative agencies must refrain, as a matter of principle, from exerting a guiding influence on future administrative action; legal

protection in the realm of future administrative activities is therefore problematical" (footnotes omitted, italics added, Lorenz [1980] p. 576). Mayntz (1978) p. 205, however, claims that in regulating air pollution the courts were doing just what Lorenz opposes. Because state and federal control were weak during the period of her study, she found that lower-level governments used court decisions to provide guidelines for action. The court rulings interpreted vague terms in the law and helped shape administrative behavior.

4. GG art. 93(4a) permits individuals to bring complaints of unconstitutionality (*Verfassungsbeschwerden*).

5. The Constitutional Court can hear cases seeking a ruling on the compatibility of a state or federal law with the Grundgesetz. Such cases can be brought only by state or federal governments or by one-third of the members of the Bundestag. They can also involve the compatibility of Land law with federal law. GG art. 93(1)2. Concrete norm-control actions under GG art. 100(1) apply only to formal laws, not to regulations. Article 100 deals with intercourt referrals of constitutional questions. Ossenbühl (1988b) p. 423. The administrative courts can invalidate Länder regulations (*Rechtsvorschriften*) through Normenkontrolle actions brought by individuals who have been damaged or who expect to be damaged. VwGO §47. Ossenbühl (1988b) p. 422; Currie (1993) pp. 255–256.

One critic of German risk regulation proposes that organized groups be permitted to bring Normenkontrolle actions against the guidelines and standards in the environmental area. Courts would review the procedures of regulatory law. Wolf (1987) p. 391.

6. Schäfer (1963) p. 178. DIN standards have no formal legal validity and cannot be challenged in court except in the context of their application in a particular instance. Gusy (1986).

7. Winter (1987); Ossenbühl (1988a), (1988b). Greve (1989) argues that no such trend can be discerned.

8. Since both cases involve nuclear power—the substantive environmental area in which the direct oversight of the central government is strongest—their general applicability is somewhat doubtful. The Länder administer the Atomic Power Law as agents of the federal government (GG arts. 74a, 87c, *Atomgesetz*—AtG §24).

9. Kalkar case, BVerfGE 49, 89 (1978). The high administrative court of North Rhine-Westphalia referred this constitutional issue to the Court. The case was brought under GG art. 100(1) which requires courts to submit constitutional questions to the relevant federal or state constitutional court for decision.

10. The judiciary's insistence that certain risks are permitted only if regulated by legislation [*Vorbehalt des Gesetzes*] may be limited to nuclear power. The High Administrative Court for the State of Hesse attempted to apply the reasoning of Kalkar to a case of government inaction. (VGH Kassel, November 6, 1989, *Neue Juristische Wochenschrift* 43:336–339 [1990].) Finding that genetic engineering research had risks similar to those of nuclear power, the court refused to permit such research to continue without a regulatory statute. The decision was widely criticized by jurists, including the chief judge of the Federal Administrative Court. The commentary suggests a narrow reading of Kalkar in which *only* the risks of nuclear power *must* be

regulated by statute (Sendler [1990] p. 231; see also Hirsch [1990]; Rose [1990]; Vitzthum [1990]; the relevant article is GG art. 74 [11a]). Nuclear power has a special status in German law because of the post-war prohibition on developing nuclear power that was ended by a constitutional amendment in 1959 (Schmidt-Aßmann [1992] p. 50).

Before the higher administrative court had a chance to overturn the decision, the Bundestag passed a statute permitting research if the risk is tolerable relative to the goal (*Gentechnikgesetz*—GenTG). The statute became law on June 20, 1990, a little more than six months after the decision was announced. The Constitutional Court has not, however, ruled directly on the question of whether this portion of Kalkar applies only to nuclear power. I am grateful to Gerald Neuman for clarifying these points.

11. Translation by Kommers (1989) pp. 154–155. The Kalkar decision does not address the tension between clear rules and discretion in individual cases. One justification for permitting rulemaking activity in the executive branch is to reduce the discretion of lower-level officials in the interest of fair treatment of similar cases. Thus even within the individual rights framework, high-level, general rulemaking can be supported—not because it is flexible but because it is relatively inflexible. It is more flexible than legislation in that it can quickly respond to changed scientific conditions, but it is less flexible than case-by-case adjudication governed only by broad statutory language.

12. Greve (1989) p. 212 argues that the case also limited the ability of individuals to challenge administrative actions as inconsistent with statute. This, however, is a controversial interpretation not shared by German commentators (interview with Rudolf Steinberg, July 1993).

13. Mülheim-Kärlich case, BVerfGE 53, 30 (1979).

14. Translation by Kommers (1989) p. 149.

15. Sasbach case, BVerfGE 61, 82 (1982).

16. The regulation was the *Atomanlagen-Verordnung*—AtAnlV of October 29, 1970, issued under AtG §7. The relevant sections are AtAnlV §§2(2)(2) and 3(1).

17. BVerfGE 61, 82, 115 (my translation). The German reads: "Die Gerichte haben solche Feststellungen und Bewertungen nur auf ihre Rechtmäßigkeit hin zu überprüfen, nicht aber ihre eigenen Bewertungen an deren Stelle zu setzen" (citations omitted).

18. BVerfGE 61, 82, 115.

19. BVerfGE 83, 130, 149–154 (1990).

20. Denninger (1990) bases his argument on the Rechtsstaat principle included in GG art. 20.

21. Id., pp. 150–151.

22. Id., pp. 169–173. See also Ossenbühl (1987) p. 37.

23. Denninger (1990) pp. 178–180.

24. Steinberg (1994) pp. 94–98.

25. He bases his constitutional argument on GG art. 2(2), which states that "everyone shall have the right to life and to inviolability of his person. The liberty of the individual shall be inviolable. These rights may only be encroached upon pursuant to a law."

26. Maunz and Zippelius (1991) p. 95; Schwarze (1992) p. 688. The basic rights are listed in the first eighteen articles of the Grundgesetz. Article 19 sets out principles for restrictions on basic rights. Article 20 establishes that the Federal Republic is a democratic and social federal state (art. 20[1]) and that executive and judiciary are bound by law and justice (Gesetz und Recht, art. 20[3]).

27. Letter from Gerd Winter, July 1993; Currie (1989) pp. 353–354; and Schwarze (1992) pp. 686–688. The principle has been applied, for example, in a case involving suspended sentences for criminals that raised questions of individual liberty under GG article 2(2) (BVerfGE 19, 342, 348–349 [1965]). A more recent case grounded the principle in fundamental rights (*Wesen der Grundrechte selbst*) BVerfGE 65,1, 44 (1983)—Volkszählung (national census case).

28. Maunz (1991) p. 16; Schwarze (1992) p. 689. In an early case the Constitutional Court upheld a price control regulation but stated that in setting prices under the statute, public officials must satisfy the proportionality principle (BVerfGE 8, 274, 310 [1958]). See also BVerfGE 34, 52, 61 (1972). The principle was used by the Federal Administrative Court to uphold the regulation of pollution from power plants (*Verordnung über Großfeuerungsanlagen*—13.BImSchV), BVerwGE 69, 37, 44–45 (1984). According to Ossenbühl (1987) p. 38, the principle also applies to informal administrative measures, such as announcements dealing with product safety.

29. Chemical Weapons case, BVerfGE 77, 170 (1987). A dissent by Justice Mahrenholz (BVerfGE 77, 170, 235ff), citing Kalkar and Mülheim-Kärlich, would impose heavier affirmative duties on federal officials in cases of life-threatening risks.

30. Currie (1989), Currie (1994) pp. 306–310, and Schwarze (1992) pp. 684–692 emphasize the link to individual rights. For an example of the Constitutional Court's reasoning, see BVerfGE 7, 377, 407 (1958).

31. VGH Mannheim, NVwZ 1988, 168. The case is included in a German casebook on administrative law to illustrate the meaning of the proportionality principle (Richter and Schuppert [1991b] pp. 163–167).

32. GG art. 2(1).

33. Furthermore, since fish are curious (*neugierig*), they are bound to be attracted to diving activity. Thus a regulation requiring divers to avoid schools of fish was too intrusive. It would make fish observation (*Fischbeobachtung*) a fundamental element of the sport of diving.

34. *Kostendeckungsprinzip*, BVerfGE 34, 52, 61 (1972), BVerfGE 42, 191, 202–204 (1976). The former case was an unsuccessful challenge to a regulation setting fees for judicial exams. The latter case deals with the cost of ambulance services. Casting doubt on the exact meaning of the principle, the court states that the fees should "at least" (*zumindest*) cover costs. The principle is discussed by Zimmerman (1989), who argues that it derives from the proportionality principle. See also Currie (1994) chapter 2 p. 81 at notes 122–123.

35. BVerwGE 81, 12 (1988). The statute is the *Pflanzenschutzgesetz*—PflSchG.

36. " . . . die nach dem Stande der wissenschaftlichen Erkenntnisse nicht vertretbar sind," PflSchG §15(1)3.

37. Currie (1982) pp. 360, 370; Kloepfer (1989) pp. 416, 425–426, 432, 620, 629, 670, 721, 753.

38. Proportionality is mentioned in *Wasserhaushaltsgesetz*—WHG §30; *Abfallgesetz*—AbfG §§3,14; *Bundes-Immissionsschutzgesetz*—BImSchG §§17, 41.

39. The Federal Immission Control Act permits the state to issue subsequent orders to pollution sources that already have a license. Orders cannot be issued, however, if they lack proportionality. (BImSchG §17(2), Kloepfer [1989] p. 432.) The similar provision in the Waste Avoidance and Waste Management Act lacks this condition (AbfG §8[1]), but Kloepfer (1989) p. 721, argues that it should be implied.

40. Currie (1982) p. 360; Kloepfer (1989) p. 416.

41. Rehbinder (1988) pp. 132–133 identifies eleven possibilities and argues for a stronger interpretation than is common in German legal judgments. Weale, O'Riordan, and Kramme (1991) pp. 115–122 summarize Rehbinder's argument. The term originated in the introduction to the 1971 Environmental Program of the federal government (id. p. 115) and is included in most German environmental statutes (Rehbinder [1988] p. 130).

42. The regulation is 13.BImSchV.

43. BVerwGE 69, 37, 44–46 (1984).

44. BVerwGE 69, 37, 45. Rehbinder (1988) p. 135 criticizes this decision for imposing too great a limitation on the Vorsorge principle. He notes with approval the more protective standard for atomic power articulated by the Federal Administrative Court's Wyhl decision, BVerwGE 72, 300, 315 (1985).

45. BVerwGE 70, 365, 368–369 (Geesthacht-Krümmel [1985]).

46. Ossenbühl (1988b) pp. 418–419 criticizes the general failure to provide justifications for rules. He points to the example of the European Community, which requires such justifications. He argues that a statement of reasons would facilitate judicial control of the implementation of rules and would protect those affected by the rule. At present, when an official prepares a statement of reasons, it is used in the internal discussions over the rule but is not part of the public record.

47. GG art. 80. See chapter 4.

48. For some examples in the environmental area, see BVerwGE 69, 37 (1984), BVerwGE 70, 365 (Geesthacht-Krümmel [1985]), BVerwGE 72, 300 (Wyhl [1985]).

49. The legality of legal regulations also occasionally comes before the administrative courts through cases in which the plaintiff alleges that his or her "subjective" rights have been violated. The administrative courts then rule on the formal legality of the administrative regulation. For example, executive discretion was upheld in a case involving a legal ordinance limiting the number of places in dentistry in the universities of North Rhine-Westphalia. The Federal Administrative Court ruled that the executive branch was simply making concrete an abstract and general norm set by the legislature. The court contended that it could not legitimately control an essentially political process. It refused to substitute its judgment for that of the government. BVerwGE 70, 318, 331–332 (1984).

50. Ossenbühl (1988a) pp. 435–438, Richter and Schuppert (1991b) pp. 93–111.

51. Ossenbühl (1988a) pp. 453–454; BVerwGE 34, 278, 281–282 (1969)—Zurückstellung vom Wehrdienst (deferral of military service).

52. Ossenbühl (1988a) pp. 454–455.

53. Ossenbühl (1988a) p. 430–431, 436–438, 455–456. The air and noise standards are called *Technische Anleitung zur Reinhaltung der Luft*—TA Luft and *Technische Anleitung zum Schutz gegen Lärm*—TA Lärm. See Kloepfer (1989) pp. 712–713 on the legal authority for the issuance of guidelines under the Waste Management Act of 1986 (*Abfallgesetz*—AbfG). A *Technische Anleitung Sonderabfall* for hazardous waste has been promulgated (*Umwelt*, January 1993, pp. 33–34). A *Technische Anleitung Siedlungsabfälle*, which came into force on June 1, 1993, approved incineration as a method for disposing of household waste (Helga Keßler, "Ein Problem wird verfeuert: Der Bundesrat hat für die Müllverbrennung votiert," *Die Zeit*, February 26, 1993).

54. Brohm (1987) pp. 267, (1988) pp. 224–226; Ossenbühl (1988a) p. 455.

55. BVerwGE 55, 250 (Voerde, 1978). A case study providing background on the case can be found in Duerksen (1983) pp. 95–100. The case challenged the siting of a coal-fired power plant in the Ruhr region. The federal court overturned an appeals court ruling that compliance with federal guidelines was not sufficient. Had the lower court decision been upheld, proponents would have had to prove to *the court* that public health and welfare would not be harmed by construction of the plant.

56. *Antizipiertes Sachverständigengutachten.* The phrase was apparently coined by Breuer (1978).

57. Brohm (1988) pp. 224–226.

58. BVerwGE 72, 300–332 (Wyhl, 1985); BVerwGE 78, 177–184 (1987).

59. Scholarly commentary provides various glosses on this basic formulation. Kimminich (1989) pp. 79–80, without explicitly discussing guidelines, argues that judges have a role in assuring that technology is controlled by legal norms and ethical principles. He urges judges to maintain the values of a free, democratic state. To do this effectively in technical areas, he recommends that judges be willing to call on scientific disciplines other than law and write their opinions so that nonlawyers can read them. Ossenbühl (1988a) p. 456 argues that such guidelines are binding on judges but require less deference than laws or legal regulations. Papier (1989) p. 159 states that legal guidelines have no external legal authority to bind the relationship between citizens and the state. The mere use of the label "normkonkretisierende" guideline should not be sufficient to produce judicial deference. He approves judicial deference to such guidelines, however, so long as the statute has delegated authority to the executive to set general standards. He points to procedural requirements, such as Bundesrat approval and consultation with concerned parties, as adding to the case for judicial deference. Nevertheless, even when a guideline is otherwise acceptable, it must be possible to challenge it in court in individual cases (id. pp. 161–165).

60. The highest administrative court has not yet explicitly ruled on the applicability of this view of legal guidelines to other areas of environmental protection. In the regulation of air or water pollution or the control of hazardous chemicals, the level of risk or damage is equally difficult to express as a purely scientific standard, but the risks are not so catastrophic as with nuclear power.

61. According to Ossenbühl (1988a) pp. 458–459, legal controls on the process of producing guidelines are not common. A few statutes, such as the Air and Noise

Pollution Law, have hearing requirements, and those with external norm-setting effects must be made public. He mentions no legal challenges to the adequacy of procedures, however.

62. Some German commentators have recommended a more procedurally based juris-prudence. Thus Papier (1989) p. 162 argues that procedural requirements in statutes enhance the legitimacy of technical guidelines. He does not, however, advocate judicial review of the adequacy of these procedures. Ossenbühl (1987) p. 37 argues that a right to a hearing is implied by the Rechtsstaatsprinzip whenever the executive acts. For him, Article 80 of the Grundgesetz does not exhaust the constitutional constraints on the administration. Instead, he argues that the constitution requires transparent administrative procedures that permit outsiders to evaluate the process, the methods employed, and the grounds of the decision. Concentrating on environ-mental and technical regulations and guidelines, Denninger (1990) pp. 166–180 makes a similar constitutional argument for broad participation that includes public interest groups and for hearings that involve a review of the substance of proposals. Von Lersner (1990) pp. 195–196 proposes a legislative change that would require public notice of proposed standards, complete with a statement of reasons. Outsiders could then record objections, which in most cases would be addressed at a public hearing. For the special case of atomic power, where even Verwaltungsvorschriften are uncommon, Steinberg (1994) pp. 97–98 proposes a similar statutory reform to give safety guidelines legal force and a more open and accountable procedural basis.

63. Denninger (1990) argues that reforms of this type have a constitutional basis. See also von Lersner (1990); Ossenbühl (1987) p. 37; Papier (1989).

64. See, for example, the legislative proposals made by Steinberg (1994), pp. 97–100 for reform of the standard-setting process in the atomic power field. He criticizes a draft statute of the Bundesregierung for ignoring concerns about the democratic legit-imacy of the largely closed-door processes currently in use.

65. Lübbe-Wolff (1991b) pp. 244–246 also suggests such borrowing. She would look both to the Administrative Procedures Act and the Federal Advisory Committee Act.

SIX   GERMAN PLANNING AND LICENSING PROCESSES

1. *Verwaltungsverfahrensgesetz*—VwVfG §§72–78.
2. Rehbinder (1985) pp. 8–9, Steinberg (1992b).
3. *Verwaltungsgerichtsordnung*—VwGO §44a, VwVfG §§45, 46, *Baugesetzbuch*—BauGB §214 ff.
4. *Bundesnaturschutzgesetz*—BNatSchG §29.
5. See *Bundes-Immissionsschutzgesetz*—BImSchG §50, Currie (1982).
6. Steinberg (1990) pp. 298–300, Steinberg (1992b). Wahl (1982) pp. 53–56 views the planning process as an objective, multifaceted weighing of a project's benefits with other concerns, but argues that the process does not always fulfill his view of its purpose. In atomic power licensing processes, only the site proposed by the utility is evaluated. When projects are licensed under the Immission Control Law, com-patibility with regional plans is not required, and many states did not even have such plans in 1982 [id. pp. 60–62].

7. Compare von Lersner (1990) p. 197, who concludes that the legitimacy of environmental standards lies in the process used to produce them, not in the substantive result.

8. VwVfG §§72–78. The *Planfeststellungsverfahren* outlined here originated in town and country planning law. As used in planning law, it produced regulations with legal force and was not limited to individual projects. Letter from Winfried Brohm, June 7, 1993.

9. VwVfG §73(1).

10. "Dessen Belange durch das Vorhaben berührt werden," VwVfG §73(4).

11. VwVfG §73(4). The plan must be open for inspection for four weeks and "shall comprise the drawings and explanations which make clear the project, the reasons behind it and the land and fixed assets *(Grundstücke und Anlagen)* affected." (VwVfG §73[1]. A translation of the VwVfG is in Dale [1977] pp. 234–266).

12. VwVfG §73(9).

13. "[Z]um Wohl der Allgemeinheit oder zur Vermeidung nachteiliger Wirkungen auf Rechte" (VwVfG §74[2]). The planning authority can also require that compensation be paid to affected persons if it is impracticable to modify the project to avoid injury (VwVfG §75[2], see Steinberg [1992b]).

14. VwVfG §74(1) which refers to VwVfG §§69, 74(5).

15. BImSchG §10. The process is elaborated in *Verordnung über das Genehmigungsverfahren*—9.BImSchV. The major difference is not the process but the standard of decision. Under the BImSchG a license must be granted if legal requirements are met. Under a Planfeststellungsverfahren, this is a necessary but not a sufficient condition. In addition the authorities must find that the benefits outweigh the harms (Schmidt-Aßmann [1992] pp. 11–14).

16. Compare the Atomic Power Law *(Atomgesetz—*AtG §7[4]) with the BImSchG §§8, 10 (1–4, 6–8, 10 sent. 2 and 18). The procedures in AtG §7(4) are in addition to other procedures specified in AtG §7 and in *Atomrechtliche Verfahrensverordnung—*AtVfV (Nelkin and Pollak [1981] pp. 32–36). Under the BImSchG a firm is entitled to a license if it complies with the requirements of the law, but under the AtG the applicant has a claim only to an error-free exercise of discretion (Schmidt-Aßmann 1992, p. 15). The law regulating the use of genetic technology *(Gentechnikgesetz—*GenTG §18[1]) adopts BImSchG §10 for licensing firms using genetic technologies. In contrast, the Water Act does not specify the procedures to be used in granting a license except to require that persons and authorities be able to make formal objections and to note that environmental impact statements must be submitted when required by law *(Wasserhaushaltsgesetz—*WHG §9). The WHG also differs with respect to the legal presumptions on which it is based. Under the BImSchG §6 applicants are entitled to a license if they comply with the legal requirements, but no such presumption exists under WHG §§1a(3), 2, 7, 8. (Steinberg [1992b] p. 1506).

17. If the application includes trade or industrial secrets, these should be noted and submitted separately (BImSchG §10[1],[2]).

18. BImSchG §10(3), (4).

19. BImSchG §10(3).

20. "Die Genehmigungsbehörde [hat] die rechtzeitig gegen das Vorhaben erhobenen

Einwendungen mit dem Antragsteller und denjenigen, die Einwendungen erhoben haben, zu erörtern" (BImSchG §10[6]).

21. BImSchG §10(6),(10). The wording is practically identical to that in the Administrative Procedures Act (VwVfG §73[6]).

22. BImSchG §10(7).

23. Those who objected may be informed through a public notice if they number more than 300 (BImSchG §10[8]).

24. BImSchG §10(8).

25. BImSchG §11, AtG §7b.

26. See BVerwGE 70, 365, 372–376 (1985) (Geesthacht-Krümmel), BVerwGE 72, 300, 303–317 (1985) [Wyhl].

27. For a description of the process as of 1980 see Nelkin and Pollak (1981) pp. 32–36, who discuss these criticisms. Duerksen (1983) pp. 89–100 provides two case studies demonstrating the difficulties that can arise in Germany from consultation failures. See also Linse, Falter, Rucht, and Kretschmer (1988). Steinberg (1990) p. 311 argues that public participation often occurs too late in the process to be effective.

28. Case studies of the local implementation process for environmental statutes found that only in a few cases did hearings change the outcome proposed by the administration. The hearing of concerned individuals came too late in the process (Hucke, Müller, and Wassen [1980] pp. 211–212, 371–372).

29. Holznagel (1990) pp. 51–102 claims that for construction projects the developer and the administration have often exchanged and commented on each other's plans and reached a consensus before the Planfeststellungsverfahren under VwVfG §§72–78 begins. Hucke, Müller, and Wassen (1980) studied cases in the fields of water pollution, and sludge and waste disposal. They conclude that the major decisions were usually made before the public hearing began, although the hearing requirement may have influenced the proposed plan (id. pp. 211–212). Based on experience in the water pollution area, Lübbe-Wolff (1992) also argues that preliminary negotiations between the authorities and businesses seeking licenses have an important impact on the final outcome. According to her, one purpose of such negotiations is to reduce the risk of a negative outcome once the formal hearing process gets underway. Third-party participation rights are thus restricted. The law's complexity also restricts the public's ability to mount effective challenges. She suggests that an independent environmental lawyer be involved in the preliminary negotiations to guard against this possibility. The lawyer would need to not only know the law but also be familiar with the technical issues. The lawyer would also play a role in assuring that all substantial interests are included in the preliminary discussions. She believes that such a reform would be of more value than the environmental impact assessment process under the *Gesetz über die Umweltverträglichkeitsprüfung*—UVPG, which can only influence the formal hearing process.

30. WHG §§14, 31; BNatSchG §§8, 29. In the past, the approval of waste disposal sites could be carried out through either a licensing or a planning process (*Abfallgesetz*—AbfG §§7–8a). The law was amended in 1993 to restrict the use of planning procedures. The approval of waste disposal sites, such as incinerators, must now be made under the licensing rules of the BImSchG. This restricts the range of issues

open to decision by the public authorities and gives the licensing applicant a legal presumption in favor of obtaining the license. Only refuse disposal sites (*Mülldeponien*) remain under the Act's planning provisions. The new law is the *Investitionserleichterungs- und Wohnbaulandgesetz*; article 6 amends the AbfG §§7–8a.

31. Currie (1982), Wahl (1982) p. 62. Comprehensive policy-making is further hampered under the air pollution statute by the presumption in favor of granting a license that must be overcome by the state (BImSchG §6).

32. Wahl (1982), Richter and Schuppert 1991b, p. 288.

33. Holznagel (1990), Nelkin and Pollak (1981) pp. 32–36. For example, in the case of the Wyhl nuclear power plant, the "Land minister of economics, politically responsible for the procedure in Wyhl, was also the acting vice-chairman of the utility's board of directors" [(1981) p. 34].

34. For a series of case studies involving nuclear plants, see Linse, Falter, Rucht, and Kretschmer (1988). Nuclear protest activities in the seventies are discussed in Nelkin and Pollak (1981). According to Halfman (1989) p. 58, the major accomplishments of the anti-nuclear movement in the seventies were symbolic and cultural.

35. Rucht (1988b) pp. 149, 271, reports that 90,000 people submitted objections in the first round of proceedings in 1974 concerning the licensing of an atomic power plant at Wyhl in West Germany. In a second proceeding held in 1983, 44,000 people raised objections. Such a volume of objections was a new phenomenon in the mid-seventies. Seven people objected in 1969 to the first German atomic power plant in Biblis, and only four objected to the beginning of construction on Block B of the complex in 1971–72 (Rucht, pp. 268–269). The number of objectors to the Wackersdorf reprocessing plant in 1983 was 53,000; 55,000 objected to Block C of Biblis; 65,000 to a proposed atomic power plant at Breisach, and 82,000 to the expansion of the Stuttgart airport. Kretschmer (1988) pp. 194, 276–277.

36. According to Duerksen (1983) p. 101, environmental disputes in Europe are often more violent than in the United States. This is attributed by "knowledgeable observers" to the failure to include European citizens in the decision-making process, "negotiations between government and industry . . . carried out in private." Although the situation appears to have improved since the time of Duerksen's study, the only legal requirement of consultation is BNatSchG §29 (to be discussed later in this chapter). See also Kitschelt (1986).

    The marginal role of public interest organizations contrasts with the influential position of economic "interest associations." The industrial peak associations founded in the nineteenth century cover most of German industry, and most employers are members of some association. At the federal level, the industrial Verbände are represented at parliamentary committees. Committees must schedule hearings at which the Verbände can testify. Anheier (1990) pp. 326–327. Such hearings are not usually open to the public.

37. VwVfG §§17, 18. If such a group has no representative, the authority may appoint one (VwVfG §§17[4], 18[1]). Only individuals—not public interest organizations—can be representatives (VfVfG §§17[1], 18[1]).

38. Baumann (1982) p. 262 argues that a similar two-month time limit in filling court challenges disadvantages complainants who are not themselves experts.

39. A study of the implementation of the air pollution laws published in 1978 reported that most citizens initiatives were single-issue groups that disbanded after that issue was no longer on the public agenda (Mayntz et al. [1978] p. 307).

40. The umbrella organization, called the Bundesverband Bürgerinitiativen Umweltschutz (BBU), was founded in 1972. In 1989 it had three professional employees and a budget of DM 120,000. Two hundred groups were members, which was down from three hundred in 1985 (Rucht [1991] p. 354). These two hundred included some one thousand local initiatives. Anheier (1990) p. 319. At the high point of organization in 1981 there were fifteen hundred groups with five million members (Paterson [1989a] p. 270).

41. Sellers (1994) table 5.10, shows that 61% of those questioned in Freiburg thought that local administrators were essentially concerned with the public good, compared with 6% for citizens groups, 24% for environmental groups, and 22% for local elected officials (the corresponding numbers for New Haven, Connecticut, are 52%, 26%, 39%, and 32%). Some German respondents viewed participatory activity as selfish (id. p. 55).

42. Mayntz et al. (1978) p. 306. They also found that officials had a generally favorable view of the impact of such groups because they provided a counterweight to lobbies on the other side [(1978) pp. 308–313].

43. Ormond (1991) p. 79.

44. Mayntz et al. (1978) pp. 635–637. The percentage of governments reporting no active Bürgerinitiativen was much higher for water than for air, ranging from 31.6% to 83%, depending on the type of government. Citizens groups also were evaluated much more negatively by public officials.

45. BNatSchG §29. Ormond (1991) pp. 79–81 describes the provision, which applies only to the following types of activities: preparation of ordinances of nature conservation authorities; preparation of landscape programs and plans, in so far as they are binding on the individual (which they are not in most Länder); granting of exemptions from mandatory provisions protecting nature reserves or national parks; and planning procedures for public works if the project interferes with nature and landscape. According to Ormond, exemptions from national park regulations are uncommon. Such parks and reserves only cover 3% of the West German land area. "Administrative decisions affecting the far more extensive 'protected landscape areas' (*Landschaftsschutzgebiete*; about 26% of the total area) are made without any participation by environmental groups" (id. p. 80). The most important category is the last one, because such planning procedures involve most large projects, such as highways, railways, and airfields, and almost always interfere with nature.

46. BNatSchG §29(2),(4). See Gassner (1991) for a list of the recognized nature protection organizations at the federal level and in each of the Länder. In the western Länder the number of recognized organizations ranges from three to eight, with the exception of Bremen, where only a single, unified group is recognized. According to Ormond (1991) p. 80, in Hesse only eight of the fifty that applied were certified.

47. Some have expressed concern that nature protection groups might accept compensation for blunting their opposition to projects that damage nature. Hoffmann-Riem (1990) pp. 20–21 reports a case in which opponents of a coal-fired power plant

accepted compensation payments. The protests against these payments centered on the belief that the opponents had made public interest claims solely to further their private interests. In contrast, the same author mentions another case in which groups obtained "ecological compensation" in the form of a nature protection area supported by the state government. In return, the groups agreed not to mount a court challenge to a planned factory. Hoffmann-Riem judges this second arrangement acceptable because no private gains were involved ("die Absprache [war] moralisch nicht oder doch weniger 'anrüchig' ").

48. Except for appeals to the administrative courts (VwVfG §70), once the planning decision is made it is final, and no additional claims can be made to discard, modify, or shut down the project. The only exceptions are unforeseeable effects that harm individuals. These can be resolved by either plan modifications or monetary compensation (WHG §11, BImSchG §14). The law also contemplates the possibility that the project may need to be modified in midstream. If the modifications are important, a new planning process is required (VwVfG §76).

49. Boehmer-Christiansen and Skea (1991) p. 153.

50. Halfman (1989) p. 81. Rehbinder (1985), p. 24, states that nuclear power cases "have seldom been successful on the merits in the first instance and never in the second and third instances." For examples of how activists have used the courts, see Linse, Falter, Rucht, and Kretschmer (1988) and Nelkin and Pollak (1981). The main direct impact of legal challenges has been to impose delays (Nelkin and Pollak, pp. 74, 155–166, 206–209).

One response to the delay imposed by court review was a federal law giving the Länder administrative courts initial jurisdiction for certain large projects that could harm the environment. This cut out the lowest courts. Critics argued that the law was designed not only to speed the process but also to remove the litigation from the young activist judges on the lower courts. Rehbinder (1985) p. 6.

51. The Administrative Judiciary Statute, VwGO §42(2), states that "unless otherwise determined by law, suit is admissible only if the plaintiff claims to be violated in his rights by the administrative act or its denial or omission." It is not enough that the government's action is illegal. In addition, the plaintiff must have been actually injured in a subjective right (Jarass [1989] and Schmidt-Aßmann [1992] pp. 25–26). Baumann (1982) discusses the application of this doctrine to atomic law.

52. Böhret (1983) p. 42; Greve (1989); Ormond (1991), pp. 82–83; Rehbinder (1976), Rehbinder (1985); Steinberg (1984), Steinberg (1992a) pp. 63–69. Wagener (1988) argues for an expansive interpretation of standing doctrine in air pollution law. Even under the WHG, where the rights of neighbors are given no explicit procedural protection, the Federal Administrative Court upheld the right of a neighbor to bring suit. The Court put together several sections of the act to find that administrative procedures must give neighbors an opportunity to claim rights violations. This requirement then gave such neighbors standing in court (BVerwG, DVBl pp. 1265–1267, December 15, 1987). The case involved a water authority that gave an individual the right to open a gravel pit, with the understanding that it would eventually be filled with water. The "neighbor" was the public utility in charge of purifying drinking water for the community.

53. Steinberg (1984) pp. 355–356. The courts have defined the neighborhood of a nuclear power station to be a zone of about 30 km around the plant (Ormond [1991] p. 82). Baumann (1982) pp. 259–260 reviews the cases up to 1982. Bizer, Ormond, and Riedel (1990) p. 30, point to the example of the open sea, where no one resides. Standing to challenge sea dumping is allowed only to fishing enterprises whose catch will be harmed.

54. BVerwG, DVBl, February 15, 1983, 183–184, NJW 1983, 1507. In that case an individual who lives 45 km from a plant argued that he should be treated as a neighbor subject to "other hazards" under the BImSchG §5. If he were judged a neighbor, then he could claim a right to participate in the licensing hearing under BImSchG §10. The court held the action inadmissible but dismissed the case on its merits. The court admitted that procedural failures could produce violations of constitutional rights, but it judged the danger of an explosion on which the claim was based to be too small a risk to merit consideration. See also Jarass (1989) pp. 60–61. Notice that the lack of class actions could play a role here because the risk of an explosion was applied only to one person, not to the entire population subject to the risk.

55. Interview with Justice Berkemann, Federal Administrative Court. See BVerwGE 61, 256 (1980) [Stade] and BVerwG 70, 365 (1985). The plaintiff in the Stade case argued that the operator of a nuclear power plant was violating its legal duty to minimize radiation. The court denied standing. It argued that the risks faced by the individual plaintiff would not be significantly changed by a higher safety standard. Steinberg (1992a) p. 67 summarizes and criticizes the argument: "It is possible that the probability of developing cancer might be increased in the population as a whole. However, this change in the so-called 'population-risk' did not affect the individual risk. The individual risk could not be modified by a higher number of persons being exposed to the risk. This increase with respect to the population-risk only would be of concern to the interests of the general welfare but not to the interests of the individual. This reasoning excludes the most important group of environmental actions from litigation by concerned third parties, namely all preventive measures taken before situations of clear and present danger arise." Baumann (1982) p. 265 points out that in some cases the smaller the danger posed by an atomic power plant, the greater the possibility of a legal challenge. If a few people's rights are injured sufficiently, they may obtain standing in court. If millions of people are each injured a small amount, no one may be granted access.

56. BVerwGE 70, 365, 371 (1985). Schmidt-Aßmann (1992) p. 26 states that "der Rechtsschutz kein Popularrechtsschutz ist, sondern eine besondere Klagebefugnis voraussetzt." According to Jarass (1989) p. 61–62, as environmental law has moved toward emissions restrictions and away from nuisance law, third-party protection is becoming less important. This has reduced the possibility of third-party lawsuits. Because such suits are one of the few ways of overcoming implementation deficits, this desirable shift in policy will have the side effect of reducing the role of courts in assuring effective implementation (id. p. 63).

57. Badura (1989) p. 9–14.

58. Bizer, Ormond, and Riedel (1990) pp. 28–29.

59. Ormond (1991) p. 83.

60. The relevant sections of the German Law on Administrative Courts are VwGO §§154–164.

61. The Administrative Courts' list of the amount in controversy by type of case is found in "Streitwertkatalog für die Verwaltungsgerichtsbarkeit" (1992). The amount in controversy depends on the identity of the plaintiff. In waste disposal, nuclear power, and air pollution cases, if the enterprise seeking a license sues, the guidelines value the case at 2.5% of the investment. If a private person complains, the case is valued at the decrease in value of that person's property or in other situations at a flat DM 20,000 or DM 10,000. Greve (1987) p. 125, n. 29, mentions a 1980 case in which the courts set the value of a lawsuit brought by environmentalists at DM 100,000: "The plaintiffs lost; some of them were subsequently imprisoned to enforce payment. The court's action apparently had a deterrent effect; the number of lawsuits filed against nuclear reactors went down."

62. In some instances, the court requires that the plaintiff pay judicial costs in advance. If the plaintiff wins the lawsuit, the costs are refunded. If the plaintiff's probability of victory is judged to be low, the court can refuse a request for legal aid to cover these costs even if the individual is poor. In upholding the Bavarian High Administrative Court's use of this practice, the German Constitutional Court found that it did not violate constitutional principles of equality and the welfare state. According to the court: "These rules require a broad assimilation of the situation of those who possess means and those who do not in the sphere of judicial protection. This requirement is satisfied by the legislator when he makes the position of the poor person equal to that of the individual of means who would not reasonably pursue a similar action after taking the costs involved into consideration." BVerfGE 10, 264, 270–271 (1960).

63. Interview with Justice Schlichter, Federal Administrative Court.

64. Rehbinder (1985) p. 14; Koch (1986) pp. 75–76, interview with Justice Schlichter.

65. Rehbinder (1985) p. 16–17, Schmidt-Aßmann (1992) p. 27. Bizer, Ormond, and Riedel (1990) pp. 55–57 summarize the contrary arguments. The most fundamental objection is based on the GG art. 19(4) which states that "should any person's right be violated by public authority, recourse to the court shall be open to him." This is taken by some to be the exclusive justification for court review. This narrow view is criticized by Bizer, Ormond, and Riedel, who argue that Verbandsklage are constitional, id. pp. 84–89. In particular, article 20 supports the use of courts to supervise the administration, and Verbandsklage can be a route to such supervision.

66. Interview with Justice Berkemann. See also Greve (1989) p. 210, n. 67; Steinberg (1992a) p. 64. BVerwGE 72, 15–28 (1985), establishes that organizations can obtain standing through the purchase of a small piece of property in the neighborhood of the challenged project. This result was confirmed in a more recent case, BVerwG, NVwZ 1991, 781–782 (decided July 27, 1990). For a recent example of a case where an organization obtained standing by land purchase see BVerwGE 92, 263 (1993).

Steinberg (1992a) p. 64 notes the risks of this strategy. In the case against the permit for the Kalkar fast breeder reactor, the only plaintiff was bought out by the respondent. Ormond (1991) p. 83 mentions another possible difficulty. The Bavarian Administrative Court of Appeal refused to grant standing to an association on the ground that it had acquired the land to block a construction project rather than to profit from its use. Bayerischer Verwaltungsgerichtshof (VGH), *Neue Zeitschrift für Verwaltungsrecht* (NVwZ) 1989, p. 684.

67. Greve (1989) p. 215; Rehbinder (1976) p. 158. Recent attempts by the opposition Greens and Social Democrats have also failed. Bizer, Ormond, and Riedel (1990) p. 18; Ormond (1991) pp. 85–86.

68. The western Länder are Berlin, Bremen, Hamburg, Hesse, Lower Saxony, Saarland, and Schleswig-Holstein. The eastern Länder are Brandenburg, Saxony, Saxon-Anhalt, and Thüringen. Three are city-states with little nature to protect. Balzer (1989); Bizer, Ormond, and Riedel (1990); Greve (1989); Ormond (1991), pp. 83–91. The Brandenburg statute, which gives nature protection organizations access to court, was enacted in the spring of 1992. (*Brandenburgisches Naturschutzgesetz*—BbNatSchG). Sections 61–64 deal with the participation of nature protection groups in the administrative process; section 65 deals with their access to the courts. The most recent statute, passed by Lower Saxony in October 1993, is apparently the most far-reaching (Niedersächsisches Naturschutzgesetz §§60a–60c).

Ormond, id. at 86–87, counted sixty-five court cases between 1979, when the first statute was enacted in Bremen, to 1990. The laws in the eastern Länder and Schleswig-Holstein are too new to have any cases. Fifty cases occurred in Hesse, which had a large number of controversial building projects during the period. The fifty suits were 0.025% of the workload of the Hesse administrative courts. For the twenty suits that overcame the admissibility hurdle, the success rate was 50%, which compares with 15% for administrative litigation in general. Bizer, Ormond, and Riedel (1990) pp. 60–83. Ormond (1991) pp. 87–91, provides an English summary.

69. BVerwGE 78, 347; NVwZ 1988, 526. The decision overruled a decision of the Berlin Administrative Court of Appeal that found Berlin's provisions for suits by associations (*Verbandsklage*)] unconstitutional. Ormond (1991) p. 85.

70. BVerwG, NVwZ 1991 162–166 (decided October 31, 1990).

71. BVerwGE 92, 263–265 (decided April 29, 1993). The court held that permitting nature protection groups standing to challenge federal government decisions would violate German principles of federalism and violate VwGO §42(2), which requires that plaintiffs allege violations of their rights. The opinion, however, takes care to reaffirm the legality of Verbandsklage within a state and accepts their role as a method of "objective-legal" control over officials. Although in the case at hand this interpretation leads the justices to conclude that suits against federal officials are prohibited, it is an acknowledgment of the legal legitimacy of state statutes that use the courts to regulate administrative processes.

72. The case dealt with a challenge to a proposed rail route between Erfurt and Bebra. For a related case rejecting a challenge by the state of Hesse to the same railway see BVerwGE 92, 258–263 decided April 29, 1993. The court found that railroads were a federal responsibility and that Hesse's rights had not been injured. Thus the state had no standing to bring a suit under VwGO §42(2).

73. Ormond (1991) p. 91.

74. VwGO §44a, VwVfG §§44, 45, 45. Purely procedural challenges are not possible except for a few formal requirements that do not involve the adequacy of participa-

tion. Procedural violations must be shown to have affected the outcome (see also BauGB §§214–216).

75. See the discussion of the Sasbach case, BVerfGE 61, 82 in chapter 5. There the Constitutional Court upheld a restriction on judicial review in the name of improving the quality of the administrative process.

76. This paragraph is based on an interview with Justice Berkemann, Federal Administrative Court.

77. BVerwGE 34, 301, 303, 309 (1969). The decision makes somewhat more specific the requirements of VwVfG §§72–78 discussed above.

78. Steinberg (1993) pp. 166–168. The Administrative Procedures Act, VwVfG §46 states: "Folgen von Verfahrens- und Formfehlern. Die Aufhebung eines Verwaltungsaktes, der nicht nach §44 nichtig ist, kann nicht allein deshalb beansprucht werden, weil er unter Verletzung von Vorschriften über das Verfahren, die Form oder die örtliche Zuständigkeit zustande gekommen ist, wenn keine andere Entscheidung in der Sache hätte getroffen werden können." ["Consequences or Defects of Procedure and Form. Quashing of an administrative act, which is not void under §44, cannot be claimed on the ground that it has been taken in violation of the provisions on procedure, form or territorial competence, if no other decision could have been taken in the matter" (translation by Singh [1985] p. 171). Section 44 lists other reasons why an act may be void.

79. VwGO §113.

80. Greve (1989), Steinberg (1993) pp. 237–249, 347–351.

81. The most recent legal changes have focused on these management problems and may further undermine the democratic legitimacy of German administrative processes. Two recent laws restrict public participation and judicial review in a number of areas. The first is the *Verkehrswegeplanungsbeschleunigungsgesetz*, December 16, 1991, a law designed to expedite the siting of highway routes and other transportation projects in the new Länder; the second is the *Investitionserleichterungs- und Wohnbaulandgesetz*, April 22, 1993, a law dealing with the facilitation of capital investment and with the provision of land for residential building. Although the second law was motivated by the need to facilitate development in the east, it applies to the country as a whole. See Bullinger (1992); Klinski and Gaßner (1992); Rehbinder (1992b) pp. 241–242; Steinberg (1993) pp. 51–53, 300–303, 380–383; and Wagner (1992).

82. Von Lersner (1990) pp. 195–196.

83. Von Lersner (1990) p. 196 points to the language of AbfG §7(2) as a model.

84. See BImSchG §51 and AbfG §16.

SEVEN   GERMAN REFORM EFFORTS

1. Kloepfer et al. (1991), cited hereafter as UGB.

2. Interview with Eckard Rehbinder, July 1993.

3. UGB §§134–144. UGB §135 states that these sections of the code would have priority over VwVfG §29. See the further discussion of the new law on public access to information in chapter 8.

4. BNatSchG §29.

5. UGB §131(2).

6. See chapter 8 for a discussion of the Environmental Impact Assessment Process required under a European Union directive.

7. UGB §§132, 152, 159.

8. UGB §133.

9. Interview with Eckard Rehbinder, July 1993.

10. UGB §§153, 159.

11. UGB §§154, 160.

12. UGB §161.

13. UGB §162(1). Exceptions are permitted if no loss of environmental protection occurs.

14. UGB §162.

15. UBG, pp. 470–471. "Danach muß eine ausreichende staatliche Kontrolle über die Vereinbarkeit des Regelwerks mit den gesetzlichen Wertungen und die Objektivität und Neutralität der Normierung gewährleistet sein" (UGB:471). ("There must be sufficient state control over the compatibility of regulations with legal requirements to guarantee the objectivity and neutrality of the norm-setting process" [my translation].)

16. UGB §§77–81, 87–90.

17. UGB, p. 364.

18. For an excellent overview of the issue with Canadian examples, see Dewees (1992). See also Jost (1993).

19. Dewees found no tort suits against major air polluters in Canada between 1975 and 1985, a time when air pollution was falling. In the United States, environmental liability has had its greatest impact on hazardous waste sites and is unimportant for air and water pollution. Dewees's Canadian case studies confirm this pattern in Canada (Dewees [1992b] pp. 432–433).

Denmark permits individual citizens to sue, not for damages but to force environmental authorities to take action against polluters. The legal cases involved problems that citizens could notice, such as noise and smell. The more serious problems of water, soil, and air pollution were ignored. After environmental organizations were permitted as plaintiffs in 1982, a better balance of cases arose. Direct inspections by the authorities, initiated only in 1985, were required to strike a balance between large and small cases. Moe (1993) p. 159.

20. If the link between discharges and harms occurs in the present, a tax can act as an incentive to cut back harmful discharges. In contrast, there is no efficiency gain if current dischargers are taxed for risks created in the past. If the harms of pollution have a long latency period, using taxes as incentive devices may not be feasible. Firms can avoid future tax liability by going out of business. For a fuller discussion of the choice between direct regulation and tort law as regulatory systems, see Rose-Ackerman (1992a) and Shavell (1987) pp. 277–290.

21. The same is true of criminal law. Individual responsibility is difficult to establish, and the standards of proof are higher in criminal than in civil law. For a discussion of criminal enforcement in the United States and a critique of current efforts, see Cohen (1992).

22. *Umwelthaftungsgesetz*—UmweltHG, Nov. 7, 1990. Overviews and critiques in English are provided in Hoffman (1991), Hoffman (1992), and Taupitz (1993). The act drew some of its provisions from the Water Resources Act §22 (*Wasserhaushaltsgesetz*—WHG). The German High Court construed the law to imply causation if the source is "inherently suited" to have caused the harm. The WHG, however, permits liability for pure economic loss, which is excluded from the UmweltHG (Hoffman [1992]).

23. One observer claims that the law is "a synthesis of pre-existing civil damage remedies into a remedy of somewhat broader scope," which imposes somewhat higher levels of liability. Hoffman (1991) p. 28. For an economic analysis of the incentives created by the law, see Jost (1993).

24. UmweltHG §6; Hoffman (1991) pp. 35–36; Taupitz (1993).

25. Jost (1993) p. 626 argues that the enforcement problems of the law are similar to the limitations of a negligence system. Information about a company's level of care is valuable, and it may be in a firm's interest to provide misleading or false information.

26. UmweltHG §7; Hoffman (1991) p. 36; Taupitz (1993).

27. Hoffman (1991) p. 32 states that the statute contemplates joint and several liability, but Taupitz (1993) p. 30 thinks that the statute is unclear. The act excludes damage caused by force majeure, excludes property damage if it is insubstantial or "reasonable," and limits liability from a single effect to DM 320 million (DM 160 million for personal injury and DM 160 million for property damage) (id. pp. 32–33, UmweltHG §§4, 5, 15).

28. Hoffman (1991) pp. 33–34. The list is in an appendix to the act. It includes about 60% of the facilities subject to the Federal Immission Control Act (*Bundes-Immissionsschutzgesetz*—BImSchG).

29. Hoffman (1991) p. 34.

30. UmweltHG §§8, 9, 10; Hoffman (1991) p. 37. These information rights are especially noteworthy given Germany's generally weak public rights to information.

31. Taupitz (1993).

32. UmweltHG §23.

33. Paul Luiki and Dale Stephenson, "European Community Waste Policy: At the Brink of a New Era," Bureau of National Affairs, *International Environment Reporter, Current Report*, 10 (July 17, 1991):403.

34. Insurance is not required, however, until the Ministry of Justice promulgates a regulation stating insurance terms and this regulation is accepted by both houses of Parliament. Until the regulation is approved, facilities are subject to liability but are not required to purchase insurance (UmweltHG §§19, 20, and Appendix 2; Hoffman [1992]).

35. In 1991 the German Casualty Insurers' Association produced a model insurance contract covering environmental liability. In spite of negotiations designed to produce an agreement, the model policy has not been accepted by the Federation of German Industry or the German Insurance Protection Association. A revised draft that met some of their objections was issued in July 1992. The model policy is outlined in Hoffman (1992). The draft does not cover "normal operations" that produce expected levels of pollutants, it excludes harms that predate the policy period, and it requires that each risk and facility be specifically declared in the policy.

The law covers "gradual" pollution impacts, and the model policy also attempts to cover these, subject to limits.

36. Wilhelm Zeller, a board member of the Cologne Reinsurance Company, recommends that reinsurance policies for environmental liability be priced separately and written to limit overall exposure. His remarks are included in *Reinsurance,* Reuters Textline-NEXIS, September 9, 1992.

37. For a similar view, see Taupitz (1993). Ott and Schäfer (1994) propose that a new institution be created to amass information on environmental problems and to levy charges and make payments to insurance funds. Their proposal gives firms an incentive to clean up and to provide accurate information to the institution. Although the authors use the language of German private law to describe their plan, they have essentially proposed a public agency much like the American independent agencies that regulate railroads, communications, and the securities markets.

38. Breuer (1990). Brohm (1991a) and Hoffman-Riem (1990) consider a range of applications, including environmental issues.

39. An overview of thinking on this subject is contained in Hoffmann-Riem and Schmidt-Aßmann (1990). Breuer (1990) emphasizes the difficulties of any simple importation of American regulatory negotiation models to the German context. Brohm (1991a) draws on the American experience but proposes an application more closely tied to the bureaucracy. Rose-Ackerman (1994b) develops the arguments presented here in the United States context.

40. Steinberg (1990) pp. 304–305 argues that negotiated solutions are not suitable for rulings that affect indeterminate numbers of people. See also Breuer (1990); Hoffmann-Riem (1990) pp. 24–26; and Winter (1985).

41. The problem of such a two-step process, however, is assuring that important options are not eliminated by technocrats and public officials before citizens are given a right to participate in a public hearing (Holznagel [1991b] p. 98, Steinberg [1990] p. 311). Breuer (1990) p. 243 argues for the early informal participation of citizens in cases where industry is already being consulted.

42. In contrast, if each party is excessively pessimistic about its position if the negotiation fails, the chance of agreement is improved. Uncertainty about the reversion point among risk-averse participants will also further agreement.

43. See Hoffmann-Riem (1990) for a general discussion of regulatory negotiation in the German legal context.

    The use of a nongovernmental mediator represents a departure from previous German attempts to increase participation. As a compromise solution, Brohm (1991) recommends using public officials as mediators. He would distinguish between mediation officials and decision-making officials. Holznagel (1990) and (1991a) recommends using private mediators to assure fairness in the planning process. He recommends incorporating a mediated negotiating process into the Planfeststellungsverfahren for such projects as waste disposal facilities. He argues that such a change in practice is generally compatible with the German Administrative Procedures Act (*Verwaltungsverfahrensgesetz*—VwVfG), although he recommends some legal modifications to make mediated negotiation more effective (Holznagel 1991a).

44. For a fuller discussion of some of these issues see Holznagel (1990).

45. Negotiated Rulemaking Act, 5 U.S.C. §§561–570 (Supp IV 1992).
46. One recent application of the law, however, demonstrates its limits in scientifically complex fields. A negotiation over rules for disinfectants and disinfection by-products in drinking water was stymied by the lack of scientific data. The negotiators themselves recommended additional spending on research. *Environmental Reporter,* October 29, 1993, p. 1201.
47. Administrative Conference of the United States (1990), Perritt (1986).
48. According to Brohm (1991a) p. 1025 infrastructure projects such as highways, waterways, airports, and railways take between ten and twenty years to reach final approval. Recent legal changes have sought to deal with these problems not by finding an alternative form of public participation and judicial review but by streamlining procedures and restricting access to the courts (*Verkehrswegebeschleunigungsgesetz,* December 16, 1991; *Investitionserleichterungs- und Wohnbaulandgesetz,* April 22, 1993, see Steinberg [1994] pp. 51–53, 300–303, 380–383).
49. Holznagel (1991b) p. 97.
50. The legality of such procedures has been the subject of commentary. Kunig (1990) concludes that the Administrative Procedures Act and the Grundgesetz can be interpreted to permit such procedures. Informal procedures are permissible subject to judicially imposed limits requiring neutrality, equal treatment, and consideration of conflicts (id. p. 52). The procedures' legitimacy is grounded not in the people's votes (*Wahlvolk*) but in individuals' willingness to participate (*Handlungswillen*) (id. pp. 56–57). Regulatory negotiation is permitted, but only if the democratic Rechtsstaat does not abdicate its authority to "concerned parties." See also Breuer (1990) and Hoffmann-Riem (1990).
51. Holznagel (1991b) pp. 95–96.
52. "Neues aus Neuss" (1992) p. 25 lists examples.
53. Striegnitz (1990).
54. "Neues aus Neuss" (1992) p. 26.
55. "Neues aus Neuss" (1992).
56. Wiedemann, Femers, and Hennen (1991).
57. Wiedemann, Femers, and Hennen (1991) p. 83. Hoffmann-Riem (1990) p. 25 points out that the German administrative authorities have difficulty accepting the resistance of third parties as a legitimate expression of concern. Instead, opponents are often classified as "adversaries" (*Gegner*), and the goal is to break or overcome their resistance.
58. Wiedemann, Femers, and Hennen (1991) p. 82.
59. Id., p. 83.
60. Kilimnik (1988) reviews German occupational safety and health regulation. Many standards, especially those involving safety and accident prevention, are set through industry-wide insurance organizations of firms and labor unions (*Berufsgenossenschaften*) with authority to promulgate legally binding health and safety standards. The associations draw heavily on the work of private technical standard-setting organizations, such as the DIN. The state thus has essentially turned over some of its regulatory functions to the insurance associations, retaining only the right to include public officials in the group charged with drafting the regulations. The

federal government has not, however, relinquished all authority over workplace health and safety. The insurance associations have done little to regulate exposure levels for chemicals. The German Research Society has filled this gap, and a federal regulation on dangerous substances in the workplace now supersedes any regulations of the insurance associations (Kilimnik, pp. 170, 184–189, 195–196, 200). Federal statutes also cover particular types of workers, such as youth, pregnant women, mothers, and the disabled (Peacock [1984] pp. 69–70).

61. For a more general discussion of the problem of matching techniques and problems, see chapter 9.

EIGHT EXTERNAL CONTROL

1. The Treaty of Maastricht establishes the European Union (EU) to replace the European Communities (EC) as the new umbrella structure for the European Coal and Steel Community, the European Atomic Energy Community, and the European Community (the new name of the European Economic Community) (Treaty on European Union, art. A, supplement to *European Report*, No. 1746, February 22, 1991).

2. Haagsma (1989); and Rehbinder and Stewart (1985) pp. 15–42, 57–108.

3. Rehbinder and Stewart (1985) pp. 16–19; Sands (1991) pp. 2512–2513.

4. Before the treaty's adoption, the European Court of Justice had held in 1985 that protection of the environment was an EC objective (Case 240/83, *Procureur de la République v. Asso. de Défense des Brûleurs d'Huiles Usagées*, 1985 ECR 531; Krämer [1993] p. 112; Sands [1991] p. 2513).

5. In addition, in crafting policies the EC should take account of costs and benefits, base its policy on scientific and technical data, and consider both environmental conditions and the state of development of various regions. Subsection VI, §25 of the Single European Act which is art. 130R of the amended Treaty of Rome.

6. These new tasks are included in article 2 of the amended Treaty of Rome. Furthermore, article 3 of the amended treaty lists one of the EU's activities as creation of a "policy in the sphere of the environment" (art. 3[K]).

7. The principle is included in the amended Treaty of Rome, article 130R(2) which reads, "Community policy on the environment shall aim at a high level of protection, taking into account the diversity of situations in various regions of the Community. It shall be based on the precautionary principle and on the principles that preventive action should be taken, that environmental damage should be a priority to be rectified at source and that the polluter should pay. Environmental protection requirements must be integrated into the definition and implementation of other Community policies." It is not clear whether this statement is stronger or weaker than the existing language. The mention of the "precautionary principle" is new, but it is unclear what it means to "take into account the diversity of situations in various regions of the Community." For example, can a country that is in the minority when the Council adopts a policy challenge that policy in the ECJ on the ground that its special situation was not taken into account? For a discussion of the diverse meanings of the precautionary principle (*Vorsorge*), see Rehbinder (1988).

8. Treaty of Rome art. 130R(4), now repealed. This paragraph stated a variant of the principle of "subsidiarity" for environmental matters. Krämer (1993) p. 113; Simitis (1993) p. 11. The principle originated in nineteenth-century Catholic thinking about the relationship of church, state, and individual (Anheier [1992] pp. 32–37).

9. Paragraph 2 of the new article 3B of the Treaty of Rome reads: "In areas which do not fall within its exclusive competence, the Community shall take action, in accordance with the principle of subsidiarity, only if and in so far as the objectives of the proposed action cannot be sufficiently achieved by the Member States and can therefore, by reason of the scale or effects of the proposed action, be better achieved by the Community" (see Krämer [1993] pp. 112–115; Simitis [1993] pp. 10–13).

10. Leonard (1988) pp. 118, 140.

11. Rehbinder and Stewart (1985) pp. 61–69, 74–85.

12. Treaty of Rome, as amended, art. 100A. The Treaty of Maastricht amends this article to give Parliament a veto and increases its role in proposing amendments to Council legislation.

13. Even if the Council approves a piece of legislation unanimously, it must send the proposal to the Parliament for a second reading if the legislation is authorized under the section of the treaty that permits passage by a qualified majority. (Case 300/89, *Commission of the European Communities v. Council of the European Communities,* judgment of June 11, 1991.)

14. Treaty of Rome, art. 130S (§25 of the Single European Act), before modification by the Treaty of Maastricht, stated: "The Council acting unanimously on a proposal from the Commission and after consulting the European Parliament and the Economic and Social Committee, shall decide what action is to be taken by the Community. The Council shall, under the conditions laid down in the preceding subparagraph, define those matters on which decisions are to be taken by a qualified majority."

15. Sands (1991) pp. 2516–2517; Smith and Hunter (1992) pp. 10–14.

16. Johnson and Corcelle (1989) pp. 133–134.

17. The revised art. 130S, para. 1, states that "the Council, acting in accordance with the procedures referred to in art. 189C and after consulting the Economic and Social Committee, shall decide what action is to be taken by the Community in order to achieve the objectives referred to in art. 130R." Article 189C permits "qualified majority voting in the Council after it has obtained the opinion of the European Parliament. The Council's position and the Commission's, if it is different, are then communicated to the Parliament. The act will be adopted if the Parliament has not acted within three months or has approved the Council's position. In contrast, within three months the Parliament can by majority rule reject the Council's position or propose amendments. If the Parliament has rejected the Council's position, then the Council can enact it into law only with a unanimous vote. Otherwise the proposal is returned to the Commission, which reexamines it in the light of the Parliament's proposed amendments. The Commission forwards the reexamined proposal to the Council plus a compilation of parliamentary amendments that it rejected. If the Council accepts the Commission's new proposal by a qualified majority, the proposal will then become law. If the Council wishes to adopt any of the

rejected parliamentary amendments or propose new amendments of its own, it must act unanimously."

According to art. 130S, para. 3, "general action programs setting out priority objectives to be attained" are to be adopted by a somewhat different procedure, which is set out in article 189B. This procedure envisages that a joint Council-Parliamentary committee will be set up in the event of disagreements between the Council and the Parliament and also gives the Parliament veto power. This procedure also applies to legislation proposed by the Council under art. 100a.

18. The exceptions that require unanimity in the Council and do not require the complex process outlined in the preceding note are listed in art. 130S, para. 2. They are provisions primarily of a fiscal nature; measures concerning town and country planning, land use with the exception of waste management and measures of a general nature, and management of water resources; and measures significantly affecting a member state's choice between different energy sources and the general structure of its energy supply.

19. The system of qualified majority rule system is described in art. 148, para. 2 of the Treaty of Rome.

20. Treaty of Rome, art. 189. For a discussion of the different sorts of directives issued by the EU, see Rehbinder and Stewart (1985) pp. 34–42, 137–142. One recent exception to the use of directives in the environmental area is an EC regulation of 1988 implementing an international protocol on the protection of the ozone layer (Jachtenfuchs [1990] p. 269). Regulations are directly binding on member states (Treaty of Rome, art. 189).

21. Commission of the European Communities (December 31, 1991). See also Krämer (1991a).

22. Smith and Hunter (1992) pp. 9–11. According to Krämer (1991a) pp. 37–38, the Commission occasionally makes site visits or undertakes fact-finding missions. These are not, however, true inspections, and they are carried out only after informing the member state and the complainant. Krämer reports that the European Parliament has been asking for environmental inspectors for years and suggests that the European Environmental Agency be given an inspection role. So far the Parliament has failed to achieve this goal, although the Council regulation establishing the agency states that it will consider the question within two years. According to Krämer (id. at 38), "At the Community level, inspectors act at present in the areas of customs, fishery, competition and nuclear energy. Furthermore, Community veterinarians, together with Member States' veterinarians, visit slaughterhouses inside the EEC and in all other countries which import meat into the EEC, in order to check hygiene conditions. If Community inspectors can act in all of these sectors, there is no institutional argument against having EEC environmental inspectors. The opposition to this proposal thus seems to be rather ideological."

23. Rehbinder and Stewart (1985) p. 145; Smith and Hunter (1992) pp. 9–11. Commission of the European Communities (December 31, 1991) provides recent examples of noncompliance (paras. 57 and 78).

24. According to Führ (1992) p. 17, even this modest enforcement authority could be severely restricted. Invoking the "subsidiarity principle," Jacques Delors, former

president of the Commission, argues that member states should themselves check whether they meet the requirements of EU law.

25. The Commission had 17,687 employees in 1992. Of the 13,484 professional and technical employees, 2,234 (or 17%) provided translation services. Most of the rest focused on agriculture and trade policy. The entire EC budget in 1992 was ECU 63 billion, or about $86 billion. The budget is capped at 1.2% of the EU's GNP. In 1992 ECU 36 billion was budgeted for agricultural subsidies. Only 0.2%, or just over ECU 100 million, was budgeted for the environment, and this money was spent on special grant programs, not the enforcement of directives (European Communities, 1992). Commission efforts to raise the budget share to 1.37 per cent of the GNP of the EU have been opposed by the Council of Ministers.

26. "Memorandum Submitted by Ken Collins, Chairman, European Parliament Committee on Environment, Public Health and Consumer Protection," 1991. Collins reports that Directorate-General XI's legal unit contained nine officials, of which four are established EC officials and the rest are "either contracted or on secondment to the Commission" (id. p. 5). Commission of the European Communities (December 31, 1991) lists 51 directives enforced by the environmental directorate (Directorate XI). Other directives with environmental impact have been promulgated under art. 100A of the treaty, which deals with the establishment of the internal market. For example, the directives dealing with air pollution from vehicles come under this category [88/76/EEC and 88/77/EEC, both promulgated on December 3, 1987, 1987 *Official Journal of the European Communities* (OJ) (L 36) 1 and (L 36) 33]. One source notes that by the mid–eighties 150 directives with environmental impact were in force (Sands [1991] p. 2512). Enforcement authority for directives promulgated under article 100A is, however, located in another area of the Commission.

27. Krämer (1991a) pp. 134. Violation of an EU directive can be part of a case in a national court. National courts are instructed to refer doubtful questions of EU law to the ECJ. Individuals who have been directly harmed can challenge national laws and practices in their own courts as inconsistent with EU directives, but broad-based public-interest challenges do not appear to be possible (Rehbinder and Stewart [1985] pp. 144–149; Hartley [1988]; Krämer [1991b] pp. 135–137). Krämer notes, however, that "no preliminary ruling of the European Court of Justice appears to have been given in an environmental case that was initiated by an environmentalist or an environmental organisation" (id. p. 136).

28. Commission of the European Communities, December 31, 1991, para. 32. "Complaints [come] from individuals, non-governmental organizations, local authorities, embassies, and even Ministers of a Member State . . ." The Commission has no other regular source of information on the application of directives (id. para. 33).

29. Krämer (1991a) p. 33. The Commission has published a standard form to make it relatively easy to lodge complaints (id. p. 37). Krämer (id. p. 49) reports that "many complaints are introduced by local, regional, national or international environmental organisations. These organisations have specific means for selecting complaints and influencing the media in order to make the complaint procedure part of their campaign." Sands (1991) pp. 2521–2522 discusses the activities of organized environmental groups, such as Greenpeace, in Brussels.

30. Commission of the European Communities (December 31, 1991) Annex 2; Krämer (1991a) p. 31; and data supplied by Ludwig Krämer. The number of environmental complaints received by year is as follows: 1981:9, 1982:10, 1983:8, 1984:9, 1985:37, 1986:165, 1987:150, 1988:216, 1989:465, 1990:480, 1991:353. In addition, the following number of violations of environmental directives were detected by the Commission in recent years: 1984:2, 1985:10, 1986:32, 1987:38 1988:33, 1989:60, 1990: 42, 1991:113. The proportion of total complaints to the Commission that dealt with environmental matters increased from 2–3% in the early eighties to just under 40% in 1989 and 1990.

31. Commission of the European Communities (December 31, 1991) para. 99.

32. The enforcement process is governed by art. 169 of the Treaty of Rome, which was not changed by the Treaty of Maastricht.

33. "The letter of formal notice and reasoned opinion are not published. Occasionally the Commission publishes a press release on such cases as it considers important. The impact of these press releases is very great, particularly in the United Kingdom with its outstanding, highly sensitive journalism." Krämer (1991a) p. 46.

34. Environmental cases are a small proportion of the court's caseload. The largest number of disputes occur in areas where the EU can take direct action, such as tariffs, agricultural policy, and antitrust violations (Hartley [1988]). Of the 278 cases (including 145 judgments) decided in 1989 under the EEC treaty, 54 involved agriculture (42 judgments), 83 competition (9 judgments), and 61 the free movement of goods and persons (50 judgments). Only 6 environmental and consumer protection cases were decided (3 judgments) (European Communities, Court of Justice [1990] p. 33, table 4). Between 1980 and 1989, 39 judgments were handed down in cases dealing with the environment (Commission of the European Communities, December 31, 1991, Annex 4). This is 2% of the 1,780 judgments issued in those years (European Communities, Court of Justice, p. 38). The number can, however, be expected to increase as the Commission's more active enforcement efforts take hold. In 1990, 10 environmental cases were decided (OJ C 338, Annex 4). If this pattern holds, it would represent more than a doubling of the environmental cases decided. The increase, however, would still leave environmental cases well under 10% of total judgments.

35. The data were supplied by Ludwig Krämer. The data for 1982 to 1990 have been published in Commission of the European Communities (December 31, 1991) Annex 3, and the data from 1981 to 1990 data are in Krämer (1991a) p. 14.

36. Commission of the European Communities (December 31, 1991) Annex 3.

37. Krämer (1991a) pp. 33–34 points to the general difficulty of relying on complaints that may not represent the most serious or urgent cases. In 1990, the Commission received 56 complaints about Germany, but only 33 about Italy and 19 about Greece, although both Italy and Greece had weaker environmental records than Germany (id. p. 32).

38. Case C-345/89, *Ministere Public v. Stoeckel,* judgment of July 25, 1992, found that a labor law directive concerning equal treatment of male and female workers was sufficiently precise and unconditional to have direct effect. A directive has direct effect only if it is unconditional, is sufficiently precise, and defines rights that an

individual can assert against the member state (Hanft, 1991–1992, p. 1256; Wägenbaur, 1988).

39. Smith and Hunter (1992) pp. 7–9.

40. Joined cases C-6/90 and C-9/90, *Andrea Francovich and Danila Bonifaci v. Italy*, judgment of November 19, 1991. The conditions for liability are that the result to be achieved by the directive involved individual rights; that the subject matter of those rights could be identified by reference to the directive; and that a causal link existed between the infringement of the member state's obligation and the damage suffered. Damages are available to the same extent that compensation would be available under national law. See Hanft (1991–1992). Simitis (1993) p. 4, in an article on labor law, argues that as a result of this development in the law, EU directives and regulations now closely resemble each other.

41. For an example of the problems, see Ashworth and Papps's (1992) analysis of the EC mercury directive. They argue that, contrary to EC practice, directives should be couched "in specific terms with respect to desired impact (on both the environment and the industry) and allow the regulating agency to be responsible for the exact pattern of controls which will meet the objectives in each time period" (id. p. 90).

42. Smith and Hunter (1992) p. 15; Westbrook (1991); Council Regulation 90/1210/EEC of May 7, 1990 on the establishment of the European Environmental Agency and the European environmental information and observation network.

43. At a special summit on October 29, 1993, EU leaders assigned the locations of nine EU institutions, including the European Environmental Agency. The most important decision was the placement of the European Central Bank in Frankfurt. "With European Union's Arrival, Fears on Economy Cast a Shadow," *New York Times*, October 30, 1993.

44. Interview with Ludwig Krämer, March 1992.

45. 85/337/EEC, 1985 OJ (L 175) 44. Annexes to the directive list one group of projects for which assessments are required and another group that can be made subject to assessment at the discretion of member states. The member state can choose to include projects in the second group in the required group or can decide on a case-by-case basis whether an assessment is warranted. Annex I, the required list, includes crude oil refineries; coal gasification or liquefaction plants; thermal and nuclear power stations; installations for the disposal of radioactive, toxic, or dangerous wastes; iron and steel works; asbestos plants; chemical installations; ports and inland waterways; and the construction of motorways, long-distance railways, and airports. The German statute is *Gesetz über die Umweltverträglichkeitsprüfung—* UVPG, February 12, 1990. It requires an environmental impact process for most of the projects in the second list (Rehbinder [1992a] p. 6).

46. 85/337/EEC, 1985 OJ (L 175) 44, art. 5.

47. Id., arts. 6.1 and 6.2. Member states have discretion to define "the public concerned" and to determine the manner in which the public is informed and consulted (art. 6.3).

48. Id., art. 9. The directive is similar in many ways to the American National Environmental Policy Act (NEPA) of 1969, which requires environmental impact assessments. The major differences are the directive's annex, which lists specific types of

projects for which the process is required, and the lack of written environmental impact statements. The directive merely mandates that a process should be followed (Bono 1991).

49. UVPG, appendix to §3, and §9.

50. Soell and Dirnberger (1990), Steinberg (1990) pp. 310–311. In 1992 the regulation governing the licensing process under the Immission Control Act was amended to incorporate the environmental impact assessment process. The regulation gives no explicit participation rights to environmental associations (*Grundsätze des Genehmigungsverfahrens*—9.BImSchV, *Bundesgesetzblatt*, 1992, Teil 1, 1002–1010; see Rehbinder [1992b]).

51. This document may, however, be available to the public under the law on public access to information about the environment. Letter from Gerd Winter, July 1993.

52. See Soell and Dirnberger (1990) and the Öko-Institut working paper by Sander, Führ, and Fendler (1990). These weaknesses, however, do not violate the language of the directive, which does not address the quality of the assessments or the use to which they are put. The European Commission, speaking in general with no particular reference to Germany, notes: "In all but the really extreme cases, the Commission refrains from taking action on the quality of impact studies and the resultant assessment, since the Directive is neutral on this point. Consequently, even where the procedure laid down by the Directive is formally complied with, impact studies are often of a mediocre quality and almost always underestimate the harm to the environment. Furthermore, the opinions expressed by the individuals at public inquiries are not validly taken into consideration by the authorities. The impact assessment thus often turns out to be a formal procedure intended to justify the implementation of a project which has been decided on in advance on the basis of economic and technical criteria" (Commission of the European Communities, December 31, 1991, para. 89).

53. Soell and Dirnberger (1990), p. 705.

54. 85/337/EEC, 1985 OJ (L 175) 44, art. 6.2.

55. UVPG §10. This provision is permitted under the directive that allows member states to restrict the right to information on the basis of administrative and legal limitations "with regard to industrial and commercial secrecy and the safeguarding of the public interest" [art. 10].

56. The member state itself can define this category (85/337/EEC, art. 6[2], [3]).

57. Bizer, Ormond, and Riedel (1990) pp. 19–20, 95–96.

58. "Straßenrechtliche Planfeststellung nach dem Verkehrswegeplanungsbeschleunigungsgesetz," BVerwG decision of October 30, 1992, *Umwelt- und Planungsrecht* 13:62–65. The court held that a suit challenging the adequacy of the environmental impact process could succeed only if the final outcome could have been affected ("wenn die sachliche planerische Entscheidung in rechtserheblicher Weise davon beeinflußt sein kann"). The plaintiff was a nature protection group, and the court found it doubtful (*zweifelhaft*) that such a third party had a legal stake in the relevant portion of the statute (UVPG §11 Satz 1). The court also questioned the group's standing to challenge the fact that not all environmental reports were available

during the hearing process (a violation of UVPG §9). See also Rehbinder (1992a) pp. 7–8, Steinberg (1993) p. 301.

The German law cannot be implemented in specific areas of law unless regulations are promulgated. In the summer of 1992 Germany revised the legal regulation implementing the licensing portion of the Clean Air Act in the light of the European Community directive (9.BImSchV as amended by *Bundesgesetzblatt,* 1992, Teil 1, 1002–1010). Several groups—among them the BBU, the Bund für Umwelt- und Naturschutz-BUND, the DNR and the Öko-Institut—supported a broad revision that would permit them to participate in the licensing process [Sander, Führ, Fendler (1990)]. The BUND and the Öko-Institut also filed an informal infringement complaint with the EC Commission [Rehbinder, 1992a, p. 5]. The regulation that was eventually adopted did not go as far as these groups wanted.

59. 90/313/EEC, 1990 OJ (L 158) 56–58.

60. Id., art. 3.2 permits member states to refuse a request for information where it affects governmental, commercial, or personal confidentiality, public security, or issues under investigation. Material voluntarily supplied by a third party may be exempt from disclosure, as well as "material, the disclosure of which would make it more likely that the environment to which such material related would be damaged." Art. 3.3 permits a request to be refused "where it would involve the supplying of unfinished documents or data or internal communications, or where the request is manifestly unreasonable or formulated in too general a manner."

61. *Verwaltungsverfahrensgesetz*—VwVfG §§29(1) and 29(2) state: "(1) The authority shall allow participants to inspect the documents connected with the proceedings where knowledge of their contents is necessary in order to enforce or defend their legal interests . . . (2) The Authority shall not be obliged to allow documents to be inspected where this would impair the authority's regular fulfillment of its tasks, knowledge of the contents of the documents would be to the disadvantage of the country as a whole or of one of the Länder or where proceedings have to be kept secret under a law or by their very nature, i.e. in the rightful interests of participants or of third parties."

62. Umweltinformationsgesetz—UIG, July 8, 1994 (Bundesgesetzblatt, I, pp. 1490–1492).

63. In addition to the UIG, I also examined a July 13, 1992, ministry draft prepared after these consultations. Bundesminister für Umwelt, Naturschutz und Reaktorsicherheit, *Z II 5–41005/1,* "Referentenentwurf, Gesetz zur Umsetzung der Richtlinie des Rates vom 7. Juni 1990 über die Umwelt (90/313/EWG)—Umweltinformationsgesetz (UIG), July 13, 1992" (hereinafter cited as Referentenentwurf, UIG). The draft, which is similar to the actual UIG, also included a *Begründung,* explaining the meaning of and justification for the proposed law. Page numbers in subsequent notes refer to the Begründung.

64. Referentenentwurf, UIG, pp. 12–14.

65. Id. pp. 16–17.

66. UIG §§7, 8. Following art. 6 of the European Union directive, the German law covers information held by private individuals or bodies with public law responsibilities (UIG §2[2]). The 1992 explanatory document mentions private waste dis-

posal organizations as an example (Referentenentwurf, UIG, p. 30). A more interesting question is whether the files of the DIN-VDI Commission on air pollution control would be included given their contractual relation with the federal government.

67. UIG §9(2) gives the federal and state governments authority to promulgate regulations specifying the law's jurisdiction. The statute defines environmental information only in general terms, UIG §3(2). UIG §8 requires the authorities to consult with (*anzuhören*) those affected by the release of information if their rights as individuals or corporate entities might be violated. Information is not to be released if it invades the privacy of individuals, is contrary to the laws of intellectual property, or would involve the release of trade or industrial secrets.

68. 90/313/EEC, art. 4.

69. UIG §4(1). The Administrative Courts must, however, determine the content of this right given the exceptions and procedural constraints imposed by the law.

70. Sands (1990) pp. 690–691. Röscheisen (1992) p. 1: "Die Möglichkeit der demokratischen Kontrolle in einer unübersichtlichen, technologisch orientierten Gesellschaft und die Notwendigkeit einer effektiven und umfassenden Umweltpolitik setzen die Öffentlichkeit sämtlicher Informationen über die Umwelt voraus."

71. Art. 21(4) of the Constitution of the State of Brandenburg, as adopted by plebiscite on June 14, 1992, to enter into force on August 21, reads: "Jeder hat das Recht auf Einsicht in Akten und sonstige amtliche Unterlagen der Behörden und Verwaltungseinrichtungen des Landes und der Kommunen, soweit nicht überwiegende öffentliche oder private Interessen entgegenstehen." See also Verfassung des Freistaates Sachsen, May 27, 1992, art. 34; and Verfassung des Landes Sachsen-Anhalt, July 16, 1992, art. 6. The State of Hesse, basing its recommendations on a proposal of Spiros Simitis, has proposed that the Commission for the Reform of the Constitution include an art. 5(2a) stating: "Jeder Mensch hat das Recht auf Zugang zu den Daten der vollziehenden Gewalt ohne den Nachweis eines Interesses. Einschränkungen dieses Rechts dürfen nur durch Gesetz oder aufgrund eines Gesetzes erfolgen, wenn öffentliche Geheimhaltungsinteressen dies zwingend gebieten oder die Geheimhaltungsinteressen Dritter überwiegen." The proposed clause is justified as a way to improve the transparency of the state administration.

72. Sands (1990) p. 698.

73. GG art. 75. In a report published in 1991 on the application of EC law, the Commission notes that water management is in the hands of the Länder, "which have in the past taken little heed of Directives such as 78/659/EEC (waters supporting fish life), 79/923/EEC (shellfish waters) and 80/68/EEC (groundwater)." Two ECJ cases decided in 1991 found that Germany had failed to implement both the groundwater and the surface water directives properly. The cases are Case 131/88, *Commission v. Germany*, judgment of February 28, 1991, and Case 58/89, *Commission v. Germany*, judgment of October 17, 1991.

In the area of nature protection the Commission finds that "some Länder are lagging seriously behind in designating special protection areas for the conservation of wild birds. [Even] . . . designated habitats continue to be threatened by construction work, contamination and day-to-day activities" (Commission of the European Communities [December 31, 1991] para. 42).

74. Case C-361/88, *Commission v. Germany*, judgment of May 30, 1991; Case C-59/89, *Commission v. Germany*, judgment of May 30, 1991.

75. The drinking-water directives are 75/440/EEC and 79/869/EEC. The case is C-58/89, *Commission v. Germany*, judgment of October 17, 1991. The wild-bird directive is 79/409/EEC, dealt with in Case C-288/88, *Commission v. Germany*, 1990 ECR I-2721.

76. Another case concerning groundwater was also a defeat for Germany. In that case, Germany argued that the combination of existing substantive and procedural statutes was sufficient to implement the directive without any need to amend its laws. The court found that none of Germany's arguments could be supported (Case C-131/88, *Commission v. Germany*, 1991 ECR I-825).

77. Germany amended the Grundgesetz in response to the Treaty of Maastricht. A new article 23(1), promulgated in December 1992, endorses German participation in a European Union that "is committed to democratic, social, and federal principles, to the rule of law, and to the principle of subsidiarity and that guarantees the protection of basic rights essentially comparable to that of this Basic Law." See Currie (1994) pp. 73–74 for a discussion. Later sections of article 23 provide an explicit role for the Bundesrat and the states in interactions with the European Union (art. 23[2], [4], [5], [6]).

78. See Brewin and McAllister (1990) pp. 455, 480. Commission of the European Communities (December 31, 1991) paras. 14–33 outlines Commission enforcement efforts and points out that, in spite of an interest in applying national provisions that implement directives, the Commission can do little more than respond to complaints.

79. Rehbinder and Stewart (1985) pp. 144–149.

80. Case C-57/89, *Commission v. Germany*, judgment of February 28, 1991. The Commission wanted a declaration from the court that the building of a dike in a protected area was contrary to Directive 79/409/EEC on the conservation of wild birds. The court, in contrast, found that the dike itself had offsetting ecological benefits.

81. National courts can also refer issues to the European Court of Justice for preliminary rulings. Of the 336 cases brought in 1988 under the EEC Treaty, 138 were for a preliminary ruling. None concerned the environment. Ninety-six involved agriculture or the free movement of goods and persons (European Communities, Court of Justice, 1990, table 3, p. 35). It is possible, however, that some of the free-movement cases had environmental aspects, because a member state will sometimes defend a trade restriction as justified on environmental grounds. See also Krämer (1991b) pp. 135–137.

82. Commission of the European Communities (December 31, 1991) paras. 21–23, 40. The Commission believes that limit values for pollutants included in directives should also be included in national legislation that implements these directives (para. 23). In paragraph 21 the report also paraphrases Case 145/82, *Commission v. Italy*, 1983 ECR 711 at p. 718 to the effect that if rights or obligations are conferred on individuals, "an internal circular which can at any time be altered at the whim of the national authorities would not incorporate a directive correctly. This also applies where a circular is not published or, having been published, may be amended by another cir-

a circular is not published or, having been published, may be amended by another circular which is not published, so that the public cannot determine what law is applicable." See Wägenbaur (1988) pp. 316–317, who supports the view that technical guidelines such as TA Luft are not appropriate methods of implementing guidelines.

83. Case C-131/88, *Commission v. Germany*, 1991 ECR I-825. The case concerned the implementation of Council Directive 80/68/EEC of December 17, 1979, on the protection of groundwater against pollution caused by certain dangerous substances.

84. German lawyers referred to an earlier case which held that "the transposition of a directive into domestic law does not necessarily require that its provisions be incorporated formally and verbatim in express, specific legislation." C-131/88, I-867, referring to Case 363/85, *Commission v. Italy*, 1987 ECR 1733.

85. C-131/88, I-868.

86. Id., I-878.

87. Id., I-880–I-881.

88. Id., I-879.

89. For a critique of the European Court of Justice's opinion in this case by a German lawyer, see Lübbe-Wolff (1991a). She echoes my concerns about the excessive formalism of ECJ jurisprudence [id. at 152–153], and claims that administrative guidelines have binding force for public officials [id. at 134]. In fact, she argues that in practice such guidelines are often more important than statutes and legal ordinances [id. at 153].

90. Case C-361/88, *Commission v. Germany*, judgment of May 30, 1991. The case deals with the implementation of Council Directive 80/779/EEC.

91. Case C-59/89, *Commission v. Germany*, judgment of May 30, 1991. The case deals with the implementation of Council Directive 82/884/EEC.

92. The court does object to the fact that the planning process is contained in an act, the BImSchG, which does not cover all sources of air pollution (C-361/88, para. 18, C-59/89, para. 17).

93. TA Luft No. 2.5.1.

94. C-361/88, para.14.

95. In German law, administrative guidelines cannot be challenged except when they have been applied in a particular case. Yet in defending the use of guidelines before the ECJ, Germany contends that such guidelines "supplement the binding legal rules in the technical field, so that they form part of the rules and legislation concerned." Case 208/85, *Commission v. Germany*, 1987 ECR 4045, 4050. The German lawyers argued that infringement of the 'Technical Rules' constituted "an infringement of the legislation which requires those rules to be observed" (id. at 4064). The ECJ rejected the claim. The case involved the packaging and labeling of waste.

96. Lübbe-Wolff (1991a) p. 153.

97. Interview Ludwig Krämer, March 1992.

NINE   ENVIRONMENTAL LAW AND ADMINISTRATIVE PROCESS

1. Compare *Daubert v. Merrell Dow Pharmaceuticals*, 113 S.Ct. 2786 (1993) at 2795–2797, which makes some "general observations" about the admissibility of scientific

evidence into trials. The Court argues that judges should ask if the theory has been empirically tested and subjected to peer review. They should consider the margin of error in the results and whether the result is "generally acceptable."

2. Compare the similar sentiment in Daubert at 2798, which contrasts the quest for truth in the courtroom with that in the laboratory. The Federal Rules of Evidence are "designed not for the exhaustive search for cosmic understanding but for the particularized resolution of legal disputes."

3. The exceptions concern cases where citizens believe that costs should be imposed on one group. For example, if voters believe that firms should end up with lower profits when occupational health and safety are controlled, a labor-management negotiation that sets the status quo as a benchmark would be politically unacceptable.

4. See chapter 7 for a discussion of the preconditions for regulatory negotiation.

5. Stewart (1975).

6. Such hybrids, however, raise their own problems. The incentives to negotiate are changed when the outcome is an input to the second stage. The objectivity of information presented at the first-stage hearing may be influenced by its use as an input in a subsequent consensual process.

7. See chapter 4 for a discussion of the complex range of institutions, including advisory committees set up by the government and private standard-setting bodies.

8. See the U.S. Administrative Conference's similar recommendation in the American context, 1 CFR chap. 3 (January 1, 1993 ed.) §305.78, "Federal agency interaction with private standard-setting organizations in health and safety regulation."

9. See chapter 4.

10. APA §553 (see chapter 1 for a brief description).

11. APA §706(2). Some statutes permit review under a substantial evidence test (see chapter 1).

12. Edley (1990), Mashaw (1994), Melnick (1983).

13. Compare Ossenbühl (1988b) pp. 414–415, 418–419.

14. See, for example, Holznagel (1991a), pp. 106–113, and Lübbe-Wolff (1992).

15. The courts have, however, given a narrow interpretation to the "policy statement" category. *Community Nutrition Institute v. Young,* 818 F.2d 943 (D.C. Cir. 1987); *State of Alaska v. U.S. Department of Transportation,* 868 F.2d 441 (D.C. Cir. 1989).

16. The Environmental Protection Agency issues technical guidelines that appear analogous to German guidelines. It also uses circulars to communicate enforcement standards to regional offices, state agencies, and pollution sources. Anthony (1992); Elliott (1992); McGarity (1992); Strauss (1992b).

17. Anthony (1992).

18. Elliott (1992); Strauss (1992b).

19. *McLouth Steel Products Co. v. Thomas,* 838 F.2d 1317, 1325 (D.C. Cir. 1988). Elliott (1992) p. 1491 claims that "the agency's failure to justify *de novo* its action casts no doubt on the validity of the nonbinding, generic policy."

20. Chapter 8 discusses the UIG, the new law implementing the EU's Freedom of Information on the Environment directive.

21. Compare Lübbe-Wolff (1991b).

22. Sellers (1994) Chapter 5, pp. 62–63 notes the strong link between the Green party

and citizen initiatives in Freiburg. He raises the important issue of funding. The Green party established an *Ökofund* (Ecological Fund), which contributed to at least one local citizen initiative in Freiburg. The fund is financed by public money granted to the party. See also Kitschelt (1989).

23. "Streitwertkatalog für die Verwaltungsgerichtsbarkeit" (1992).

24. See chapter 1. The Öko-Institut recommends one-sided fee shifting as part of its proposed EU directive on "Access to Justice." The draft directive provides legal standing in environmental matters for environmental associations. The fee-shifting provisions are in article 8. Martin Führ, Betty Gebers, Thomas Ormond, and Gerhard Roller, "Access to Justice: Legal Standing for Environmental Associations in the European Community," *Environmental Law Network International Newsletter* 1/94, pp. 3–9.

25. In other words, the plaintiffs' lawyers would be paid by the defendant government in the event of a victory, but the plaintiffs would pay neither their own lawyers nor the government's counsel if they lost. The contingent nature of the plaintiffs' lawyers' reward would discourage frivolous suits.

26. Rose-Ackerman (1992b) pp. 33–42. In the American context my proposal is consistent with a recent decision of the U.S. Court of Appeals for the District of Columbia (*International Union, UAW v. OSHA*, 938 F. 2d 1310, 1318–1321 [1991]). If upheld or extended to other statutory provisions, the decision provides a way for American courts to police congressional-bureaucratic relations in the aftermath of Supreme Court decisions requiring judicial deference to clear statutory language and to agency interpretations of the law. *Chevron, U.S.A. Inc. v. Natural Resources Defense Council, Inc.*, 467 U.S. 837 (1984).

27. See chapter 5.

28. *Verwaltungsgerichtsordnung*—VwGO §§35–37, Singh (1985) p. 110.

29. A system of effluent charges for water pollution does exist. The state began to collect charges in 1981 (Salzwedel and Preusker [1982] pp. 98–100). It is not a true market system, however, because the authorities also issue licenses to individual dischargers telling them what they can emit. See Rehbinder (1993) pp. 72–74 and chapter 2.

30. Treaty of Rome as amended, art. 130R, para. 2.

31. See also Rehbinder (1993). The 1991 Annual Report of the European Commission reports on the conclusions reached by an EC-sponsored expert group that examined the scope for the greater use of economic and fiscal instruments in environmental policy: "Three conclusions emerge from its report, namely that the use of economic incentives and market mechanisms to attain environmental policy objectives is consistent with the philosophy underlying the internal market; there is a need at European level to develop economic and fiscal instruments which can contribute to environmental protection; and it is particularly important to take environmental considerations into account in the harmonization of indirect taxation. This report also showed that, in the long run, the introduction of environmental levies and taxes could generate considerable resources at [the] national level." The report goes on to state that the Council has "expressed the wish that such instruments should be introduced in support of the current rules." (Commission of the European Communities [1991], p. 215, para. 501).

32. Exhaust from motor vehicles and diesel engines is controlled under directives 88/76/EEC, December 3, 1987, OJ L 36/1; 88/436/EEC, June 16, 1988, 1988 OJ L 214; 89/458/EEC, July 18, 1989, 1989 OJ L 226; 89/491/EEC, July 17, 1989, 1989 OJ L 238; and 91/542/EEC, October 1, 1991, 1991 OJ L 295 (amending 88/77/EEC, December 3, 1987, OJ L 36/33). These directives were adopted under article 100A of the treaty on establishing the internal market. The process that led to the adoption of the 1987 directives and the role of the Single European Act in permitting the measures to pass by a qualified majority are described in Johnson and Corcelle (1989) pp. 124–136.

    Early enforcement activity in the environmental area was based on the fear that the member state environmental statutes would have protectionist effects. For example, the Commission mounted a legal challenge against Germany's compulsory deposit scheme for bottles (Brewin and McAllister, p. 480). See also Rehbinder and Stewart (1985).

33. Interview with Carlo Ripa di Meana, *Der Spiegel*, July 15, 1992.

34. The arguments in this section are also presented in Rose-Ackerman (1994a).

35. Kagan (1992), Mashaw (1994).

36. According to Werham (1992) pp. 586–587, judges believed that "hybrid" procedures requiring judicialized procedures like testimony and cross-examination in rulemaking were best suited for resolving factual disputes.

37. O'Leary (1989) pp. 551–552 provides a list through the mid-1980s.

38. On the EPA, see especially O'Leary (1989).

39. Both sides of the debate are canvassed in O'Leary (1989). She concluded that the overall impact has been mixed. The problem is a result of the nature of the judicial process, the overreaching of a few judges, and the unrealistic way Congress has drafted statutes that the courts must interpret.

40. See the critique of several Clean Air Act cases in Melnick (1983).

41. This view is in contrast to administrative proceedings involving the granting or denial of such individual benefits as welfare or social security. There the preservation of individual rights has been a concern of the courts in the face of pressures for the inexpensive processing of massive numbers of applicants and appeals.

42. Strauss (1992a), for example, shows how the highway-siting decision at issue in *Citizens to Preserve Overton Park v. Volpe*, 401 U.S. 402 (1971), was the result of a political balancing of interests at the local level. According to him, judicial review was unnecessary to assure democratic legitimacy; the court should have deferred to the political resolution.

43. Scalia (1981); Strauss (1989); Strauss (1992b).

44. Mendeloff (1979); Mendeloff (1988). In a recent case the EPA picked up Mendeloff's language and argued that time pressure led it to both underregulate and overregulate. *Shell Oil Co. v. E.P.A.* 950 F.2d 741 (D.C. Cir. (1991).

45. 54 Fed. Reg. 2332–2983 (January 19, 1989).

46. *AFL-CIO v. Occupational Safety and Health Administration*, 965 F.2d. 962 (11th Cir. 1992).

47. Mashaw and Harfst (1990); Scanlon and Rogowsky (1984).

48. Pierce (1991). Pierce argues that part of the problem is the increased number of

federal judges. A decision remanded to the agency may be reviewed by a new judicial panel with a different view of the law.

49. Anthony (1992).

50. *Lujan v. National Wildlife Federation,* 497 U.S. 871 (1990); *Lujan v. Defenders of Wildlife,* 112 S.Ct. 2130 (1992). See also *Air Courier Corp. v. American Postal Workers Union,* 111 S.Ct. 913 (1991), which denies standing to postal workers seeking to challenge U.S. Postal Service policy.

51. 497 U.S. 871.

52. Id. at 886–889.

53. Id. at 891.

54. See id. at 913 (Justice Blackmun dissenting).

55. 112 S.Ct. 2130 (1992).

56. Id. at 2137–2140.

57. Id. at 2140–2142.

58. Id. at 2142–2143.

59. Id. at 2142, n. 7.

60. Id. at 2145. Sunstein (1992) argues that the opinion, though wrongly decided, holds all citizen suit provisions unconstitutional. Sunstein's view is an overly strong reading of the holding, given the concurrence which states: "Congress has the power to define injuries and articulate chains of causation that will give rise to a case or controversy when none existed before, and I do not read the Court's opinion to suggest a contrary view." (Id. at 2146–2147 [concurring opinion of Justice Kennedy, joined by Justice Souter]).

61. 112 S.Ct. 2130, 2158.

62. Id. at 2160.

63. GG arts. 80, 84, 85.

64. See chapter 5.

65. Rose-Ackerman (1992b) pp. 33–42.

66. Rose-Ackerman (1992b) pp. 43–62 argues for this type of review.

67. GG art. 93 (1)2: "The Federal Constitutional Court shall decide: . . . in case of differences of opinion or doubts on the formal and material compatibility of federal law or Land law with this Basic Law, or on the compatibility of Land law with other federal law, at the request of the Federal Government, of a Land Government, or of one third of the Bundestag members." See also Bundesverfassungsgerichtsgesetz— BVerfGG §§76–79.

68. Linde (1988) claims that state judges are more involved in policy than federal judges are. He reports that justices in at least twelve states can give advisory opinions in some situations to the legislative and executive branches. The states are Alabama, Colorado, Delaware, Florida, Louisiana, Maine, Massachusetts, Michigan, New Hampshire, North Carolina, Rhode Island, and South Dakota (id. p. 118).

69. Giving informal advice to the President and Congress is a long-standing practice; Marcus and Van Tassel (1988) pp. 43–50. See generally Katzman, ed. (1988). The federal judiciary has been remarkably reticent on some major issues, even those which clearly affect it, such as the creation of the United States Sentencing Commission (Stith and Koh 1993).

70. Marcus and Van Tassel (1988) pp. 41–42 argue that advisory opinions are not prohibited by the text of the Constitution. The doctrine originated in a letter from the Supreme Court justices to George Washington in 1793 in which they refused to issue an advisory opinion on a foreign policy matter, arguing that they could not be officially required to render such a service.

REFERENCES

Aberbach, Joel D., *Keeping a Watchful Eye: The Politics of Congressional Oversight*, Washington, D.C.: Brookings Institution, 1990.

Ackerman, Bruce, and William Hassler, *Clean Coal/Dirty Air*, New Haven: Yale University Press, 1981.

Administrative Conference of the United States, "Agency Experience with Negotiated Rulemaking," *Negotiated Rulemaking Sourcebook*, Washington, D.C.: GPO, 1990, pp. 327–343.

Allen, Christopher S., "Political Consequences of Change: The Chemical Industry," in Peter Katzenstein, ed., *Industry and Politics in West Germany: Toward the Third Republic*, Ithaca: Cornell University Press, 1989, pp. 157–184.

Anheier, Helmut, "An Elaborate Network: Profiling the Third Sector in Germany," in B. Gidron, R. Kramer and L. M. Salamon, eds., *Government and the Nonprofit Sector: Emerging Relationships in Welfare States*, San Francisco: Jossey-Bass, 1992, pp. 31–56.

——, "A Profile of the Third Sector in West Germany," in H. Anheier and W. Seibel, eds., *The Third Sector: Comparative Studies of Nonprofit Organizations*, Berlin: Walter de Gruyter, 1990, pp. 313–332.

Anthony, Robert A., "Interpretive Rules, Policy Statements, Guidances, Manuals, and the Like—Should Federal Agencies Use Them to Bind the Public?" *Duke Law Journal* 41:1311–1384 (1992).

Aronson, Adam L., "From 'Cooperator's Loss' to Cooperative Gain: Negotiating a Greenhouse Gas Abatement," *Yale Law Journal* 102:2143–2174 (1993).

Ashe, A. Marice, "The Low-Level Radioactive Waste Policy Act and the Tenth Amendment: A 'Paragon of Legislative Success' or a Failure of Accountability," *Ecology Law Quarterly* 20: 267–312 (1993).

Ashworth, John, and Ivy Papps, "Should Environmental Legislation Set the Rules Constraining Polluters? Defining the Ends and Assessing the Means of Environmental Policy: An Examination of the EC Mercury Directive," *International Review of Law and Economics* 12:79–93 (1992).

Badaracco, Joseph L., Jr., *Loading the Dice: A Five-Country Study of Vinyl Chloride Regulation*, Boston: Harvard Business School, 1985.

Badura, Peter, "Schutz Dritter durch Nebenbestimmungen einer Planfeststellung oder

Genehmigung," in Herbert Leßmann, Bernhard Großfeld, and Lothar Vollmer, eds., *Festschrift für Rudolf Lukes zum 65. Geburtstag,* Cologne: Carl Heymanns, 1989, pp. 3–23.

Balzer, Susanne, "Rechtliche Ausgestaltung und Rechtswirklichkeit der Verbandsklage von Naturschutzverbänden in der Bundesrepublik Deutschland," *Natur und Landschaft* 64:26–28 (1989).

Barrett, Scott, "The Problem of Global Environmental Protection," in Dieter Helm, ed., *Economic Policy Towards the Environment,* Oxford: Blackwell, 1991, pp. 137–155.

Bartik, Timothy, "The Effects of Environmental Regulation on Business Location in the United States," *Growth and Change* 19:22–44 (1988).

Bauer, Rudolph, Sebastian Klinke, and Stefan Pabst, *Meeting People's Needs in Germany,* 2d edition, Bremen: University of Bremen, Institute for Local Social Policy and Nonprofit Organizations, 1992.

Baumann, Wolfgang, "Betroffensein durch Großvorhaben—Überlegungen zum Rechtsschutz im Atomrecht," *Bayerische Verwaltungsblätter* 28:257–266 (1982).

Bennett, Graham, and Konrad von Moltke, "Integrated Permitting in the Netherlands and the Federal Republic of Germany," in Nigel Haigh and Frances Irwin, eds., *Integrated Pollution Control in Europe and North America,* Washington, D.C.: Conservation Foundation, 1990, pp. 105–146.

Bizer, Johann, Thomas Ormond, and Ulrike Riedel, *Die Verbandsklage im Naturschutzrecht,* Taunusstein: Eberhard Blottner, 1990.

Blair, Philip, "Federalism, Legalism and Political Reality: The Record of the Federal Constitutional Court," in Charlie Jeffery and Peter Savigear, eds., *German Federalism Today,* Leicester: Leicester University Press, 1991, pp. 63–83.

Blankenburg, Erhard, "The Waning of Legality in the Concept of Policy Implementation," *Law and Policy* 7:481–491 (1985).

Boehmer-Christiansen, Sonja, "Anglo-German Contrasts in Environmental Policy-Making and Their Impacts in the Case of Acid Rain Abatement," *International Environmental Affairs* 4:295–322 (1992).

Boehmer-Christiansen, Sonja, and Jim Skea, *Acid Politics: Environmental and Energy Policies in Britain and Germany,* London and New York: Belhaven, 1991.

Bohne, Eberhard, *Politics and Markets in Environmental Protection: Reforming Air Pollution Regulation in the United States of America and the Federal Republic of Germany,* Report to the German Marshall Fund of the United States, Washington, D.C., (draft) 1987.

——, "Recent Trends in Informal Environmental Conflict Resolution," in Wolfgang Hoffmann-Riem and Eberhard Schmidt-Aßmann, eds., *Konfliktbewältigung durch Verhandlungen,* vol. 1, Baden-Baden: Nomos, 1990, pp. 217–230.

Böhret, Carl, "Public Administration in a Democracy," in Klaus König, Hans Joachim von Örtzen, and Frido Wagener, *Public Administration in the Federal Republic of Germany,* Antwerp: Kluwer-Deventer, 1983, pp. 33–47.

Bono, Louis L., "The Implementation of the EC Directive on Environmental Impact Assessments with the English Planning System: A Refinement of the NEPA Process," *Pace Environmental Law Review* 9:155–186 (1991).

Bosso, Christopher J., *Pesticides and Politics: The Life Cycle of a Public Issue*, Pittsburgh: University of Pittsburgh Press, 1987.

Breton, Albert, "A Theory of Government Grants," *Canadian Journal of Economics and Political Science* 31:175–87 (1965).

Breuer, Rüdiger, "Die rechtliche Bedeutung der Verwaltungsvorschriften nach Art. 48 BImSchG im Genehmigungsverfahren," *Deutsches Verwaltungsblatt* 93:28–37 (1978).

——, "Verhandlungslösungen aus der Sicht des deutschen Umweltschutzrechts," in Wolfgang Hoffmann-Riem and Eberhard Schmidt-Aßmann, eds., *Konfliktbewältigung durch Verhandlungen*, vol. 1, Baden-Baden: Nomos, 1990, pp. 231–252.

Brewin, Christopher, and Richard McAllister, "Annual Review of the Activities of the European Community in 1989," *Journal of Common Market Studies* 28:451–496 (1990).

Brickman, Ronald, Sheila Jasanoff, and Thomas Ilgen, *Controlling Chemicals: The Politics of Regulation in Europe and the United States*, Ithaca: Cornell University Press, 1985.

Brohm, Winfried, "Alternativen zum einseitigen hoheitlichen Verwaltungshandeln," in Wolfgang Hoffmann-Riem and Eberhard Schmidt-Aßmann, eds., *Konfliktbewältigung durch Verhandlungen*, volume I, Baden-Baden: Nomos, 1990a, pp. 253–258.

——, "Beschleunigung der Verwaltungsverfahren—Straffung oder konsensuales Verwaltungshandeln? *Neue Zeitschrift für Verwaltungsrecht* 10:1025–1033 (1991a).

——, "Planungs- und Entwicklungsverwaltung am Beispiel der Stadt- und Raumplanung," in Manfred Löwisch, Dieter Grimm, and Gerhard Otte, eds., *Funk-Kolleg Recht*, vol. 2, Frankfurt am Main: Fischer, 1985, pp. 95–120.

——, "Sachverständige Beratung des Staates," in Josef Isenee and Paul Kirchhof, eds., *Handbuch des Staatsrechts*, vol. 2, Demokratische Willensbildung—Die Staatsorgane des Bundes, Karlsruhe: C. F. Müller, 1988, pp. 207–248.

——, "The Status of Administrative Judges," in *Reports on German Public Law*, Rudolf Bernhardt and Ulrich Beyerlin, eds., XIIIth International Congress of Comparative Law, Montreal, 1990b, Heidelberg: C. F. Müller, pp. 221–240. A revised version in German appeared as "Stellung und Funktion des Verwaltungsrichters," *Die Verwaltung* 24: 137–167 (1991b).

——, "Verwaltung und Verwaltungsgerichtsbarkeit als Steuerungsmechanismen in einem polyzentrischen System der Rechtserzeugung," *Die Öffentliche Verwaltung* 40:265–271 (1987).

Brown, Gardner M., Jr., and Ralph W. Johnson, "Pollution Control by Effluent Charges: It Works in the Federal Republic of Germany, Why Not in the U.S.," *Natural Resources Journal* 24:929–966 (1984).

Brüggemeier, Gert, and Josef Falke, "Product Safety Policy in the Federal Republic of Germany," in Christian Joerges, ed., *European Product Safety, Internal Market Policy and the New Approach to Technical Harmonisation and Standards*, EUI Working Paper in Law no. 91/12, Florence: European University Institute, 1991, pp. 1–87.

Bullinger, Martin, "Aktuelle Probleme des deutschen Verwaltungsverfahrensrechts: Das Beschleunigungsgebot und seine Vereinbarkeit mit rechtsstaatlichen und demokratischen Verfahrensprinzipien" *Deutsches Verwaltungsblatt* 107:1463–1468 (1992).

Burtraw, Dallas, and Paul R. Portney, "Environmental Policy in the United States," in
Dieter Helm, ed., *Economic Policy Towards the Environment*, Oxford: Blackwell,
1991, pp. 289–320.

Cavender, Jeannine, and Jill Jager, "The History of Germany's Response to Climate
Change," *International Environmental Affairs* 5:3–18 (1993).

Christian, Amy C., "Designing a Carbon Tax: The Introduction of the Carbon-Burned
Tax (CBT)," *Journal of Environmental Law and Policy* 10:221–281 (1992).

Church, Thomas W., and Robert T. Nakamura, *Cleaning Up the Mess: Implementation
Strategies in Superfund*, Washington, D.C.: Brookings Institution, 1993.

——, "Cooperative and Adversary Regimes in Environmental Policy: Hazardous Waste
Cleanup in Europe and the United States," Albany: Rockefeller College of Public
Affairs, State University of New York at Albany (draft), June 19, 1994.

Cohen, Mark A., "Criminal Penalties," in Thomas Tietenberg, ed., *Innovation in Environmental Policy*, Hants, England: Edward Elgar, 1992, pp. 75–108.

Commission of the European Communities, *XXIVth General Report on the Activities of
the European Communities, 1990*, Brussels, 1991.

Commission of the European Communities, "Monitoring the Application by Member
States of Environmental Directives," Annex C, Eighth Report to the European
Parliament on Monitoring the Application of Community Law, printed in *Official
Journal* C 338 (December 31, 1991).

Crandall, Robert, and Paul Portney, "Environmental Policy," in Paul Portney, ed., *Natural Resources and the Environment*, Washington, D.C.: Urban Institute, 1984, pp.
47–82.

Cropper, Maureen L., and Wallace E. Oates, "Environmental Economics: A Survey,"
Journal of Economic Literature 30:675–740 (1992).

Currie, David, "Air Pollution Control in West Germany," *University of Chicago Law
Review* 49:355–393 (1982).

——, *The Constitution of the Federal Republic of Germany*, Chicago: University of Chicago Press, 1994.

——, "Lochner Abroad: Substantive Due Process and Equal Protection in the Federal
Republic of Germany," *Supreme Court Review* 1989: 333–372 (1989).

——, "Separation of Powers in the Federal Republic of Germany," *American Journal of
Comparative Law* 41:201–260 (1993).

Czada, Roland, "Konfliktbewältigung und politische Reform in vernetzten Entschei-
dungsstrukturen: Das Beispiel der kerntechnischen Sicherheitsregulierung," in
Roland Czada and Manfred G. Schmidt, eds., *Verhandlungsdemokratie, Interessen-
vermittlung, Regierbarkeit: Festschrift für Gerhard Lehmbruch*, Opladen: Westdeutscher, 1993, pp. 73–98.

Dale, Sir William Leonard, *Legislative Drafting, a New Approach: A Comparative Study
of Methods in France, Germany, Sweden, and the United Kingdom*, London: Butter-
worths, 1977.

Davis, Charles E., and James P. Lester, "Federalism and Environmental Policy," in
James P. Lester, ed., *Environmental Politics and Policy: Theories and Evidence*, Durham: Duke University Press, 1989, pp. 57–84.

Davis, Gary, and Joanne Linnerooth, "Government Ownership of Risk: Guaranteeing a

Treatment Infrastructure," in Bruce Piasecki and Gary Davis, eds., *Review of America's Future in Toxic Waste Management: Lessons from Europe*, Westport, Conn.: Quorum Books, 1987, pp. 95–130.

Denninger, Erhard, *Verfassungsrechtliche Anforderungen an die Normsetzung im Umwelt- und Technikrecht*, Baden-Baden: Nomos, 1990.

Deutsches Institut für Normung, *Verweisung auf technische Normen in Rechtsvorschriften: Symposium*, Berlin: Beuth, 1982.

Dewees, Donald, "The Efficacy of Environmental Regulation," Toronto: Faculty of Law, University of Toronto, 1992a.

——, "The Efficiency of the Common Law: Sulphur Dioxide Emissions in Sudbury," *University of Toronto Law Journal* 42:1–21 (1992b).

Dower, Roger C., "Hazardous Waste," in Paul Portney, ed., *Public Policies for Environmental Protection*, Washington, D.C.: Resources for the Future, 1990, pp. 151–194.

Duerksen, Christopher, *Environmental Regulation of Industrial Plant Siting: How to Make It Work Better*, Washington, D.C.: Conservation Foundation, 1983.

Eads, George, and Michael Fix, *Relief or Reform? Reagan's Regulatory Dilemma*, Washington, D.C.: Urban Institute, 1984.

Edley, Christopher F., Jr., *Administrative Law: Rethinking Judicial Control of Bureaucracy*, New Haven: Yale University Press, 1990.

Elliott, E. Donald, "Re-Inventing Rulemaking" *Duke Law Journal* 41:1490–1496 (1992).

Elliott, E. Donald, Bruce Ackerman, and John Millian, "Toward a Theory of Statutory Evolution: The Federalization of Environmental Law, *Journal of Law, Economics, and Organization* 1:313–340 (1985).

European Communities, *Final Adoption of the General Budget of the European Communities' Budget for Fiscal Year 1992*, L 26, February 3, 1992, 92/41/EEC, Euratom, ECSC.

European Communities, Court of Justice, *Synopsis of the Work of the Court of Justice of the European Communities, 1988–1989*, Luxembourg, 1990.

European Union, "Treaty on European Union," supplement to *European Report*, no. 1746, February 22, 1991.

Farber, Daniel A., "State Regulation and the Dormant Commerce Clause," *Constitutional Commentary* 3:395–414 (1986).

Fishbein, B. K. *Germany, Garbage, and the Green Dot*, New York: INFORM, 1994.

Fogt, Helmut, "The Greens and the New Left: Influences of Left-Extremism on Green Party Organisation and Policies," in Eva Kolinsky, ed., *The Greens in West Germany: Organisation and Policy Making*, Oxford: Berg German Studies Series, 1989, pp. 89–121.

Freeman, A. Myrick, III, "Water Pollution Policy," in Paul Portney, ed., *Public Policies for Environmental Protection*, Washington, D.C.: Resources for the Future, 1990, pp. 97–150.

Führ, Martin, "Implementation of EC Environmental Legislation No Longer Subject to Review in Brussels," *Environmental Law Review, International Newsletter* 2/1992, pp. 17–19.

——, "Technische Normen in demokratischer Gesellschaft," *Zeitschrift für Umweltrecht*, 4:99–102 (1993).

Gallagher, Anne, "The 'New' Montreal Protocol and the Future of International Law for Protection of the Global Environment," *Houston Journal of International Law* 14:267–364 (1992).

Garrett, Theodore L., and Sonya D. Winner, "A Clean Air Act Primer: Parts I, II, III," *Environmental Law Reporter: News and Analysis* 23:10159–10189, 10235–10262, 10301–10329 (1992).

Gassner, Erich, "Zur Mitwirkung von Naturschutzverbänden in Verwaltungsverfahren: Zugleich eine Besprechung von Waskows Untersuchung," *Natur und Recht* 12: 211–215 (1991).

Germany, Bundestag, 12th Voting Period, Enquete Commission on the "Protection of Humanity and the Environment—Assessment Criteria and Prospects for Environmentally Sound Product Cycles in Industrial Society," *Responsibility for the Future: Options for Sustainable Management of Substance Chains and Material Flows*, Interim Report, Bonn: Economica, 1994.

Germany, Federal Environmental Agency, *Facts and Figures on the Environment of Germany: 1988/89*, Berlin, 1990.

Germany, Federal Ministry for the Environment, "An Overview of the Research Programme: Costs of Environmental Pollution, Advantages of Environmental Protection," Information Sheet, Bonn, September 1991.

——, *Environmental Protection in Germany: National Report of the Federal Republic of Germany for the United Nations Conference on Environment and Development in June 1992 in Brazil*, Bonn, 1992.

Gey, Steven G., "The Political Economy of the Dormant Commerce Clause," *Review of Law and Social Change* 17:1–80 (1989–1990).

Grefen, Klaus, "Harmonization of Technical Rules for Clean Air in View of the European Internal Market," presented at the First European Conference on Cooperation in Environmental Technology, Cologne, November 13–15, 1991. Kommission Reinhaltung der Luft im VDI und DIN, Düsseldorf, 1991.

Greve, Michael S., *Environmentalism and the Rule of Law: Administrative Law and Movement Politics in West Germany and the United States*, Ph.D. diss., Cornell University; Ann Arbor, Mich.: University Microfilms International, 1987.

——, "The Non-Reformation of Administrative Law: Standing to Sue and Public Interest Litigation in West German Environmental Law," *Cornell International Law Journal* 22:197–244 (1989).

Grundgesetz für die Bundesrepublik Deutschland, text as of October 1990, Bonn: Deutscher Bundestag-Verwaltung-Referat Öffentlichskeitsarbeit, 1991.

Gurlit, Elke, *Die Verwaltungsöffentlichkeit in Umweltrecht*, Düsseldorf: Werner, 1989.

Gusy, Christoph, "Wertungen und Interessen in der technischen Normung," *Umwelt- und Planungsrecht* 6:241–250 (1986).

Haagsma, Auke, "The European Community's Environmental Policy: A Case-Study in Federalism," *Fordham International Law Review* 13: 311–359 (1989).

Hahn, Robert W., and Gordon L. Hester, "Where Did All the Markets Go? An Analysis of EPA's Emissions Trading Program," *Yale Journal of Regulation* 6:109–153 (1989).

Halfmann, Jost, "Social Change and Political Mobilization in West Germany," in Peter Katzenstein, ed., *Industry and Politics in West Germany: Toward the Third Republic,* Ithaca: Cornell University Press, 1989, pp. 51–86.

Hanft, James E., *"Francovich and Bonifaci v. Italy:* EEC Member State Liability for Failure to Implement Community Directives," *Fordham International Law Journal* 15:1237–1274 (1991–1992).

Hansmann, Klaus, *TA Luft: Technische Anleitung zur Reinhaltung der Luft,* annotated edition, Munich: C. H. Beck, 1987.

Hansmeyer, Karl-Heinrich, and Erik Gawel, "Schleichende Erosion der Abwasserabgabe?" *Wirtschaftsdienst* 73:325–332 (1993).

Harris, Richard, and Sidney Milkis, *The Politics of Regulatory Change: A Tale of Two Agencies,* New York: Oxford University Press (1989).

Harrison, David, Jr., "Controlling Automotive Emissions: How to Save More than $1 Billion Per Year and Help the Poor Too," *Public Policy* 25:527–553 (1977).

Hartkopf, Günter, and Eberhard Bohne, *Umweltpolitik 1: Grundlagen, Analysen und Perspektiven,* Opladen: Westdeutscher, 1983.

Hartley, T. C., *The Foundations of European Community Law: An Introduction to the Constitutional and Administrative Law of the European Community,* 2d ed., Oxford: Clarendon, 1988.

Hausker, Karl, "The Politics and Economics of Auction Design in the Market for Sulfur Dioxide Pollution," *Journal of Policy Analysis and Management* 11:553–572 (1992).

Hirsch, Guenter, "Keine Gentechnik ohne Gesetz?" *Neue Juristische Wochenschrift* 43:1445–1448 (1990).

Hoffman, William C., "Germany: A Look at the Development of Environmental Liability Insurance in Germany," *Reinsurance,* Reuters Textline-LEXIS, March 9 and April 9, 1992.

——, "Germany's New Environmental Liability Act: Strict Liability for Facilities Causing Pollution," *Netherlands International Law Revue* 38:27–41 (1991).

Hoffmann-Riem, Wolfgang, "Verhandlungslösungen und Mittlereinsatz im Bereich der Verwaltung: Eine vergleichende Einführung," in Wolfgang Hoffmann-Riem and Eberhard Schmidt-Aßmann, eds., *Konfliktbewältigung durch Verhandlungen,* vol. 1, Baden-Baden: Nomos, 1990, pp. 13–41.

Hoffmann-Riem, Wolfgang, and Eberhard Schmidt-Aßmann, eds., *Konfliktbewältigung durch Verhandlungen,* vols. 1 and 2, Baden-Baden: Nomos, 1990.

Holzapfel, Klaus-J., ed., *Kürschners Volkshandbuch Deutscher Bundestag: 12.Wahlperiode 1990,* Rheinbreitbach: Neue Darmstädter, 1991.

Holznagel, Bernd, *Konfliktlösung durch Verhandlungen,* Baden-Baden: Nomos, 1990.

——, "Mittlerunterstützte Aushandlungsprozesse aus Anlaß abfallrechtlicher Planfeststellungsverfahren," in Kathrin Becker-Schwarze, Wolfgang Köck, Thomas Kuycka, and Matthias von Schwanenflügel, eds., *Wandel der Handlungsformen im Öffentlichen Recht,* Stuttgart: R. Boorberg, 1991a, pp. 99–120.

——, "Uses of Environmental Mediation when Siting Hazardous Waste Facilities," *National Law School Journal* 3:95–107 (1991b).

Hucke, Jochen, Axel Müller, and Peter Wassen, *Implementation kommunaler Umweltpolitik,* Frankfurt am Main: Campus, 1980.

Jachtenfuchs, Markus, "The European Community and the Protection of the Ozone Layer," *Journal of Common Market Studies* 28:261–278 (1990).

Jacob, Herbert, *German Administration Since Bismarck: Central Authority Versus Local Automony*, New Haven: Yale University Press, 1963.

Jarass, Hans D., "Drittschutz im Umweltrecht," in Herbert Leßmann, Bernhard Groß-feld, and Lothar Vollmer, eds., *Festschrift für Rudolf Lukes*, Cologne: Carl Heymanns, 1989, pp. 57–72.

Jarass, Hans D., and Joseph DiMento, "Through Comparative Goggles: A Primer on German Environmental Law," *Georgetown International Law Review* 6:47–72 (1993). (This article has also been published as Hans Jarass and Joseph DiMento, "German Environmental Law in Comparison to U.S. Environmental Law," *Zeitschrift für vergleichende Rechtswissenschaft* 92:420–442 [1993].)

Johnson, Stanley P., and Guy Corcelle, *The Environmental Policy of the European Communities*, London: Graham and Trotman, 1989.

Jost, Peter J., "Economic Analysis of Procedural Aspects in the German Environmental Liability Law," *Journal of Institutional and Theoretical Economics* 149:609–633 (1993).

Kagan, Robert, "Adversarial Legalism and American Government," *Journal of Policy Analysis and Management* 10:369–406 (1991).

Katzenstein, Peter J., *Policy and Politics in West Germany: The Growth of a Semisovereign State*, Philadelphia: Temple University Press, 1987.

Katzman, Robert A., ed., *Judges and Legislators: Toward Institutional Comity*, Washington, D.C.: Brookings Institution, 1988.

Kilimnik, Kenneth S., "German Occupational Safety and Health Regulation From an American Perspective," *Dickinson Journal of International Law* 6:143–235 (1988).

Kimminich, Otto, "Das Verhältnis von Recht und Technik im Umweltschutz," in Herbert Leßmann, Bernhard Großfeld, and Lothar Vollmer, eds., *Festschrift für Rudolf Lukes*, Berlin: Carl Heymanns, 1989, pp. 73–86.

Kitschelt, Herbert, *The Logic of Party Formation: Ecological Politics in Belgium and West Germany*, Ithaca: Cornell University Press, 1989.

——, "Political Opportunity Structures and Political Protest: Anti-Nuclear Movements in Four Democracies," *British Journal of Political Science* 16: 57–85 (1986).

Klinski, Stefan, and Hartmut Gaßner, "Das Gesetz zur Beschleunigung der Verkehrswegeplanung: Planungsrecht auf Abwegen," *Neue Zeitschrift für Verwaltungsrecht* 11:235–239 (1992).

Kloepfer, Michael, *Umweltrecht*, Munich: C. H. Beck, 1989.

Kloepfer, Michael, Eckard Rehbinder, Eberhard Schmidt-Aßmann, with Philip Kunig, *Umweltgesetzbuch—Allgemeiner Teil*, Berlin: Erich Schmidt, 1991.

Koch, Harald, "Class and Public Interest Actions in German Law," *Civil Justice Quarterly* 5: 66–77 (1986).

Kommers, Donald, *The Constitutional Jurisprudence of the Federal Republic of Germany*, Durham: Duke University Press, 1989.

Kommission Reinhaltung der Luft im VDI und DIN, *Aufbau, Aufgaben, Ergebnisse*, Düsseldorf, 1991.

Kraemer, R. Andreas, "Implementation of the Montreal Protocol in Industrialised Countries," *Environmental Law Network International Newsletter* 2/92, 11–16.

Kraft, Michael E., and Norman Vig, "Environmental Policy in the Reagan Presidency," *Political Science Quarterly* 99:415–439 (1984).

Krämer, Ludwig, "Environmental Protection and Article 30 EEC Treaty," *Common Market Law Review* 30:111–143 (1993).

——, "The Implementation of Environmental Laws by the European Economic Communities," *German Yearbook of International Law* 34:9–53 (1991a).

——, "Participation of Environmental Organisations in the Activities of the EEC," in Martin Führ and Gerhard Roller, eds., *Participation and Litigation Rights of Environmental Associations in Europe*, Environmental Law Network International, Frankfurt am Main: Peter Lang, 1991b, pp. 129–140.

Kretschmer, Winfried, "Wackersdorf: Wiederaufarbeitung im Widerstreit," in U. Linse, R. Falter, D. Rucht, and W. Kretschmer, eds., *Von der Bittschrift zur Platzbesetzung: Konflikte um technische Großprojekte*, Berlin: J. H. W. Dietz, 1988, pp. 165–218.

Kunig, Philip, "Alternativen zum einseitig-hoheitlichen Verwaltungshandeln," in Wolfgang Hoffmann-Riem and Eberhard Schmidt-Aßmann, eds., *Konfliktbewältigung durch Verhandlungen*, volume I, Baden-Baden: Nomos, 1990, pp. 43–66.

Kvistad, Gregg, "Radicals and the State: The Political Demands on West German Civil Servants," *Comparative Political Studies* 21:95- 125 (1988).

Lamb, Irene, "Die Bedeutung technischer Normen im Umweltrecht," *Zeitschrift für Umweltrecht*, 4:97–99 (1993).

Landy, Marc K., Marc J. Roberts, and Stephen Thomas, *The Environmental Protection Agency: Asking the Wrong Questions*, New York: Oxford University Press, 1990.

Langbein, John, "The German Advantage in Civil Procedure," *University of Chicago Law Review* 52:823–866 (1985).

Lazarus, Richard J., "The Neglected Question of Congressional Oversight of EPA: *Quis Custodiet Ipsos Custodes* (Who Shall Watch the Watchers Themselves?)," *Law and Contemporary Problems* 54:205–239 (1991).

Leonard, Dick, *Pocket Guide to the European Community*, Oxford and London: Basil Blackwell and the Economist, 1988.

Leonardy, Uwe, "The Working Relationship between Bund and Länder in the Federal Republic of Germany," in Charlie Jeffrey and Peter Savigear, eds., *German Federalism Today*, Leicester: Leicester University Press, 1991, pp. 40–62.

Linde, Hans A., "Comment on the Constitutional Supervision of the Administrative Agencies in the Federal Republic of Germany," *Southern California Law Review* 53:601–609 (1980).

——, "Observations of a State Court Judge," in Robert A. Katzman, ed., *Judges and Legislators: Toward Institutional Comity*, Washington, D.C.: Brookings Institution, 1988, pp. 117–128.

Linse, Ulrich, Reinhard Falter, Dieter Rucht, and Winfried Kretschmer, *Von der Bittschrift zur Platzbesetzung: Konflikte um technische Großprojekte*, Berlin: J. H. W. Dietz, 1988.

Lorenz, Dieter, "The Constitutional Supervision of the Administrative Agencies in the Federal Republic of Germany," *Southern California Law Review* 53:543–582 (1980).

Lowry, William R., *The Dimensions of Federalism: State Governments and Pollution Control Policies,* Durham: Duke University Press, 1992.

Lübbe-Wolff, Gertrude, "Die Bedeutung des EG-Recht für den Grundwasserschutz," in Peter Behrens and Hans-Joachim Koch, eds., *Umweltschutz in der Europäischen Gemeinschaft,* Baden-Baden: Nomos, 1991a, pp. 127–156.

——, "Das Kooperationsprinzip im Umweltrecht: Rechtsgrundsatz oder Deckmantel des Vollzugsdefizits?" in Arthur Benz and Wolfgang Seibel, eds., *Zwischen Kooperation und Korruption: Abweichendes Verhalten in der Verwaltung,* Baden-Baden: Nomos, 1992, pp. 209–232.

——, "Verfassungsrechtliche Fragen der Normsetzung und Normkonkretisierung im Umweltrecht," *Zeitschrift für Gesetzgebung* 6:219–248 (1991b).

——, "Vollzugsprobleme der Umweltverwaltung," *Natur und Recht* 15:217–229 (1993).

McConnell, Virginia D., and Robert M. Schwab, "The Impact of Environmental Regulation on Industry Location Decisions: The Motor Vehicle Industry," *Land Economics* 66:67–81 (1990).

McGarity, Thomas O., "Some Thoughts on 'Deossifying' the Rulemaking Process," *Duke Law Journal* 41:1385–1462 (1992).

McInnis, Daniel F., "Ozone Layers and Oligopoly Profits," in Michael Greve and Fred L. Smith, Jr., eds., *Environmental Politics: Public Costs, Private Rewards,* New York: Praeger, 1992, pp. 129–154.

Manne, Alan S., and Richard G. Richels, "International Trade in Carbon Emission Rights: A Decomposition Procedure," *American Economic Review—Papers and Proceedings* 81:135–139 (1991).

Mansfield, Marla E., "The 'New' Old Law of Judicial Access: Toward a Mirror-Image Nondelegation Theory," *Administrative Law Review* 45:65–105 (1993).

Marburger, Peter, "Die gleitende Verweisung aus der Sicht der Wissenschaft," in Deutsches Institut für Normung, ed., *Verweisung auf technische Normen in Rechtsvorschriften: Symposium,* Berlin: Beuth, 1982, pp. 27–39.

Marcus, Maeva, and Emily Field Van Tassel, "Judges and Legislators in the New Federal System, 1789–1800," in Robert A. Katzman, ed., *Judges and Legislators: Toward Institutional Comity,* Washington, D.C.: Brookings Institution, 1988, pp. 31–53.

Markusen, James R., Edward R. Morey, and Nancy D. Olewiler, "Competition in Regional Environmental Policies When Plant Locations Are Endogenous," *Journal of Public Economics,* forthcoming.

——, "Environmental Policy when Market Structure and Plant Location are Endogenous," *Journal of Environmental Economics and Management* 24:69–86 (1993).

Mashaw, Jerry L., "Improving the Environment of Agency Rulemaking: An Essay on Management, Games, and Accountability," *Law and Contemporary Problems* 57:185–257 (1994).

Mashaw, Jerry L., and David L. Harfst, *The Struggle for Auto Safety,* Cambridge, Mass.: Harvard University Press, 1990.

Mashaw, Jerry L., and Susan Rose-Ackerman, "Federalism and Regulation," in George Eads and Michael Fix, eds., *The Reagan Regulatory Strategy: An Assessment,* Washington, D.C.: Urban Institute, 1984, pp. 111–52.

Maunz, Theodor, "Article 80," in T. Maunz and G. Dürig et al., *Grundgesetz: Kommentar*, Munich: C. H. Beck, 1991.

Maunz, Theodor, and Reinhold Zippelius, *Deutsches Staatsrecht*, Munich: C. H. Beck, 1991.

Mayntz, Renate, "Intergovernmental Implementation of Environmental Policy," in Kenneth Hanf and Fritz W. Scharpf, eds., *Interorganizational Policymaking: Limits to Coordination and Central Control*, London: Sage, 1978, pp. 201–214.

Mayntz, Renate, and Fritz Scharpf, *Policy-Making in the German Federal Bureaucracy*, Amsterdam: Elsevier, 1975.

Mayntz, Renate, and associates, *Vollzugsprobleme der Umweltpolitik*, Stuttgart: Kohlhammer, 1978.

Melnick, R. S., *Regulation and the Courts: The Case of the Clean Air Act*, Washington, D.C.: Brookings Institution, 1983.

Mendeloff, John, *Regulating Safety: An Economic and Political Analysis of Occupational Safety and Health Policy*, Cambridge, Mass.: MIT Press, 1979.

——, *The Dilemma of Toxic Substance Regulation: How Overregulation Causes Underregulation*, Cambridge, Mass.: MIT Press, 1988.

Miller, Jeffrey G., *Citizen Suits: Private Enforcement of Federal Pollution Control Laws*, New York: John Wiley, 1987.

Moe, Mogens, "Implementation and Enforcement in a Federal System," *Ecology Law Quarterly* 20: 151–164 (1993).

Morgenstern, Richard, "Toward a Comprehensive Approach to Global Climate Change," *American Economic Review-Papers and Proceedings* 81:140–145 (1991).

Müller, Edda, *Innenwelt der Umweltpolitik*, Opladen: Westdeutscher, 1986.

——, "Sozial-liberale Umweltpolitik: Von der Karriere eines neuen Politikbereichs," *Das Parlament* (Supplement, Aus. Politik und Zeitgeschichte), November 17, 1989, pp. 3–15.

——, "Umweltreparatur oder Umweltvorsorge? Bewältigung von Querschnittsaufgaben am Beispiel des Umweltschutzes, *Zeitschrift für Beamtenrecht* 38:165–174 (1990).

National Academy of Public Administration, *Congressional Oversight of Regulatory Agencies: The Need to Strike a Balance and Focus on Performance*, Washington, D.C.: NAPA, 1988.

Nelkin, Dorothy, and Michael Pollak, *The Atom Besieged*, Cambridge, Mass.: MIT Press, 1981.

"Neues aus Neuss," *WZB-Mitteilungen* 58:24–27 (December 1992).

Neumann, Horst, Hans-Joachim Schultz-Wildelau, and Jan Schilling, "Wasserwirtschaftliche Rahmenpläne und Bewirtschaftungspläne (§§36, 36b Wasserhaushaltsgesetz) als Beitrag zum Umweltschutz in Niedersachsen," in Werner Schenkel and Peter-Christoph Storm, eds., *Umwelt: Politik, Technik, Recht*, Berlin: Erich Schmidt, 1990, pp. 257–272.

Nordhaus, William, "A Sketch of the Economics of the Greenhouse Effect," *American Economic Review-Papers and Proceedings* 81:146–150 (1991).

Oates, Wallace E., *Fiscal Federalism*, New York: Harcourt Brace Jovanovich, 1972.

Oates, Wallace E., and Robert M. Schwab, "Economic Competition Among Jurisdictions: Efficiency Enhancing or Distortion Inducing?" *Journal of Public Economics* 35: 333–354 (1988)

O'Leary, Rosemary, "The Impact of Federal Court Decisions on the Policies and Administration of the U.S. Environmental Protection Agency," *Administrative Law Review* 41:549–574 (1989).

Olson, Mancur, Jr. "The Principle of 'Fiscal Equivalence': The Division of Responsibilities Among Different Levels of Government," *American Economic Review— Papers and Proceedings* 69:479–87 (1979).

Openchowski, Charles, *A Guide to Environmental Law in Washington, D.C.*, Washington, D.C.: Environmental Law Institute, 1990.

Organization for Economic Co-operation and Development, *OECD Environmental Data, Compendium 1991*, Paris, 1991a.

——, *OECD in Figures*, Paris, 1991b.

Ormond, Thomas A., "Environmental Group Actions in West Germany," in Martin Führ and Gerhard Roller, eds. *Participation and Litigation Rights of Environmental Associations in Europe*, Environmental Law Network International, Frankfurt am Main: Peter Lang, 1991, pp. 77–92.

Ossenbühl, Fritz, "Autonome Rechtsetzung der Verwaltung," in Josef Isenee and Paul Kirchhof, eds. *Handbuch des Staatsrechts der Bundesrepublik*, Vol. III, Karlsruhe: C. F. Müller, 1988a, pp. 425–462.

——, "Informelles Hoheitshandeln im Gesundheits- und Umweltschutz," *Jahrbuch des Umwelt- und Technikrechts* 3:27–48 (1987).

——, "Rechtsverordung" in Josef Isenee and Paul Kirchhof, eds. *Handbuch des Staatsrechts der Bundesrepublik*, Vol. III, Karlsruhe: C. F. Müller, 1988b, pp. 387–424.

Ott, Claus, and Hans-Bernd Schäfer, "Unternehmenspublizität, Umweltschadensbilanz und Haftung für Umweltschäden," in Claus Ott and Hans-Bernd Schäfer, eds., *Ökonomische Analyse des Unternehmensrechts*, Heidelberg: Physica, 1994, pp. 217–256.

Pakuscher, Ernst K., "The Use of Discretion in German Law," *University of Chicago Law Review* 44:94–109 (1976).

Palinkas, Peter, "Comments on Environmental Protection: Problems and Prospects in East and West Germany," in Paul J. J. Welfens, ed., *Economic Aspects of German Unification*, Berlin: Springer, 1992, pp. 208–229.

Palmer, Matthew, "Constitutional Design and Law: The Political Economy of Cabinet and Congressional Government," J.S.D. diss., Yale Law School, 1994.

Papier, Hans-Jürgen, "Bedeutung der Verwaltungsvorschriften im Recht der Technik," in Herbert Leßmann, Bernhard Großfeld, and Lothar Vollmer, eds., *Festschrift für Rudolf Lukes*, Berlin: Carl Heymanns, 1989, pp. 159–168.

Pashigian, B. Peter, "Environmental Protection: Whose Self-Interests Are Being Protected?" *Economic Inquiry* 23:551–584 (1985).

Paterson, William, "Environmental Politics," in G. Smith, W. Paterson, P. Merkl, eds., *Developments in West German Politics*, Durham: Duke University Press, 1989a, pp. 267–288.

——, "Environmental Protection, the German Chemical Industry and Government: Self-Regulation under Pressure," in Simon Bulmer, ed., *The Changing Agenda of West German Public Policy*, Aldershot: Dartmouth, 1989b, pp. 73–89.

Peacock, Alan, ed., *The Regulation Game: How British and West German Companies Bargain with Government*, Oxford: Blackwell, 1984.

Pearce, David W., "An Economic Approach to Saving the Tropical Forests," in Dieter Helm, ed., *Economic Policy Towards the Environment*, Oxford: Blackwell, 1991, pp. 239–262.

Pehle, Heinrich, *Analyse und Bewertung von Umweltverwaltungen: Das Beispiel Bundesumweltministerium (BMU)*, unofficial discussion paper, AK Umweltpolitik der DVPW (1988a).

——, "Das Bundesumweltministerium: Neue Chancen für den Umweltschutz? Zur Neuorganisation der Umweltpolitik des Bundes," *Verwaltungsarchiv II* 13:184–202 (1988b).

——, "Das Bundesministerium für Umwelt, Naturschutz und Reaktorsicherheit (BMU)—alte Politik im neuen Gewand?" *Gegenwartskunde* 37:259–287 (1988c).

Perritt, Henry, Jr., "Negotiated Rulemaking in Practice," *Journal of Policy Analysis and Management* 5:482–495 (1986).

Pierce, Richard, Jr., "The Unintended Effects of Judicial Review of Agency Rules: How Federal Courts Have Contributed to the Electricity Crisis of the 1990s," *Administrative Law Review* 43:7–29 (1991).

Portney, Paul, "Air Pollution Policy," in Paul Portney, ed., *Public Policies for Environmental Protection*, Washington, D.C.: Resources for the Future, 1990a, pp. 27–96.

——, "Economics and the Clean Air Act," *Journal of Economic Perspectives* 4:173–181 (1990b).

Portney, Paul, ed., *Public Policies for Environmental Protection*, Washington, D.C.: Resources for the Future, 1990c.

Pratt, Gregory C., "Air Toxics Regulation in Four European Countries and the United States," *International Environmental Affairs* 4:79–100 (1992).

Raiczyk, Glenn, "Montreal Protocol on Substances That Deplete the Ozone Layer: Conference Calling for Accelerated Phase-out of Ozone-depleting Chemicals Is Planned for 1992," *Temple International and Comparative Law Journal* 5:363–378 (1991).

Ramsauer, Ulrich, "Article 80," in R. Wassermann, ed., *Reihe Alternativkommentare: Kommentar zum Grundgesetz für die Bundesrepublik Deutschland*, 2d ed., Neuwied: Luchterhand, 1989, pp. 554–598.

Rat von Sachverständigen für Umweltfragen, *Abfallwirtschaft*, Sondergutachten, Stuttgart: Metzler-Poeschel, 1991.

——, *Auftrag-Mitgliedschaft-Arbeitsprogramm*, Wiesbaden, 1992.

——, *Stellungnahme zum Entwurf die Rückstands- und Abfallwirtschaftsgesetzes (RAWG)*, Wiesbaden, 1993.

——, *Waldschäden und Luftverunreinigungen*, Stuttgart: Kohlhammer, 1983.

Rehbinder, Eckard, "Argumente für der Verbandsklage im Umweltrecht, *Zeitschrift für Rechtspolitik* 9:157–163 (1976a).

——, "Controlling the Environmental Enforcement Deficit: West Germany," *American Journal of Comparative Law* 24:373–390 (1976b).

——, "Environmental Regulation Through Fiscal and Economic Incentives in a Federalist System," *Ecology Law Quarterly* 20:57–83 (1993).

——, "General Report on the Status of Transposition and Implementation of the Directive on Environmental Impact Assessment," *Environmental Law Network International Newsletter* 2/1992a, pp. 5–8.

——, "Private Recourse for Environmental Harm—Federal Republic of Germany," in Stephen C. McCaffrey and Robert E. Lutz, eds., *Environmental Pollution and Individual Rights*, Deventer: Kluwer, 1978, pp. 37–66.

——, "Rethinking Environmental Policy," in G. Smith, W. Paterson, P. Merkl, and S. Padgett, eds., *Developments in German Politics*, Basingstoke/London: Macmillan, 1992b, pp. 227–243.

——, "The Role of Administrative Courts in West Germany," J. W. Goethe University, Law Faculty, Frankfurt am Main, 1985.

——, "Vorsorgeprinzip im Umweltrecht und präventive Umweltpolitik," in Udo Ernst Simonis, ed., *Präventive Umweltpolitik*, Frankfurt am Main: Campus, 1988, pp. 129–141.

Rehbinder, Eckard, and Richard Stewart, *Environmental Protection Policy, Integration Through Law: Europe and the American Federal Experience*, Vol. 2, Berlin and New York: Walter de Gruyter, 1985.

Renzsch, Wolfgang, "Föderale Finanzbeziehungen im Parteienstaat. Eine Fallstudie zum Verlust politischer Handlungsmöglichkeiten," *Zeitschrift für Parlamentsfragen* 24:331–345 (1989).

Revesz, Richard L., "Rehabilitating Interstate Competition: Rethinking the 'Race-to-the-Bottom' Rationale for Federal Environmental Regulation," *New York University Law Review* 67:1210–1254 (1992).

Richter, Ingo, and Gunnar Folke Schuppert, *Casebook Verfassungsrecht*, 2d edition, Munich: C. H. Beck, 1991a.

Richter, Ingo, and Gunnar Folke Schuppert, *Casebook Verwaltungsrecht*, Munich: C. H. Beck, 1991b.

Rissberger, Steven, "On the Brink of an Ecological Calamity: Acid Rain, Transboundary Air Pollution and Environmental Law in West Germany," *Syracuse Journal of International Law and Commerce* 12:325–358 (1985).

Rohrschneider, Robert, "New Party versus Old Left Realignments: Environmental Attitudes, Party Politics, and Partisan Affiliations in Four West European Countries," *Journal of Politics* 55: 682–701 (1993).

Röscheisen, Helmut, "Recht auf Umweltinformationen: Chance für die Umweltverbände?" Paper presented at the conference "Besserer Umweltschutz durch mehr Informationen? Die Umsetzung des EG-Rechts zum Recht auf freien Zugang zu Umweltinformationen," Hamburg, April 25, 1992.

Rose, Matthias, "Gentechnik und Vorbehalt des Gesetzes," *Deutsches Verwaltungsblatt* 105:279–282 (1990).

Rose-Ackerman, Susan, "American Administrative Law Under Siege: Is Germany a Model?" *Harvard Law Review* 107:1279–1302 (1994a).

——, "Consensus versus Incentives: A Skeptical Look at Regulatory Negotiation," *Duke Law Journal* 43:1206–1220 (1994b).

——, "Environmental Liability Law," in Thomas Tietenberg, ed., *Innovation in Environmental Policy*, Hants, England: Edward Elgar, 1992a, pp. 245–260.

——, "Inefficiency and Reelection," *Kyklos* 33:287–306 (1980a).

——, "Does Federalism Matter?" *Journal of Political Economy* 89:152–65 (1981).

——, *Rethinking the Progressive Agenda: The Reform of the American Regulatory State*, New York: The Free Press, 1992b.

——, "Risk Taking and Reelection: Does Federalism Promote Innovation?" *Journal of Legal Studies* 9:593–616 (1980b).

Rosen, Bernard, *Holding Government Bureaucracies Accountable*, 2d ed., New York: Praeger, 1989.

Rucht, Dieter, "Gegenöffentlichkeit und Gegenexperten: Zur Institutionalisierung des Widerspruchs in Politik und Recht," *Zeitschrift für Rechtssoziologie* 9:290–305 (1988a).

——, "Von der Bewegung zur Institution? Organisationsstrukturen der Ökologiebewegung," in Roland Roth and Dieter Rucht, eds., *Neue soziale Bewegungen in der Bundesrepublik Deutschland*, 2d ed., Bonn: Bundeszentrale für politische Bildung, 1991, pp. 334–358.

——, "Wyhl: Der Aufbruch der Anti-Atomkraftbewegung," in U. Linse, R. Falter, D. Rucht, and W. Kretschmer, eds., *Von der Bittschrift zur Platzbesetzung: Konflikte um technische Großprojekte*, Berlin: J. H. W. Dietz, 1988b, pp. 128–164.

Russell, Clifford S., "Monitoring and Enforcement," in Paul Portney, ed., *Public Policies for Environmental Protection*, Washington, D.C.: Resources for the Future, 1990, pp. 243–274.

Russell, Irma S. "The Role of Public Opinion, Public Interest Groups, and Political Parties in Creating and Implementing Environmental Policy," *Environmental Law Reporter* 23:10665–10674 (1993).

Salzwedel, Jürgen, and Werner Preusker, *The Law and Practice Relating to Pollution Control in the Federal Republic of Germany*, 2d ed., London: Graham & Trotman for the Commission of the European Communities, 1982.

Sander, Andrea, Martin Führ, and Roland Fendler, "Stellungnahme zum Entwurf der Neuen Verordnung zur Durchführung des Bundes-Immissionsschutzgesetzes (Verordnung über das Genehmigungsverfahren)," working paper, Freiburg: Öko-Institute, October 1990.

Sands, Philippe, "European Community Environmental Law: The Evolution of a Regional Regime of International Environmental Protection," *Yale Law Journal* 100: 2511–2523 (1991).

——, "European Community Environmental Law: Legislation, the European Court of Justice and Common-Interest Groups," *Modern Law Review* 53:685–698 (1990).

Scalia, Antonin, "Back to Basics: Making Law without Making Rules," *Regulation* 5:25–28 (July / August 1981).

Scanlon, Terrence, and Robert Rogowsky, "Back-Door Rulemaking: A View from the CPSC," *Regulation* 8:27–30 (July / August 1984).

Schäfer, Hans, "Verfassungs- und Verwaltungsgerichtsbarkeit," in Helmut R. Külz and Richard Naumann, eds., *Staatsbürger und Staatsgewalt*, Vol. I, Karlsruhe: C. F. Müller, 1963, pp. 159–182.

Scharpf, Fritz, Bernd Reissert, and Fritz Schnabel, "Policy Effectiveness and Conflict Avoidance in Intergovernmental Policy Formation," in Kenneth Hanf and Fritz W.

Scharpf, eds., *Interorganizational Policymaking: Limits to Coordination and Central Control,* London: Sage, 1978, pp. 57–112.

Schmidt-Aßmann, Eberhard, "Die gerichtliche Kontrolle administrativer Entscheidungen im deutschen Bau-, Wirtschafts- und Umweltverwaltungsrecht," in Jürgen Schwarze and Eberhard Schmidt-Aßmann, eds., *Das Ausmaß der gerichtlichen Kontrolle im Wirtschaftsverwaltungs- und Umweltrecht,* Baden-Baden: Nomos, 1992, pp. 9–61.

Schmölling, Jürgen, "Grenzwerte in der Luftreinhaltung: Entscheidungsprozesse bei der Festlegung," in Gerd Winter, ed., *Grenzwerte: Inderdisziplinäre Untersuchungen zu einer Rechtsfigur des Umwelt-, Arbeits- und Lebensmittelschutzes,* Düsseldorf: Werner, 1986, pp. 73–85.

Schnapf, David, "State Hazardous Waste Programs Under the Federal Resource Conservation and Recovery Act, *Environmental Law* 12:679–743 (1982).

Schulz, Werner, and Erika Schulz, *The Uses of Environmental Benefits Estimates in Decisionmaking—The Case of Germany,* mimeograph, Berlin, 1991.

Schwarze, Jürgen, *European Administrative Law,* Luxembourg: Office for Official Publications of the European Communities, Sweet and Maxwell, 1992.

Seibel, Wolfgang, "Government-Nonprofit Relationships in a Comparative Perspective: The Cases of France and Germany," in K. McCarthy, V. Hodgkinson, R. Summariwalla et al., *The Nonprofit Sector in the Global Community: Voices from Many Nations,* San Francisco: Jossey-Bass, 1992a, pp. 205–229.

——, "Theoretische und methodologische Perspektiven der Analyse 'abweichenden' Verwaltungshandelns," in Arthur Benz and Wolfgang Seibel, eds., *Zwischen Kooperation und Korruption: Abweichendes Verhalten in der Verwaltung,* Baden-Baden: Nomos, 1992b, pp. 327–367.

Sellers, Jefferey M., "Comparing Courts in Context: Legality and Land Use Litigation in a French, German and an American Metropolitan Area," Paper prepared for delivery at the Annual Meeting of the American Political Science Association, September 1992, manuscript, Yale University, 1992.

——, "Grounds of Democracy: Public Authority and Metropolitan Land Use in Three Societies," Ph.D. diss., Yale University, 1994.

Sendler, Horst, "Gesetzes- und Richtervorbehalt im Gentechnikrecht," *Neue Zeitschrift für Verwaltungsrecht* 9:231–236 (1990).

Ševčenko, Catherine B., "Fundamentalism or Realism: The Future of the Greens in West German Politics," *The Fletcher Forum* (1986) 10:133–157.

Shapiro, Michael, "Toxic Substances Policy," in Paul Portney, ed., *Public Policies for Environmental Protection,* Washington, D.C.: Resources for the Future, 1990, pp. 195–242.

Shavell, Steven, *Economic Analysis of Accident Law,* Cambridge, Mass.: Harvard University Press, 1987.

Simitis, Spiros, "Europäisierung oder Renationalisierung des Arbeitsrechts?" draft, Faculty of Law, Goethe University, Frankfurt, 1993.

Singh, Mahendra P., *German Administrative Law in Common Law Perspective,* Berlin: Springer, 1985.

Skowronek, Stephen, *Building a New American State: The Expansion of National Capacities, 1877–1920,* Cambridge: Cambridge University Press, 1982.

Smith, Turner T., Jr., and Roszell D. Hunter, "The European Community Environmental Legal System," in Environmental Law Institute, *European Community Deskbook,* Washington, D.C.: Environmental Law Institute, 1992, pp. 1–32. Also printed in *Environmental Law Reporter News and Analysis,* 22:10106–10135 (1992).

Soell, Hermann, and Franz Dirnberger, "Wieviel Umweltverträglichkeit garantiert die UVP? Bestandsaufnahme und Bewertung des Gesetzes zur Umsetzung der EG-Richtlinie über die Umweltverträglichkeitprüfung," *Neue Zeitschrift für Verwaltungsrecht* 9:705–713 (1990).

Steinberg, Rudolf, *Fachplanung: Das Recht der Fachplanung unter Berücksichtigung des Nachbarschutzes und der Umweltverträglichkeitsprüfung,* Baden-Baden: Nomos, 1993.

——, "Judicial Review of Environmentally Related Administrative Decision-Making," *Tel Aviv University Studies in Law* 11: 61–78 (1992a).

——, "Kritik von Verhandlungslösungen, insbesondere von mittlerunterstützten Entscheidungen," in Wolfgang Hoffmann-Riem and Eberhard Schmidt-Aßmann, eds., *Konfliktbewältigung durch Verhandlungen,* vol. 1, Baden-Baden: Nomos, 1990, pp. 295–315.

——, "Neue Entwicklung in der Dogmatik des Planfeststellungsrechts," *Deutsches Verwaltungsblatt* 107:1501–1507 (1992b).

——, "Parlament und organisierte Interessen," in Hans-Peter Schneider and Wolfgang Zeh, eds., *Parlamentsrecht und Parlamentspraxis in der Bundesrepublik Deutschland,* Berlin: Walter de Gruyter, 1989, pp. 217–259.

——, "Untergesetzliche Regelwerke und Gremien," in Rudolf Steinberg, ed., *Reform des Atomrechts,* Baden-Baden: Nomos, 1994, pp. 82–100.

——, "Verwaltungsgerichtlicher Umweltschutz: Voraussetzungen und Reichweite der egoistischen Umweltschutzklage," *Umwelt- und Planungsrecht* 4:350–359 (1984).

Stewart, Richard, "The Reformation of American Administrative Law," *Harvard Law Review* 88:1667–1711 (1975).

Stith, Kate, and Steve Y. Koh, "The Politics of Sentencing Reform: The Legislative History of the Federal Sentencing Guidelines," *Wake Forest Law Review* 28:223–290 (1993).

Strauss, Peter L., *An Introduction to Administrative Justice in the United States,* Durham: Carolina Academic Press, 1989.

——, "Revisiting *Overton Park:* Political and Judicial Controls over Administrative Actions Affecting the Community," *UCLA Law Review* 39:1251–1329 (1992a).

——, "The Rulemaking Continuum," *Duke Law Journal* 41:1463–1489 (1992b).

Streibel, Günther, "Environmental Protection: Problems and Prospects in East and West Germany," in Paul J. J. Welfens, ed., *Economic Aspects of German Unification,* Berlin: Springer, 1992, pp. 183–207.

"Streitwertkatalog für die Verwaltungsgerichtsbarkeit," *Die Öffentliche Verwaltung* 45: 257–261 (1992).

Striegnitz, Meinfried, "Mediation: Lösung von Umweltkonflikten durch Vermittlung: Praxisbericht zur Anwendung in der Kontroverse um die Sonderabfalldeponie Münchehagen," *Zeitschrift für angewandte Umweltforschungen* 3:51–62 (1990).

Sunstein, Cass R., *After the Rights Revolution: Reconceiving the Regulatory State,* Cambridge, Mass.: Harvard University Press, 1990.

——, "What's Standing After *Lujan?* Of Citizen Suits, 'Injuries,' and Article III," *Michigan Law Review* 91:163- 236 (1992).

Taupitz, Jochen, "The German Environmental Liability Law of 1990: Continuing Problems and the Impact of European Regulation," *Syracuse Journal of International Law and Commerce* 19:13–37 (1993).

Thiem, V., "Environmental Law in the Federal Republic of Germany—The Position at April 1976," in S. Ercman, ed., *European Environmental Law: A Legal and Economic Appraisal,* Bern: Bubenberg, 1977, pp. 345–377.

Tietenberg, Thomas, "Economic Instruments for Environmental Regulation," in Dieter Helm, ed., *Economic Policy Towards the Environment,* Oxford: Blackwell, 1991, pp. 86–110.

Tilmann, Winfried, "TRK-Werte für krebsverdächtige Stoffe?" *Jahrbuch des Umwelt- und Technikrechts,* 3:245–269 (1987).

Tribe, Laurence H., *American Constitutional Law,* Mineola, N.Y.: Foundation, 1988.

"Twenty-Third Annual Administrative Law Issue," *Duke Law Journal* 41:1311–1507 (1992).

Umweltbundesamt, *Annual Report 1991, English Summary,* Berlin, 1992a.

——, *Daten zur Umwelt: 1990/91,* Berlin: Erich Schmidt, 1992b.

——, *Jahresbericht, 1990,* Berlin, 1991.

"UNCED: Rio Conference on Environment and Development," *Environmental Policy and Law* 22:204–225 (1992), cited as UNCED.

United Nations, Convention on Biological Diversity. Reprinted in *Environmental Policy and Law* 22:251–258 (1992).

United Nations Framework Convention on Climate Change, Reprinted in *Environmental Policy and Law* 22:258–264 (1992).

United States Environmental Protection Agency, *Enforcement Accomplishment Reports,* Washington D.C.: GPO, 1988–1992.

——, Office of Water and Office of Policy, Planning and Evaluation, *The Benefits and Feasibility of Effluent Trading Between Point Sources: An Analysis in Support of Clean Water Act Reauthorization,* Washington, D.C., May 1992. (Prepared by Industrial Economics.)

United States President's Council on Environmental Quality, *Environmental Quality: 21st Annual Report,* Washington, D.C.: U.S. GPO, 1991.

United States President's Council on Environmental Quality, *Environmental Quality: 23d Annual Report,* Washington, D.C.: U.S. GPO, 1993.

Van Dijk, P., *Judicial Review of Governmental Action and the Requirement of an Interest to Sue,* Alphen aan den Rijn, The Netherlands: Sijthoff and Noordhoff, 1980.

Vitzthum, Wolfgang Graf, "Gentechnik und Grundrechtsschutz," *Verwaltungsblätter für Baden-Württemberg* 11:48–51 (1990).

Von Lersner, Heinrich, "Verfahrensvorschläge für umweltrechtliche Grenzwerte," *Natur und Recht* 12:193–197 (1990).

Wägenbaur, Rolf, "Die Umsetzung von EG-Recht in deutsches Recht und ihre gesetzgeberische Problematik," *Zeitschrift für Gesetzgebung* 3:303–318 (1988).

Wagener, Heiko, "Der Anspruch auf Immissionsschutz: Plädoyer für einklagbares Recht," *Natur und Recht* 2:71–78 (1988).

Wagner, Jörg, "Verfahrensbeschleunigung durch das Verkehrswegeplanungsbeschleunigungsgesetz," *Neue Zeitschrift für Verwaltungsrecht* 11:232–235 (1992).

Wahl, Rainer, "Genehmigung und Planungsentscheidung: Überlegungen zu zwei Grundmodellen des Verwaltungsrechts und zu ihrer Kombination," *Deutsches Verwaltungsblatt* 97:51–62 (1982).

Wallich, Henry C., "The American Council of Economic Advisers and the German Sachverständigenrat: A Study in the Economics of Advice," *Quarterly Journal of Economics* 72:349–379 (1968).

Warren, Melinda, and Kenneth Chilton. "Higher Budgets for Federal Regulators." *Regulation* 13:21–25 (Fall 1990).

Weale, Albert, "Vorsprung durch Technik? The Politics of German Environmental Regulation," in Kenneth Dyson, ed., *The Politics of German Regulation*, Aldershot: Dartmouth, 1992, pp. 159–183.

Weale, Albert, Timothy O'Riordan, and Louise Kramme, *Controlling Pollution in the Round: Change and Choice in Environmental Regulation in Britain and West Germany*, London: Anglo-German Foundation, 1991.

Weidner, Helmut, *Air Pollution Control Strategies and Policies in the Federal Republic of Germany*, Berlin: Wissenschaftszentrum Berlin für Sozialforschung, 1986.

——, "Die Umweltpolitik der konservativ-liberalen Regierung," *Das Parlament* (Supplement, Aus Politik und Zeitgeschichte), November 17, 1989, pp.16–28.

Weimer, David, and Aidan Vining, *Policy Analysis: Concepts and Practice*, second edition, Englewood Cliffs, N.J.: Prentice-Hall, 1992.

Werham, Keith, "The Neoclassical Revival in Administrative Law," *Administrative Law Review* 44:567–627 (1992).

Westbrook, David A., "Environmental Policy in the European Community: Observations on the European Environmental Agency," *Harvard Environmental Law Review* 15:257–273 (1991).

Wetstone, Gregory S., and Armin Rosencranz, *Acid Rain in Europe and North America: National Responses to an International Problem*, Washington, D.C.: Environmental Law Institute, 1983.

Wiedemann, Peter Michael, Susanne Femers, and Leonhard Hennen, *Bürgerbeteiligung bei entsorgungswirtschaftlichen Vorhaben*, Berlin: Erich Schmidt, 1991.

Winter, Gerd, "Die Angst des Richters bei der Technikbewertung," *Zeitschrift für Rechtspolitik* 20:425–431 (1987).

——, "Bartering Rationality in Regulation," *Law and Society Review* 19:219–250 (1985).

——, "Gesetzliche Anforderungen an Grenzwerte für Luftimmissionen," in Gerd Winter, ed., *Grenzwerte: Interdisziplinäre Untersuchungen zu einer Rechtsfigur des Umwelt-, Arbeits- und Lebensmittelschutzes*, Düsseldorf: Werner, 1986, pp. 127–141.

Wolf, Rainer, "Zur Antiquiertheit des Rechts in der Risikogesellschaft," *Leviathan* 15: 357–391 (1987).

Wood, B. Dan, and Richard Waterman, "The Dynamics of Political Control of the Bureaucracy," *American Political Science Review* 85:801–828 (1991).

Zimmerman, Franz, "Grundrechtsbindungen bei der Finanzierung öffentlicher Sach- und Dienstleistungen durch spezielle Entgelte," *Deutsches Verwaltungsblatt* 104: 901–907 (1989).

INDEX

Ackerman, B., 158, 159, 165, 171
Administrative courts, 12–13, 131, 138–139; and cost-benefit analysis, 76–77; representative of the public interest, 131, 145
Administrative guidelines. *See also* Administrative law; Rulemaking
—Germany, 60–61, 127–128; and EU directives, 117–119; and informal agreements, 68–69; judicial review of, 78–80
—United States, 128
Administrative law, 1–3, 121–125; Germany, 9–13, 125–126; U.S., 13–16, 133–138. *See also* Administrative guidelines; Judicial review, in administrative law; Rulemaking
Administrative Procedures Act: German, 8, 59–60, 143; U.S., 1, 14–15, 59, 67, 126–127
Advisory committees, Germany, 65–66
Air pollution, 20–23, 38
—Germany, 20–31, 69–70, 189; acid rain, 28–29, 34; "bubbles," 153; citizen suits, role of, 87; hearings, 67
—United States, 20–31, 32, 35, 48–49
Anheier, H., 148, 191, 192, 203
Anthony, R. A., 213, 216
Atomic power. *See* Nuclear power

Baumann, W., 191, 193, 194
Biodiversity, 37, 53
Bizer, J., 194, 195, 196, 208
Blankenburg, E., 168
Boehmer-Christiansen, S., 145, 148, 154, 157, 158, 159, 160, 161, 167, 180, 193
Bohne, E., 155, 157, 161, 167, 179, 180, 181, 212

Böhret, C., 146, 172, 182, 193
Bosso, C. J., 151, 159, 161
Breuer, R., 176, 179, 181, 187, 200, 201
Brickman, R., 146, 147, 159, 167, 176, 179, 180
Brohm, W., 144, 147, 149, 176, 180, 187, 189, 200, 201
Brüggemeier, G., 176, 178
Building and Planning Law, Germany, 97, 149, 188, 189, 197
Bundesrat, role of, 8–9, 58–59
Bundestag, 8–9; veto, 59
Bund für Umwelt und Naturschutz Deutschland, 67, 180, 209
Bureaucracy: Germany, 9–12, 144–145; United States, 13–15
Bürgerinitiativen, 11, 86–87, 89; *BBU*, 67, 148, 180, 192, 209

Canada: environmental torts in, 198; government structure, 145, 150
Chemicals, regulation of, Germany, 9, 30, 65, 68–69
Church, T. W., 167, 168, 203
Citizens' groups. *See* Environmental groups; *Bürgerinitiativen*
Citizen suits: in Germany, 89; in United States, 16, 130, 136
Constitutional law. *See also* Federalism and environment; Judicial review, in administrative law; Rights, individual
—Germany, 1; *Bundesrat*, role of, 57, 58–59; courts, role of, 12–13; delegation doctrine, 57–58; parliamentary structure, 8; regulation of risks, 73–75; separation of powers, 57; states, role of, 8. *See also* Rights, individual; Proportionality principle

LEGAL MATERIALS
Abbreviations used are listed on pp. ix–xi.